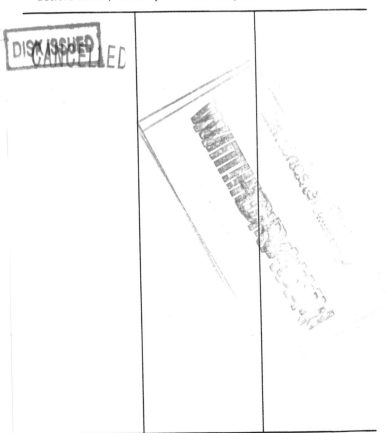

Virtual Music

Virtual Music
Computer Synthesis of Musical Style

David Cope

With commentary by Douglas Hofstadter
And with perspectives and analysis by Eleanor Selfridge-Field, Bernard Greenberg,
Steve Larson, Jonathan Berger, and Daniel Dennett

The MIT Press
Cambridge, Massachusetts
London, England

Excerpts from *Nineteen Eighty-Four* by George Orwell (copyright © George Orwell 1949) reproduced by permission of AM Heath & Co. Ltd on behalf of Bill Hamilton as the Literary Executor of the Estate of the Late Sonia Brownell Orwell and Martin Secker & Warburg Ltd. Excerpts from *The Joy of Music* by Leonard Bernstein (copyright © 1954, 1955, 1956, 1957, 1958, 1958 by Amberson Holdings, LLC) reproduced by permission of the Estate of Leonard Bernstein (The Joy Harris Literary Agency, Inc.), 1980 edition, A Fireside Book.

This book was set in Times New Roman in 3B2 by Asco Typesetters, Hong Kong, and was printed and bound in the United States of America.

Library of Congress Cataloging-in-Publication Data

Cope, David.
   Virtual music : computer synthesis of musical style / David Cope.
      p.   cm.
   Includes bibliographical references (p.   ) and index.
   ISBN 0-262-03283-X (hc. : alk. paper)
   1. Composition (Music)—Computer programs. 2. Cope, David. Experiments in musical intelligence (Computer file) I. Title.
MT56.C69   2000
781.3′4—dc21   00-035506

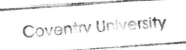

Contents

Preface

On November 8 and 9, 1997, as a part of a series of colloquia on computers and creativity, Douglas Hofstadter, in conjunction with the Center for Computer Assisted Research in the Humanities (CCARH) and Stanford University, presented a weekend of papers, panels, concerts, and discussions centered around the works of the Experiments in Musical Intelligence program. Presenters included Douglas Hofstadter, Eleanor Selfridge-Field, Bernard Greenberg, Steve Larson, Jonathan Berger, Daniel Dennett, and myself. *Virtual Music: Computer Synthesis of Musical Style* serves as a document to this colloquium, an extension of many of the thoughts presented there, and an annotated publication of sample musical output of the Experiments in Musical Intelligence computer music composing program.

With the exception of the last two chapters, the presentation order of this book closely follows that of the colloquium. Readers will note that both Doug Hofstadter and I discuss the basic principles that Experiments in Musical Intelligence follows. This apparent redundancy proved very effective at the Stanford colloquium in that Doug's informal view of the program effectively serves as an introductory tutorial to my more in-depth presentation.

Virtual Music: Computer Synthesis of Musical Style is divided into four main parts. The first part provides a background of Experiments in Musical Intelligence. It cites precedents such as the eighteenth-century *Musikalisches Würfelspiel* and other composing algorithms and presents a version of what I call The Game—a reader participation–style recognition test. This is followed by a general overview of Experiments in Musical Intelligence as seen and heard through the eyes and ears of Douglas Hofstadter, a renowned cognitive scientist and Pulitzer Prize–winning author of *Gödel, Escher, Bach*. I then respond to Doug's commentary which leads to a description of the fundamental principles upon which the Experiments in Musical Intelligence program operates.

The second part follows the composition of an Experiments in Musical Intelligence work from the creation of a database to the completion of a new work in the style of Mozart. This presentation includes, in sophisticated laypersons' terms, relatively detailed explanations of how each step in the composing process contributes to the final composition, with an example of ineffective as well as effective output.

The third part provides perspectives and analyses of the Experiments in Musical Intelligence program. These scholarly commentaries include analyses, critical evaluation, and relevant history and documentation, as appropriate. These chapters also discuss the implications of the program's compositions. The scholars include Eleanor Selfridge-Field (musicologist, associate director of the Center for Computer Assisted Research in the Humanities at Stanford University), Bernard Greenberg (Bach scholar and co-inventor of the Symbolics Lisp machine), Steve Larson (music theorist), Jonathan Berger (noted composer and theorist), Daniel Dennett (cognitive scientist and author of *Darwin's Dangerous Idea*), and Douglas Hofstadter.

The fourth part provides my response to the commentaries presented in the third part along with thoughts on a variety of implications I see as a result of my work with Experiments in Musical Intelligence. These implications include reflections on artificial intelligence, music cognition, aesthetics, intention, and the future of both Experiments in Musical Intelligence and, indirectly, the use of computers in the new millennium.

Appendix A includes the music of the databases used to create a new Mozart-style movement which appears in appendix B. Appendix C contains a rejected Mozart-style movement, as discussed in chapter 10. Appendix D provides extended musical examples referred to and discussed in *Virtual Music*. The music covers styles from a four-hundred-year span of classical music history and includes such composers as Scarlatti, Bach, Mozart, Beethoven, Schubert, Chopin, Rachmaninoff, Prokofiev, Joplin, Bartók, and others. Each music example is preceded by a brief documentation of its composition or thoughts on its aesthetic value. Appendix E presents the key to The Game in chapter 1 (see figures 1.11–1.13).

I have written *Virtual Music* using nontechnical terminology and in a style which I feel will appeal to the layperson with an interest in classical music, as well as to individuals knowledgeable about artificial intelligence. Since many of the examples are musical scores, an ability to read music will be beneficial. Those unable to play these examples on the piano will find the music available on the accompanying compact disk or on commercially available CDs of Experiments in Musical Intelligence's music: *Bach by Design*, *Classical Music Composed by Computer*, and *Virtual Mozart* (Cope 1994, 1997b, 1999).

Like most computer applications, Experiments in Musical Intelligence has had many incarnations. The program has been revised continually over many years. Therefore, the music from the mid-1980s was created by a substantially different program from the one that exists now. There are definite commonalities among the various forms of the program, and I tend to emphasize these features in my writings and discussions. I mention these versions for several reasons. First, individuals who have followed my work through various writings can become confused by the variations in the descriptions of Experiments in Musical Intelligence they encounter. While I try not to contradict earlier publications, I tend to emphasize important, newer aspects of the program in current writings, aspects which may not have even existed in earlier versions. Readers should be aware of the distinctions of the various incarnations of the program. Second, I do not want listeners of Experiments in Musical Intelligence's music to be searching for compositional processes which, by virtue of the period in which they were created, do not exist. Finally, I mention these versional differences in Experiments in Musical Intelligence because the approach I take in describing the program in this book is a *current* version, which has only existed in this form since about 1993. Most of the Experiments in Musical Intelligence program's output, therefore, cannot be understood to have been composed using *all* of the processes described in this book. However, the works composed *specifically* for this book in appendixes B and C were created using this version.

I wish to thank the many individuals who have contributed so very much to this body of work, particularly Douglas Hofstadter, who created the series of colloquia on computers and creativity at Stanford University in 1997 which led to the creation of this book. I also wish to thank the Center for Computer Assisted Research in the Humanities, particularly Eleanor Selfridge-Field, Don Anthony, and Walter Hewlett. Without the moral support and advice of colleagues such as these, this book could not have been completed.

The CD

The CD which accompanies this book contains two sets of music. The first set contains some of the musical examples of *Virtual Music: Computer Synthesis of Musical Style*. Each example is named and numbered according to the text for easy reference. The second set contains performances of many of the works presented in the appendixes of *Virtual Music*, especially those not already available on commercial recordings.

The music of both of these sets is performed here by a computer algorithm I developed called, simply, Performance. Like Experiments in Musical Intelligence, Performance relies on a database of already performed music for analysis which it then uses as a model. Performance does not use recombinancy, however, but rather uses its analyses as temporally flexible templates. Performance alters only the rhythm, articulation, and dynamics of the works it performs.

Music on the CD

Figures	Track
1.1–4	1
1.7–9	2
1.11a	3
1.11b	4
1.11c	5
1.11d	6
1.12a	7
1.12b	8
1.12c	9
1.12d	10
1.13a	11
1.13b	12
1.13c	13
1.13d	14
4.1–2	15
4.5–7	16
4.9–13	17

Music Not on the CD

Works in this book not on the accompanying CD appear on the following commercial recordings where BBD is *Bach by Design* (Centaur Records CRC 2184) and CMCC is *Classical Music Composed by Computer* (Centaur Records CRC 2329):

Bach-style inventions

1 appears as 2 on BBD

2 appears as 1 on CMCC

5 appears as 2 on CMCC

6 appears as 4 on BBD

7 appears as 3 on CMCC

8 appears as 3 on BBD

10 appears as 5 on BBD

12 appears as 1 on BBD

Beethoven-style sonata movements 1&2 on CMCC
Joplin-style rag on CMCC
Prokofiev-style sonata on BBD
Chopin-style mazurka on CMCC
Rachmaninoff-style suite on CMCC

I FUNDAMENTALS

Much of what happens in the universe results from recombination. The recombination of atoms, for instance, produces new molecules. Complex chemicals derive from the recombination of more rudimentary particles. Humans evolve through genetic recombination and depend on recombination for communication, since language itself results from the recombining of words and phrases. Cultures thereby rely on recombination to establish and preserve their traditions. Music is no different. The recombinations of pitches and durations represent the basic building blocks of music. Recombination of larger groupings of pitches and durations, I believe, form the basis for musical composition and help establish the essence of both personal and cultural musical styles. As will be seen, recombination also plays a significant role in my Experiments in Musical Intelligence program.

1 Virtual Music

Virtual music represents a broad category of machine-created composition which attempts to replicate the style but not the actual notes of existing music (Cope 1993). As will be seen, virtual music has existed in one form or another for centuries. With the advent of computers. however, the potential for virtual music has multiplied exponentially. In this chapter, I provide a brief background of virtual music and then ask you to participate in three listening tests which will challenge your ability to recognize human-composed vs. computer-composed music and to recognize actual Bach and Chopin vs. computer-composed music in their styles.

Early Examples

The figured bass, popular during the Baroque period of music history (1600–1750), demonstrates how composers and performers use combinations of notated music, period style constraints, and performer choice to produce a diversity of results and yet adhere to a composer's style. As in other examples of virtual music, each performance differs, yet each retains its stylistic integrity.

Figured basses constitute the notation for most Baroque basso continuos, the combination of a keyboard instrument (clavier or organ) and a reinforcing sustaining instrument (bass gamba, violoncello, or bassoon). Typically the keyboardist uses a notated bass line, or a bass-line and treble-line depending on the ensemble requirements, above which they freely but stylistically improvise.

Figure 1.1 shows a very simple figured bass in C major. The arabic numerals below certain notes indicate inversions of chords. Performers assume root position or 5/3 intervals above the bass-note unless otherwise instructed. The bass gambist or cellist plays the line as written. The keyboardist, however, must complete the implied chords in the proper key in a manner consistent with the style, yet original in spirit. In essence, the figured bass represents an algorithm or recipe, the realization of which depends upon the application of performance practice and performer style improvisation.

Figure 1.2 provides a very simple realization of the figured bass of figure 1.1. The chords here consist of triads (three-note chords built in thirds) or seventh chords (four-note chords built in thirds) with some notes doubled in octaves. The Baroque period constraints governing which notes should be doubled, as well as how notes should move, one to another, are quite strict and too numerous to present here. The important thing, at least for our purposes, is to understand that the music in figure 1.2 represents only one of many possible realizations of the figured bass of figure 1.1.

Figure 1.3 shows another possible correct realization of the figured bass shown in figure 1.1. Again, the music here consists of triads and seventh chords with some

Figure 1.1
A simple figured bass in C major.

Figure 1.2
One possible realization of the figured bass in figure 1.1.

Figure 1.3
Another correct realization of the figured bass shown in figure 1.1.

notes doubled. Comparing figure 1.3 with figure 1.2 demonstrates both their similarity (same note names in each chord) and differences (notes in different registers). In essence, then, we have two different examples of music, in similar block chord style, derived from the same core figured bass.

Figure 1.4 presents a more Baroque-style realization of the figured bass in figure 1.1. In fact, the melody shown in this example might typically be one of the provided elements. While this example tends to resemble figure 1.2 in chord spacing it nonetheless represents a third and distinctly different realization of the figured bass in figure 1.1. In all of these cases, the music has adhered to the constraints of the period using a combination of given music and performer choice, as well as a recombination of right notes and motives.

The *Musikalisches Würfelspiel*

One of the first formal types of algorithms in music history, and another good example of virtual music, is the eighteenth-century *Musikalisches Würfelspiel*, or musical dice game. The idea behind this musically sophisticated game involved

Figure 1.4
A more typical realization of the figured bass presented in figure 1.1.

composing a series of measures of music that could be recombined in many different ways and still be stylistically viable—virtual music. Following this process, even a very simple piece becomes a source of innumerable new works. A typical *Würfelspiel* of sixteen measures, for example, yields 11^{16}, or roughly forty-six quadrillion works, with each work, although varying in aesthetic quality, being stylistically correct (Cope 1996). Composers of *Musikalische Würfelspiele* included Johann Philipp Kirnberger, C. P. E. Bach, Franz Josef Haydn, Wolfgang Amadeus Mozart, Maximilian Stadler, Antonio Callegari, and Pasquale Ricci, among others (see Cope 1996).

Figure 1.5 provides an example of a matrix from a typical *Musikalisches Würfelspiel*, this one attributed to Franz Josef Haydn. The numbers down the left side of the matrix in figure 1.5 represent the eleven possible results of the toss of two dice (2–12). Each number in the matrix links to a previously composed measure of music. Each vertical column of the matrix indicates successive measure choices (A–H here representing an eight-measure phrase). To get a first measure of music, one tosses the dice, locates the resulting number on the left of the matrix, and then looks up the corresponding measure in vertical column A in an associated list of measures of music (not shown here due to space limitations). Subsequent tosses for columns B through H complete an initial phrase, with further phrases produced in the same way using different matrices and musical correlates. A resulting minuet appears in figure 1.6.

Composers of *Musikalische Würfelspiele* created the various measures in such a way that any of the measures in one vertical column would successfully connect with any of the measures in the column to their immediate right. This becomes fairly clear when the actual music for each measure is aligned as in the matrix. However, the music of a *Musikalisches Würfelspiel* is typically arranged arbitrarily so that it is not at all clear that the choices for each measure have the same general musical function. These apparently random arrangements no doubt made such games seem all the more fantastic in the eighteenth-century parlor where they were often played.

A number of composers employed *Würfelspiel* combinatorial techniques to create large-scale works. For example, Josef Riepel (1755) developed "melodic combinations in the construction of minuets, concertos, and symphonies. Within a given model

	A	B	C	D	E	F	G	H
2	96	22	141	41	105	122	11	30
3	32	6	128	63	146	46	134	81
4	69	95	158	12	153	66	110	24
5	40	17	113	85	161	2	159	100
6	148	74	163	45	80	97	36	107
7	104	157	27	167	154	68	118	91
8	152	60	171	53	99	133	21	127
9	119	84	114	50	140	86	169	94
10	98	142	42	156	75	129	62	123
11	3	87	165	61	135	47	147	33
12	54	130	10	103	28	37	106	5

Figure 1.5
A matrix for a first phrase from a *Musikalisches Würfelspiel* attributed to Franz Josef Haydn.

he seeks to achieve optimum effects by substituting figures, phrases, and cadences"
(Ratner 1970, p. 351).

The popularity of *Musikalische Würfelspiele* was extensive during the eighteenth century, particularly in Germany. Each game was capable of producing so much new music that the "entire population of eighteenth-century Europe, working a lifetime on these games could not exhaust the combinations" (Ratner 1970, p. 344). The creation of *Musikalische Würfelspiele*, however, did not extend beyond the Classical period nor did the form have much serious consequence. (For more on the *Musikalisches Würfelspiel*, see Eleanor Selfridge-Field's discussion in chapter 11.)

More Recent Examples

Popular music retains many of the same notational properties of the previously discussed Baroque period figured bass and shares a similar objective for virtual music: the ability to create music in many different guises while maintaining the style intended by the composer. Most popular music notation provides only a single line and chord symbols from which performers improvise their own versions of the music within the constraints provided by the implied chords. Figure 1.7 gives an example of this. Note that popular music uses a melody rather than a bass-line and note names representing chords instead of arabic numerals for inversions. However, the same kind of recombinatory principles pertain as those in figured bass.

As with Baroque figured bass, the performer of popular music is expected to supply a large number of the actual notes for the resulting music. Performers are

Figure 1.6
A resulting minuet derived from the *Musikalisches Würfelspiel* attributed to Franz Josef Haydn.

Figure 1.7
An example of popular twelve-bar blues music shorthand notation.

also expected to adhere to a logical style implied by the music as well as (often) by the title and lyrics. Thus, many different realizations can occur. Figure 1.8 presents an extremely vanilla example. Here the chords are simply iterated, much as they were in figure 1.2, the first realization of the figured bass of figure 1.1. The intended style of music barely survives this rather stagnant interpretation. On the other hand, figure 1.9 gives a much more plausible realization. Here, the left-hand figuration and the right-hand chords provide much of what audiences know as blues style. Both figures 1.8 and 1.9 are correct. The latter example, however, adheres to the style implied by the rhythm and notes of the original notation in figure 1.7.

In the Baroque figured bass and contemporary popular music we find many notational and conceptual similarities. First, both notations provide two types of information: musical notation which requires accurate performance and a shorthand for realization or improvisation. Second, both forms have constraints. In the figured bass examples, these constraints take the form of voice-leading rules and the recombination of relevant motives and musical ideas. In the popular music example, these constraints result from recombinations of possible chord notes in various registers and relevant stylistic limitations. Lastly, both examples provide performers with a fairly wide range of freedom regarding what and how many actual notes will occur and when. In short, these examples have a given part, a derived or implied rules part,

Figure 1.8
One realization of the notation in figure 1.7.

and a free part. Combined, these three elements foster the creation of innumerable style-specific realizations of the same basic given materials.

In the past fifty years or so, computers have provided the principal source for virtual music. One of the pioneers of using computers in this way was Lejaren Hiller who, in collaboration with Leonard Isaacson, wrote programs for the Illiac computer. Hiller and Isaacson's work led to the composition of the *Illiac Suite for String Quartet* in 1956 (Hiller and Isaacson 1959), one of the first such works written using computers. This innovative composition incorporates numerous experiments involving style simulation.

Iannis Xenakis uses mathematical models such as probability laws, stochastics (a mathematical theory that develops predictability from laws of probability), game theory, and Markov chains (Xenakis 1971) to compose his music. Xenakis's works often interweave his own intuitive composition with passages created by his various algorithmic computer programs which ultimately contribute to his overall musical

Figure 1.9
A much more stylistic realization of the notation in figure 1.7.

style. Considered by many as the progenitor of computer composition, Xenakis often alters computer-generated material to fit his musical needs.

Kemal Ebcioğlu (1987, 1992) used predicate calculus to develop more than 350 rules of voice-leading for creating chorales in the style of J. S. Bach. His program effectively portrays the basic techniques of four-part writing. William Schottstaedt created Counterpoint Solver (1989) which closely follows the exposition of species counterpoint as given by J. J. Fux around 1725. Schottstaedt's program produces logical counterpoint in a generic sixteenth-century style.

Charles Ames's Cybernetic Composer (1992) creates music in popular and jazz styles. Unlike the programs by Ebcioğlu and Schottstaedt which harmonize given melodies, Cybernetic Composer creates coherent melodies over basic chord progressions. Whether composing rock or ragtime, Cybernetic Composer often produces quite musical results. Christopher Fry's program Flavors Band (1993) produces generic jazz improvisations. Paul Hodgson's software, called Improvisor, mimics, in particular, the styles of Charlie Parker and Louis Armstrong. Improvisor composes in real time and because it mixes rhythmic and melodic patterns includes an element of improvised performance in its output.

Ulf Berggren's doctoral dissertation, *Ars Combinatoria: Algorithmic Construction of Sonata Movements by Means of Building Blocks Derived from W. A. Mozart's Piano Sonatas* (1995), takes snippets of music from sonatas by Mozart and recombines them according to what the program interprets as sensible musical orders. While the music produced often reveals both its sources and the seams by which these sources connect, the program does create occasional moments of interest. Figure 11.7 shows the opening of a first movement Mozart-like sonata as presented in Berggren's dissertation.

Christopher Yavelow's *Push Button Bach* program produces two-part inventions, arguably in the style of J. S. Bach. Figure 1.10 shows one of the works produced by this program. New output is rendered directly in music notation, one of the most attractive features of Push Button Bach. Purists will no doubt argue that this program's output falls far short of being truly Bach-like in style. Its simplicity and accessibility make it nonetheless one of the first such programs freely available over the Internet.

More recently, Dominik Hörnel and Wolfram Menzel (1998) have used neural nets to create music with stylistic similarities to composers of the Renaissance and Baroque periods, focusing primarily on harmonization and melodic variation. Their work departs from previous approaches based on programmed rules. Hörnel and Menzel provide their program with one or more examples of music which the neural network then "learns" through a process called backpropagation.

Figure 1.10
A two-part invention arguably in the style of J. S. Bach by Christopher Yavelow's Push Button Bach program.

The Game

To initiate this current study of virtual music I will use a version of what I have called since my youth The Game. The Game requires players to identify styles and composers of complete examples of music. In each of the three versions of The Game played here, four examples of music are used in both musical notation and in performance on the CD accompanying this book. Game players may listen to each work as many times as desired. The only rule requires players to not review music by the original composers (e.g., the Bach chorales or the Chopin mazurkas here). Players who recognize one or more of the examples should disqualify themselves from playing that particular version of The Game.

The first example of The Game involves recognizing human-composed music as distinct from machine-composed music. At least one of the four examples shown in figure 1.11 was composed by a human composer and at least one was composed by the Experiments in Musical Intelligence program. I have removed articulations, dynamics, and trills from the human-composed example(s) since the version of Experiments in Musical Intelligence that composed its example(s) did not have the capability of including these elements in its output. Many ornamentations aside from trills have been included but appear as normal rhythmic notation rather than as smaller notes. In all cases, these ornaments occur *before* the beat rather than on the beat, which may or may not be the best performance practice for this music.

I have chosen works from the literature that are not generally well known. I have also tried to limit my choices to music which I judge as average rather than exemplary in quality so as not to give either type of music an advantage. Mixing weak human-composed music with strong virtual music would simply fool listeners, whereas my real objective here is to determine whether listeners can truly tell the difference between the two types of music. A score of 50 percent thus represents a more significant indicator of listener lack of discrimination than a score of 100 percent in *either* direction.

As mentioned previously, each of the examples appears on the CD accompanying this book. For readers having the ability to perform the examples at the keyboard, playing through each example in the figure may also provide hints as to the origins of the works. Be careful, however; human composers often have different hand sizes and capabilities and thus awkward fingerings and so on do not necessarily indicate machine composition. All impossible-to-play chords should be rolled from bottom to top rather than played simultaneously. Other indicators, such as large leaps, unusual key signatures or accidentals, metric changes, and so on, may or may not be part of a

Figure 1.11
Four examples of music, at least one of which was composed by a human composer and at least one of which was composed by the Experiments in Musical Intelligence program.

Work 2

Figure 1.11 (continued)

Figure 1.11 (continued)

Work 3

Figure 1.11 (continued)

Figure 1.11 (continued)

Work 4

Figure 1.11 (continued)

Figure 1.11 (continued)

composer's style and should not be taken here as easy indicators of computer composition. The answers to this game appear in appendix E at the end of this book.

The second example of The Game involves four short chorales in the style of J. S. Bach. One or more of the chorales shown in figure 1.12 is by Bach and one or more by the Experiments in Musical Intelligence program. This particular game requires readers to determine not only which works are human-composed but also which ones best follow the style of Bach. As with the previous version of The Game, looking for simple indicators here will disappoint readers. The machine-composed example(s) do not break the commonly recognized rules of Bach four-part writing, nor do they exceed standard vocal ranges. As previously mentioned, the correct responses to this game appear in appendix E at the end of this book.

The third example of The Game presents four mazurkas in the style of Frédéric Chopin. One or more of the mazurkas in figure 1.13 is by Chopin and one or more by the Experiments in Musical Intelligence program. As I initially indicated, ornamentation, with the exception of trills, appears in standard rhythm and occurs in the preceding beat. There are far fewer mazurkas than any of the types of music used in previous versions of The Game and looking in a book of Chopin mazurkas may be tempting. Please avoid doing so, however. Readers who recognize one or more of the mazurkas presented here should disqualify themselves from playing this version of The Game. As with the other versions of The Game, the answers to this game appear in appendix E.

With a total of twelve possible results for all three games, a score of six indicates a difficulty in differentiating between the human and the computer sources for these works, as well as a difficulty in separating virtual music from originals. Scores of greater than eight or less than four indicate a failure on the part of the computer program to effectively imitate human composers. Readers who scored high (8–12) on these versions of The Game, particularly those who have musical backgrounds and thus used more than luck, should try and identify those characteristics which gave the machine-composed examples away. Readers who scored particularly low (0–4) on these versions of The Game might try to discover what led the machine-composed examples to sound as if they were human-composed. Remember that expert musicologists have failed to recognize many examples of Experiments in Musical Intelligence music, while musical amateurs have randomly identified such examples correctly. Results from previous tests with large groups of listeners, such as 5000 in one test in 1992 (see Cope 1996, pp. 81–2), typically average between 40 and 60 percent correct responses.

Figure 1.12
Four chorales in the style of J. S. Bach, at least one of which was composed by Bach and at least one of which was composed by the Experiments in Musical Intelligence program.

Chorale 3

Chorale 4

Figure 1.12 (continued)

Mazurka 1

Figure 1.13
Four mazurkas in the style of Chopin, at least one of which was composed by Chopin and at least one of which was composed by the Experiments in Musical Intelligence program.

Figure 1.13 (continued)

Mazurka 2

Figure 1.13 (continued)

Figure 1.13 (continued)

Mazurka 3

Figure 1.13 (continued)

Figure 1.13 (continued)

Mazurka 4

Figure 1.13 (continued)

Figure 1.13 (continued)

Whatever the scores of your attempts at The Game, two conclusions should be clear. First, all of the music presented is interesting and, on at least some level, convincing. I do not make this assertion lightly. I make it having seen many people play The Game and witnessed the controversy it often creates. Second, distinguishing human-composed music from that created by the Experiments in Musical Intelligence program is often quite difficult, if at all possible. The following descriptions of the program and evaluations of the results of its programming should help to clarify how such results are possible.

2 Staring Emmy Straight in the Eye—And Doing My Best Not to Flinch

Douglas Hofstadter

Editor's Introduction

Doug Hofstadter describes himself modestly as professor of cognitive science at the College of Arts and Sciences at Indiana University Bloomington (where he also directs the Center for Research on Concepts and Cognition) and someone who has had a life-long love for and involvement in music. Beyond this, of course, Hofstadter is an undisputed major figure in cognitive science and especially in the study of creativity. His Pulitzer Prize–winning book Gödel, Escher, Bach *and numerous more recent books cover vast areas of interdisciplinary studies of the visual arts, artificial intelligence, language, music, and mathematics.*

Hofstadter here offers a number of critical insights into what he believes are the implications and challenges of the Experiments in Musical Intelligence program. He shares with us his angst *over the program's apparent ability to fool people with its virtual music and to often provide convincing musical experiences which he heretofore believed only human-composed music could inspire.*

As Doug states, he and I have had many discussions about Experiments in Musical Intelligence. His article here demonstrates a keen understanding of the basic fundamentals of the program. However, Doug's interpretation of the program does not include a discussion of earmarks, transformation, and so on due either to their recent appearance in the program or the unnecessary complication their inclusion would create. He nonetheless gives a compelling description of how Experiments in Musical Intelligence works.

For the record, Doug refers to Experiments in Musical Intelligence using the familiar name "Emmy" in his prose and "EMI" or "E.M.I." in his poetry. I have preserved the latter acronym for purposes of rhyme but wish to make clear that there is no relationship between the EMI or E.M.I. acronyms and the Thorne EMI Corporation.

Good artists borrow; great artists steal.
—Douglas Hofstadter[1]

How Young I Was, and How Naive

I am not now, nor have I ever been, a card-carrying futurologist. I make no claims to be able to peer into the murky crystal ball and make out what lies far ahead. But one time, back in 1977, I did go a little bit out on a futurologist's limb. At the end of

Chapter 19 ("Artificial Intelligence: Prospects") of my book *Gödel, Escher, Bach* (1979), I had a section called "Ten Questions and Speculations," and in it I stuck my neck out, venturing a few predictions about how things would go in the development of AI. Though it is a little embarrassing to me now, let me nonetheless quote a few lines from that section here:

Question: Will there be chess programs that can beat anyone?

Speculation: No. There may be programs which can beat anyone at chess, but they will not be exclusively chess players. They will be programs of *general* intelligence, and they will be just as temperamental as people. "Do you want to play chess?" "No, I'm bored with chess. Let's talk about poetry." That may be the kind of dialogue you could have with a program that could beat everyone ...

We all know today how very wrong that speculation was. What was it that so misled the author of *Gödel, Escher, Bach* back then?

Well, when I wrote those words, I was drawing some of my ideas from a fascinating article that I had read by my soon-to-be colleague at Indiana University, the psychologist and chess master Eliot Hearst (formerly vice president of the U.S. Chess Federation [USCF], member of the U.S. Chess Olympics team, and once a frequent playing partner of Bobby Fischer). In his article (1977), Hearst (who clearly knew infinitely more about chess than I ever could hope to) eloquently expressed the conviction that deep chess-playing ability depends in an intimate manner on such cognitive skills as the ability to sort the wheat from the chaff in an intuitive flash, the ability to make subtle analogies, and the ability to recall memories associatively. All of these elusive abilities seemed to lie so close to the core of human nature itself that I jumped to the conclusion that profoundly insightful chess-playing draws intrinsically on central facets of the human condition, and that mere brute-force searching of the rapidly branching look-ahead tree, no matter how fast, broad, or deep, would not be able to circumvent or shortcut that fact.

I didn't realize—and perhaps no one did at the time—that the USCF rankings of the best computer chess programs (all of which used brute-force search algorithms) were pretty much creeping up linearly with time, so that a simple-minded linear extrapolation on a plot of chess prowess vs. time would, even back then, have suggested that computers would take over from humans somewhere around the year 2000. The first time I actually saw such a graph was in an article in *Scientific American* in the mid-1990s (written by the creators of Deep Blue, by the way), and I vividly remember thinking to myself, when I looked at it, "Uh-oh! The handwriting is on the wall!" And so it was.

Chess Tumbles to Computational Power . . .

We now know that world-class chess-playing ability can indeed be achieved by brute-force techniques—techniques that in no way attempt to replicate or emulate what goes on in the head of a chess grandmaster. Analogy-making is not needed, nor is associative memory, nor are intuitive flashes that sort wheat from chaff—just a tremendously wide and deep search, carried out by superfast, chess-specialized hardware using ungodly amounts of stored knowledge. And thus, thanks to the remarkable achievements of the past decade, one can no longer look at a subtle, elegant, and stunning midgame chess move and say with confidence, "Only a genius could have spotted that move!" because the move could just as well have emanated from a mindless, lightning-fast full-width search as from the silent machinations of an insightful human mind.

I cannot say what goes on in the brain of a Bobby Fischer or a Garry Kasparov when they play championship-level chess. I have no idea whether their phenomenal chess-playing ability draws in some subtle way on their entire human existence, on their prior struggles with life and death, on their striving for personal identity, on their coping with dashed romances, on their hopes and fears in domains apparently remote from chess—or, contrariwise, whether their chess-playing skill is in some sense totally isolated from the rest of their minds, fully contained in some little localized region of their brains that, at least in principle, could be neatly excised by a neurosurgeon, leaving the rest of their brains fully intact so that they could go on living normal lives while the little module, safely preserved and nourished in a vat, happily kept on playing world-level chess.

Eliot Hearst's article had led me to believe that the image of an isolated chess-playing module is wrong, and that, to the contrary, great chess-playing skill is of necessity deeply intertwined with all that being human is about. But as Deep Blue has taught us, that certainly need not be the case. Topnotch chess-playing does not necessarily depend on the full mental complexities that come from living life, facing death, and all those messy things that we experience. Topnotch chess playing *can* come from a pure chess engine, full stop. As for topnotch *human* chess-playing ability, one might still plausibly believe that it is necessarily tightly integrated with the rest of the brain and with the whole kit and caboodle of being human—but ever since Deep Blue's appearance on the scene, there is reason to doubt that romantic vision. Perhaps it is the case, but perhaps not.

I, in any case, have had to eat humble pie with respect to my 1977 speculation. But, I must say, having to swallow my words about chess doesn't upset me all that much, since, aside from writing that one speculation, I personally have never had any emotional stake in the notion that chess skill lies very near the pinnacle of that which is most truly human, and so I'm not crushed that my speculation was refuted. And even though people say that the game of Go is far less computer-tractable than chess is, I don't think I'd care to rewrite my speculation substituting Go for chess. I'll just admit my mistake.

So ... chess-playing fell to computers? I don't feel particularly threatened or upset; after all, sheer computation had decades earlier fallen to computers as well. So a computer had outdone Daniel Shanks in the calculation of digits of π—did it matter? Did that achievement in any way lower human dignity? Of course not! It simply taught us that calculation is more mechanical than we had realized. Likewise, Deep Blue taught us that chess is more mechanical than we had realized. These lessons serve as interesting pieces of information about various domains of expertise, but to my mind they hardly seem to threaten the notion, which I then cherished and which I still cherish, that human intelligence is extraordinarily profound and mysterious.

It is not, I hasten to add, that I am a mystic who thinks that intelligence intrinsically resists implantation in physical entities. To the contrary, I look upon brains themselves as very complex machines, and, unlike John Searle and Roger Penrose, I have always maintained that the precise nature of the physicochemical substrate of thinking and consciousness is irrelevant. I can imagine silicon-based thought as easily as I can imagine carbon-based thought; I can imagine ideas and meanings and emotions and a first-person awareness of the world (an "inner light," a "ghost in the machine") emerging from electronic circuitry as easily as from proteins and nucleic acids. I simply have always run on faith that when "genuine artificial intelligence" (sorry for the oxymoron) finally arises, it will do so precisely because the same degree of complexity and the same overall kind of abstract mental architecture will have come to exist in a new kind of hardware. What I do *not* expect, however, is that full human intelligence will emerge from something far simpler, architecturally speaking, than a human brain.

... and so, Is Musical Beauty Next in Line?

My "Ten Questions and Speculations" section in *GEB* was an attempt to articulate just these kinds of pieces of faith, and at the time I wrote it, I was particularly proud of another one of them, which I now reproduce here in full:

Question: Will a computer program ever write beautiful music?

Speculation: Yes, but not soon. Music is a language of emotions, and until programs have emotions as complex as ours, there is no way a program will write anything beautiful. There can be "forgeries"—shallow imitations of the syntax of earlier music—but despite what one might think at first, there is much more to musical expression than can be captured in syntactical rules. There will be no new kinds of beauty turned up for a long time by computer music-composing programs. Let me carry this thought a little further. To think—and I have heard this suggested—that we might soon be able to command a preprogrammed mass-produced mail-order twenty-dollar desk-model "music box" to bring forth from its sterile [sic!] circuitry pieces which Chopin or Bach might have written had they lived longer is a grotesque and shameful misestimation of the depth of the human spirit. A "program" which could produce music as they did would have to wander around the world on its own, fighting its way through the maze of life and feeling every moment of it. It would have to understand the joy and loneliness of a chilly night wind, the longing for a cherished hand, the inaccessibility of a distant town, the heartbreak and regeneration after a human death. It would have to have known resignation and world-weariness, grief and despair, determination and victory, piety and awe. In it would have had to commingle such opposites as hope and fear, anguish and jubilation, serenity and suspense. Part and parcel of it would have to be a sense of grace, humor, rhythm, a sense of the unexpected—and of course an exquisite awareness of the magic of fresh creation. Therein, and therein only, lie the sources of meaning in music.

In recent years, when lecturing about Dave Cope's work, I have read this paragraph aloud so many times that I practically know it by heart. And what do I make of it now? Well, I am not quite sure. I have been grappling for several years now with these issues, and still there is no clear resolution. That, perhaps, is why I have been so fascinated by Cope's Emmy and the issues raised thereby. Let me explain.

In the spring of 1995, I was conducting a cognitive science seminar at Indiana University called "AI: Hype versus Hope," whose purpose was for me and my students, working together, to try to sort the wheat from the chaff in this field so rife with brazen claims of human-level performance in one domain or another, most of which I knew were groundless, or nearly so. I was willing to concede, however, that even in a hopelessly hyped project, there might somewhere reside a nugget of value, and it was my idea that we would uncover those nuggets while at the same time chucking out the overblown claims. We discussed computer driving of cars, speech recognition, story understanding, machine translation, face recognition, and many other topics. One topic that particularly interested me was music, because I was convinced, a priori, that claims I'd heard here and there about high-quality music emanating from computers were hugely exaggerated, and I wanted to confirm this hunch. And so when a student in the seminar told me she had run across a book called *Computers and Musical Style* in the music library and wondered if she could present it to the seminar, I enthusiastically encouraged her to do so.

A couple of days later in class, this student described to us the ideas behind the program—Emmy, to be specific—but I found myself not terribly interested. It sounded like Emmy was dealing only with the surface level of music—with patterns,

artistic creativity; hardly anyone seemed threatened or worried at all. I felt kinship with but a few souls in the world who also were bewildered by similar triumphs. One of them was none other than Garry Kasparov, who had said, a year before being trounced by Deep Blue:

> To some extent, this match is a defense of the whole human race. Computers play such a huge role in society. They are everywhere. But there is a frontier that they must not cross. They must not cross into the area of human creativity. It would threaten the existence of human control in such areas as art, literature, and music.   (Kasparov 1996)

On one level, Kasparov's words sounded ridiculous to me. Saying computers "must not cross into ... human creativity" seemed hopelessly naive, almost like saying, "We must not let them do certain things, because they'll beat our pants off if we do, and won't that be dreadful!" And Kasparov's last sentence, even sillier, raises the specter of computers trying to wrest control away from human beings, as if on the surface of our planet there were already raging some terrible battle between alien species for control of culture. Such a weird scenario may possibly come to be in the next few decades or next few centuries—who can say for sure?—but certainly it is not happening already. Today we control computers, and that is beyond doubt or dispute.

And yet ... and yet ... something of Kasparov's worried tone resonated with me. It was as if he had felt, and I now felt, something about the profundity of the human mind's sublimity being taken away, being robbed, by the facile victories of programs that seemed totally out of touch with the essence of the domains in which they were operating so well. It seemed somehow humiliating, even nightmarish, to me.

But no matter how I tried, I could not get my own sense of confusion and worry across to my audience. One thing I learned fairly soon was that few people have a visceral feeling about the centrality and depth of music. Indeed, I discovered that there is a rough trichotomy of people. There are some who, like me, feel that music is the most powerful drug in the world, and that it reaches in and touches one's innermost core like almost nothing else—more powerfully than art, than literature, than cinema, and so on. But such people are few and far between. A much more common attitude is, "Sure I like music, but it doesn't touch me at my very core. It's just fun to listen to, to dance to, and so forth." And then another attitude that came up surprisingly often in question-and-answer sessions after my lectures was this: "I'm kind of tone-deaf, and music's okay but I can take it or leave it, so I don't really relate to your deep love of music, but ..."

I soon realized that I was probably not going to reach the third group no matter what I said, and wondered if the "music enthusiasts" of the middle group were also beyond reach. But to my greater chagrin, even most people in the *first* group often couldn't relate to my worry! This I found utterly baffling.

In pondering how I might more effectively transmit my admittedly nonscientific, totally emotional concerns to a wide audience and gain their sympathy, I somehow came up with the idea of putting my ideas into rhyming quatrains. And so, before long, I had converted a great deal of the lecture into verse. As I tried it out on audiences, I found that the serious ideas in my message, now "leaner and meaner," seemed to reach more people. Perhaps part of the reason for this is that I put on a kind of artistic persona in my rhymes, which allowed me to express myself in a more personal manner than I would dare to do in prose.

The first time I gave my versified lecture was, amusingly, in a back-to-back pair of lectures with Dave Cope right on his home turf in Santa Cruz, and our complementary talks went over very well. I might add that Dave himself—as one might expect, since music is his profession—belongs to that first category (the most intense lovers of music), and he and I even share a great deal in musical taste. This makes the discrepancy in our attitudes toward Emmy all the more striking, and, needless to say, thought-provoking.

Is Music Just Splicings of Licks, and No More?

Without further ado, let me now proceed to describe Emmy a little bit, and then begin giving my reactions in verse form. The basic idea behind Emmy is what Dave Cope terms "recombinant music"—the identification of recurrent structures of various sorts in a composer's output, and the reusing of those structures in new arrangements, so as to construct a new piece "in the same style." One can thus imagine feeding in Beethoven's nine symphonies, and Emmy coming out with Beethoven's Tenth (or Brahms' First, if you subscribe to the claims of some musicologists that in his First Symphony, Brahms carried on the Beethoven spirit beyond the grave).

Toward the beginning of *Computers and Musical Style*, his first book about Emmy, Cope says this about his personal pathway of exploration:

In 1981, during a moment of recklessness, I wrote the following in a daily journal:

> *I envision a time in which new works will be convincingly composed in the styles of composers long dead. These will be commonplace and, while never as good as the originals, they will be exciting, entertaining, and interesting. Musicians and non-musicians alike will interact with programs that allow them to endlessly tinker with the styles of the composing programs ... I see none of this as problematic. Machines, after all, only add and subtract. Programs that benefit from those operations are only as good as their creators.*

This book describes many aspects of a program I have since devised for the replication of musical styles ... If there is a discovery here, it is that one way of defining style is through pattern recognition and that musical style can be imitated if one can find what constitutes musical patterns.   (Cope 1991a, p. xiii)

Here, then, is my opening salvo of quatrains in reaction to Cope's characterization of musical style as patterns.

Is music a craft,
Or is it an art?
Does it come from mere training,
Or spring from the heart?

Is music just notes,
Merely patterns combined
By a cocktail-bar pianist
With a wandering mind?

Though Fats Waller's ticklin'
Suggests profound joy,
Might it all be illusion
From a practiced riff-boy?

Does music, like poetry,
Cry from one's core,
Or is it just splicings
Of licks, and no more?

Do the études by Chopin
Reveal his soul's mood,
Or was Frédéric Chopin
Just some slick "pattern dude"?

Was Chopin a zombie with
The gift of piano gab?
Did he toss off mazurkas
Much as party bores blab?

Could he turn off his brain
And continue to sing
In true heart-rending fashion—
Or would one miss some zing?

Was Bach a musician
Or mere *Musikant*?
Did Johann his passion
Express—or just cant?

In the furnace of Bach,
Did there burn a pilot light,
Or did Joh. Seb. compose
On cool autopilot flight?

There's music that's trite,
And there's music that's deep—
Or is that the truth?
Does all music come cheap?

Can one bypass the soul,
Can one sidestep all strife,
And produce wondrous music
Without living life?

That's the crux of my talk;
The idea, I hope, 's clear.
And until recently,
I myself had no fear.

A skeptic shot through,
But then one day I heard
Some not half-bad tunes
From a program. My word!

So can style be learned
By mechanical means?
Can Rodgers be churned
Out by Hart-less machines?

Soul-fire in Cole Porter
Began his Beguine;
Can we order more Porter
From a Cole-less machine?

Well, so begins my commentary—making no bones about setting forth an emotional point of view. But if one is to form an educated opinion of Emmy, one's first duty is obviously to familiarize oneself with how the program works. Cope, naturally, has his own ways of explaining Emmy, but I have found it useful to rephrase what I have learned over these past few years, and I think that hearing it from an outsider's viewpoint may help to clarify certain difficult points. Moreover, I found more than once, in talking with Dave, that he would provide highly revelatory answers to key questions—questions that were not answered anywhere in his writings, and in fact in most cases were not even posed in his books. Such interchanges gave me a kind of personal insight into some aspects of Emmy that I believe may be useful to share, and so, with that as my excuse, I now present my amateur's capsule portrait of Emmy's innards.

A Personal View of How Emmy Works

Emmy's central modus operandi, given a set of input pieces (usually all by a single composer and belonging to the same general form, such as *mazurka*) is:

(1) chop up; (2) reassemble.

This, in three words, is what Cope means by the phrase "recombinant music." Caveat: The assembly phase, in contrast to Mozart's famous *Musikalisches Würfelspiel*, which produced waltzes by random shuffling of 3/4 measures, is anything but haphazard or willy-nilly (as if by throwing dice). There are significant principles constraining what can be tacked onto what, and these principles are formulated so as to guarantee coherence (at least to the extent that the input pieces themselves are coherent!). I summarize these two principles as follows:

1. Make the *local flow-pattern* of each voice similar to that in source pieces.
2. Make the *global positioning* of fragments similar to that in source pieces.

These could be likened to two types of constraints that a jigsaw-puzzle solver naturally exploits when putting together a jigsaw puzzle:

1. The *shape* of each piece meshes tightly with those of neighboring pieces.
2. The *stuff* shown on each piece makes sense in the context of the picture.

The former of these constraints might be characterized as *syntactic meshing*, or meshing based solely on *form*, while the latter could be characterized as *semantic meshing*, or meshing based solely on *content*. In isolation, perhaps neither of them would be too impressive, but when used together, they form a powerful pair of constraints. But how does my jigsaw-puzzle metaphor translate into specific musical terms?

Syntactic Meshing in Emmy: Voice-Hooking and Texture-Matching

Let me first consider the first of these constraints—that involving form, or what one might call "coherence of flow." This constraint in fact breaks down into two facets:

(1) voice-hooking; (2) texture-matching.

To understand these two distinct facets of syntactic meshing, one has to imagine that a new piece is being put together note by note, in sequence, and that to this end, short fragments of input pieces are being selected so as to mesh with the current context. Imagine that we have just inserted a fragment f_1, and are considering whether to insert fragment f_2 right after it, drawn from somewhere in the input. Voice-hooking would be the requirement that *the initial note of the melodic line of fragment f_2 should coincide with the next melodic note to which fragment f_1 led in its original context.* In other words, a given fragment's melodic line should link up smoothly with the melodic line of its successor fragment. This is very much like saying that two puzzle pieces should fit together physically.

Of course, here I referred only to the melodic, or soprano, line of a piece. One can also insist on voice-hooking of the bass-line, and of intermediate lines as well (tenor, alto, and so on). Ideally, voice-hooking can be carried out successfully on all voices at once, but if not, then the most logical voices to sacrifice are the inner ones, then the bass-line, and last of all, the melodic line. Usually, provided there is a sufficient quantity of input pieces, it will be possible to achieve a good deal of satisfaction in voice-hooking.

In addition, there is *texture-matching*, which is basically the idea that *the notes in a chord can be moved up or down pitchwise by full octaves and can be spread out time-wise so as to match some preexistent local pattern in the piece being composed.* Most typically, these two operations result in the "spinning-out" of a simple chord into an arpeggio that matches some preestablished arpeggiation pattern. Thus, a purely vertical C–E–G triad could be spun out, for instance, into a C–G–E–G figure to be incorporated into an Alberti-type bass-line, or into a very wide E–C–G arpeggio to match the widely arpeggiated pattern of the bass-line of a Chopin-like nocturne. It could even be turned into the very long sequence of notes "C–E–G–C–E–G–C–E; C–E–G–C–E–G–C–E," which you may recognize as the melody in the first measure of the C major Prelude of Book I of Bach's *Well-Tempered Clavier*. Basically, the pattern of that piece is so regular that it is a mechanical act to spin out a triad into a whole sixteen-note sequence.

Semantic Meshing in Emmy: Tension–Resolution Logic and SPEAC Labels

We now turn to the second constraint—that involving content, or what one might call "tension–resolution logic." This is where ideas devised by Cope as part of Emmy may in fact constitute a significant new contribution to music theory. The basic idea is that one wishes to insert a fragment into a new piece only if *the "location" of the insertion is similar to the "location" of the fragment where it occurred in some input piece.* The word "location" is put in quotes here because it is not clear what it means. Indeed, the italicized phrase forces one to ask the puzzling question, "How can a given fragment be 'in the same location' with respect to two different pieces? How can one compare 'locations' inside totally different pieces? What, indeed, might 'location' inside a piece be taken to mean (since, self-evidently, using measure number would be a pathetic travesty of an answer)?"

Cope decided that "location" must be defined in a way that involves both global and local contexts—in fact, a series of nested contexts, ranging from very local (notes, measures), to medium-range (phrases), to large-scale (periods), to global (sections). To a fragment on any of these distinct hierarchical levels (and there can be any number of such structural levels), Cope attaches a label—one of the five letters *S, P, E, A, C*—which attempts to capture what I have chosen to call the *tension–resolution status* of that fragment. These letters stand for the following words: *statement, preparation, extension, antecedent, consequent.* The label-assignment process proceeds from most local to most global, with the labels of larger sections dependent upon the labels already assigned to their component pieces.

Unfortunately, the details of the label-assignment process are unclear to me, but in essence it starts at the most local level, where the presence of specific scale degrees in the various voices is used as the main diagnostic for the labeling of a chord (co-presence of tonic and dominant, for instance, or tonic and mediant, suggests an *S* label at that level). From there on out, certain characteristic sequences of local labels are telltale cues that suggest specific higher-level labels, and so on, always moving upward hierarchically. In the end one winds up with SPEAC labels attached to sections of many different sizes and, perforce, at many different structural levels.

The upshot of this many-leveled labeling process carried out by Emmy is that any local fragment of an input piece winds up with a set of labels—its own label, that of the larger fragment inside which it sits, then that of the next-larger fragment in which that one sits, and so on, and so on. Thus hypothetically, a given chord in an input piece could have the following set of labels (proceeding from most local to most global): A–C–C–E–P–A–S, and another chord might have the hierarchical series of labels E–S–C–S, and so on. In either case, such a series of letters basically tells you, on several different hierarchical levels, just what the tension–resolution status of the piece is at the chord concerned. And that—provided it really works well—would seem about as good a way of saying "where you are" in a piece as any I could imagine, since tension and resolution on many levels really do constitute the crux of musical meaning.

Now the trick is to use these labels to guide composition, and the basic idea is fairly straightforward. Suppose that in our piece-under-construction we find ourselves in a location whose tension–resolution status is PACSCS (moving from most local to most global). The letters *P-A-C-S-C-S* tell us "where we are," so to speak, inside our new piece. And so, in choosing a fragment to borrow from an input piece and to insert right here, our main criterion will naturally be that the chosen fragment's tension–resolution status inside its original piece was exactly PACSCS—in other words, that the fragment we are going to quote lies in "the same place" inside its original piece as in the new piece.

If in the input corpus we find several such "same-location" fragments, that is good, since it gives us a choice of how to continue, but we of course also want to satisfy the syntactic voice-hooking constraint. We thus throw away any fragments that do not match in this manner. If after this paring-down, there are still several potential fragments surviving and vying with each other for insertion, then we can choose one at random.

Suppose, on the other hand, that there is no input fragment that has exactly the desired multilevel tension–resolution status—how then to proceed? The only solution is to sacrifice something—but what? Cope decided that in such circumstances, global status is more sacrificeable than local, and so we lop off the final letter, leaving us with PACSC, and now we try again to find an appropriate fragment in the input corpus. If this fails, we lop off one more letter (thus giving PACS), and we search again in the input corpus. Since through such lopping-off we are loosening ever further the constraint of matching tension–resolution status, we will eventually find one or more input fragments that match the labels that we seek, and then we can choose randomly among those fragments, provided that voice-hooking also works. And thus the piece gets extended a little bit. At this point, we restart the constrained search process and extend the growing composition a little bit more—and so forth and so on. Thus, like a crystal growing outward, is built up a piece of music by Emmy.

In summary, here, in my own words, is the core of Emmy's composition process:

Sequential assembly of fragments that have the highest possible degree of agreement of SPEAC labels on all hierarchical levels

Stitching-together of fragments so as to respect voice-hooking constraints and so as to match local textures

Signatures

The preceding is the true core of Emmy, but in addition there are two other important mechanisms that should be described here as well. The first is what Cope calls *signatures*. A signature is a characteristic intervallic pattern that recurs throughout a composer's oeuvre, the use of which lends a high degree of seeming authenticity to a freshly composed piece. To find signatures, Cope has Emmy scour all input pieces for pairs of short note-sequences (say, between four and twelve notes, although there is no strict cutoff) whose intervallic patterns match either exactly or approximately. Thus, for instance, C–B–C–G would *exactly* match F–E–F–C, and would be a *near* match for D–C–D–A (the difference being that the first and second intervals are semitones in C–B–C–G, and whole-tones in D–C–D–A). Emmy scours the input for exact matches, and then gradually loosens up the search (relaxing the criteria governing interval-matching), until a satisfactory number of recurrent patterns have been found.

The variable numerical parameters in the computer code that determine whether a potential match is judged satisfactory or not are called "controllers," and during a search for signatures, one must adjust the controllers until just the right number of signatures is found—not too few but not too many either. I know that in the past, Cope tended to do this adjustment of controllers himself in order to increase the effectiveness of Emmy's search for signatures, but perhaps by now he has managed to automate that aspect of the process. In any case, among the subtlest of controllers are those that winnow "insignificant" notes out of a given passage, leaving just "significant" ones; thanks to such controllers, Emmy can then match a highly embellished melodic fragment that contains, say, twenty very rapid notes with another melodic fragment that contains only four slow notes, and can discover the core signature that they share. Thus signatures found by Emmy can be very subtle indeed.

An important point is that such matching of intervallic patterns must take place *across* pieces, rather than *within* a given piece—for the obvious reason that any given piece will reuse its own motives many times, and Cope is not trying—indeed, he does not wish—to get Emmy to reproduce the melodic lines of a given piece, but rather he wishes Emmy to pick up on and to exploit the recurrent (but less obvious) melodic patterns that a composer tends to reuse from piece to piece, probably without even being aware of doing so.

It may not seem a priori evident, needless to say, that all composers do have signature motives, but this has turned out to be the case. One might tend to think that the existence of many signatures would show that a composer is rut-bound, and perhaps it does, but in any case, it is a universal fact, revealed in undeniable fashion by Cope's work on Emmy, that each composer does employ interval-pattern motives that recur in piece after piece.

Once such signatures have been identified in the input, they are stored in a database, with each diverse instance of a given signature being stored *together with its underlying harmonies*, thus all ready for insertion *as a whole* inside a new piece. You might suppose that the insertion of prepackaged, precisely quoted chunks would risk producing passages that sound like pure plagiarism, but surprisingly, these prepackaged chunks are usually so generic-seeming and so small that, even to a highly astute listener, they don't shout from the rooftops which precise piece they came from; they merely sound like the given composer in a nonspecific, nonpinpointable manner.

Templagiarism

The second mechanism that I wish to describe here is what I dub "templagiarism," short for "template plagiarism"—a fascinating, more abstract version of the signature concept. If, in scanning a given input piece, Emmy notes that a motive appears in quick succession two or more times (again with some liberty taken in the matching, thus allowing variants of a given motive, such as tonal entries of a fugue theme, to be counted as "equal" to each other), it records the following data for these entries: (1) the *pitch displacement* of the new occurrence relative to the previous occurrence, and (2) the *temporal displacement* of the new occurrence relative to the previous occurrence. In short, Emmy records, for any repeated motive, the "where-and-when" pattern that characterizes the motive's repetitions. Emmy then detaches this abstract pattern from the specific motive in question, and takes it to be characteristic of the composer's style. Note that this is a higher-order architectural stylistic feature than a mere signature, because it is concerned not with any motive itself but with how that motive recurs within a piece.

Templagiarism can be an astonishingly effective style-evoking device, as I found out one day when listening, in Cope's living room, to "Prokofiev's Tenth Sonata for

Piano" (as Dave humorously, or perhaps hubristically, dubs one of Emmy's pieces, about which more later). As the second movement started, I heard a very striking chromatically descending eight-note motive in midrange, then moments later heard the same motive way up high on the keyboard, then once again a few notes lower, and then one last time very deep down in the bass-line. These widely spread entries gave an amazing feeling of coherence to the music. Indeed, for me the passage reeked of Prokofievian impishness, and I thought, "Good God, how in the world did Emmy do *that*?" It sounded so well calculated (not in the computer sense of the term!), so inventive, so full of musical intelligence.

Astonished, I asked Dave what was going on, and he replied, "Well, somewhere in one of the input movements on which this movement is drawing, there must be some motive—totally different from *this* motive, of course!—that occurs four times in rapid succession with exactly these same timing displacements and pitch displacements." Then he spelled out more explicitly the concept of templagiarism to me. It would have been pleasing if at that point we had scoured Prokofiev's scores until we found exactly such an episode, but we didn't take the trouble to do so. I'll take Dave's word for it that we would find it somewhere or other.

Cope's idea of templagiarism is itself brilliant and devilishly impish: it borrows a touch of genius from the composer at such a high level of abstraction that when the pattern is simply quoted lock, stock, and barrel—plagiarized, no more, no less— it once again sounds like a touch of genius, but an utterly fresh and new one. The reason it sounds fresh and new is, of course, that in order to quote the template, you need to supplement it with a new "low-level" ingredient—a new motive—and so the quotation, though exact on the *template* level, sounds truly novel on the *note* level, even if one is intimately familiar with the input piece from which the template was drawn. New filler material has been spliced into an old template that bears the unmistakable stamp of a specific genius, and so the whole passage has a powerfully compelling feel to it—a deep musical mind seems to lie behind it.

It's a bit as if one were to use fancy speech-synthesis technology to make the very familiar voice and accent of, say, John Kennedy come out with utterances that Kennedy himself never made—perhaps nonsense statements, perhaps cheap rabble-rousing inanities that he would have despised, whatever. Despite their falsified content, they would still sound for all the world like Kennedy (at the voice level, at least), and such statements probably would seem genuine to most people.

I must admit that I don't have a clear understanding of how the very complex operation of templagiarism (or, for that matter, the somewhat simpler operation of insertion of signatures) is made to coexist harmoniously with the previously described syntactic and semantic meshing-operations, because I can easily imagine them conflicting with each other. Nor do I understand how Emmy composes a "motive" and deems it worthy of use as such in an extended movement. But of course, how could I? It would probably take many months of intense study of Emmy to understand such matters. I remain an intrigued outsider, and hope and expect that over time, Dave will explain Emmy's principles ever more lucidly.

The Acid Test: Hearing and Voting

The foregoing provides a summary of what I myself have absorbed about the workings of Emmy, both from reading Cope's books and from a good number of one-on-one conversations with him. We now continue with a few more of my quatrains about Emmy.

David Cope, a composer
At UCSC,
Has a program make music
From S, P, E, A, C.

Cope's "EMI" takes scores
By, say, Bach—scores of scores!
Then it scours these scores
For Bach-style "signatures."

From a "style-free" scaffolding
(A pattern of "SPEAC" 's),
The program hangs signatures,
And lo! Old Bach speaks!

So is music an art,
Or is it merely a craft?
Remember at whom it was
That they all laughed.

The proof's in the pudding
(In this case, the ears);
If you've not heard EMI,
Don't prejudge it with sneers.

At this juncture in my lecture, I have almost always had a live pianist—sometimes Dave's wife Mary Jane Cope, who is on the music faculty at UC Santa Cruz—perform a handful of small two-voice pieces for the audience. The listeners are forewarned that there is at least one piece by Johann Sebastian Bach in the group, and at least one by Emmy in the style of Johann Sebastian Bach, and they should try to figure out which ones are by whom (or by what).

As a prelude and to set the proper tone, I first read aloud the following two short excerpts from Cope's *Computers and Music Style* (Cope 1991a), the first one describing a very simplified version of Emmy which Cope devised solely for pedagogical purposes, and the second one ushering in the chapter in which the full-strength Emmy—at least the Emmy of that vintage—is carefully discussed (though it is certainly not described in full detail):

It will create small two-part inventions similar in nature (not in quality) to those created by Bach.   (p. 98)

For the true inheritance of Bach's style to take place, a much more elaborate program would be necessary. This more elaborate program is presented in the description of Emmy in the next chapter.   (p. 136)

Make of that telling little phrase "the true inheritance" what you will . . .

After the pieces have been performed, I tell the audience that they are now going to vote (with the proviso that anyone who has recognized a piece from their knowledge of the classical repertoire is disenfranchised). The result has usually been that most of the audience picks the genuine Bach as genuine, but usually it is only about a two-thirds majority, with roughly one third getting it wrong. And it is not by any means always the less sophisticated audience members who make the wrong classification. In any case, once people have made their vote, I then return to my verse, as follows:

Well, now you've heard EMI,
Perhaps you feel had.
In your shoes, so would I.
When one's fooled, one feels bad.

And if you were right,
Not a single guess wrong,
You've the right to feel smug
For a while—but how long?

So you told Bach from EMI,
So you've got quite keen ears;
But EMI's evolving—
Just wait a few years.

To Sound like Bach and to Speak like Bach

It is indeed true that Emmy is evolving—it is a moving target. Cope began work on his program in 1981, and in all these years he has not let up on it. Emmy's early pieces are, like any fledgling composer's, pretty amateurish affairs, but her later output sounds increasingly impressive, and Cope has grown more and more ambitious over time. Whereas initially he was proud of Emmy's production of short two-part inventions and short mazurkas, he now has Emmy producing entire sonatas, concertos, and symphonies. There is even a "Mahler opera" under way or in the works—something that would certainly be a challenge for any human composer to carry off.

What exactly is the difference between stylistic imitation as carried out by a human being and stylistic imitation carried out by a computer program? My friend Bernard Greenberg has been writing music in the style of J. S. Bach (and other composers, but Bach most of all) for decades. Indeed, among my life's most amazing memories are of visits to Bernie's apartment, where, as I listened to him play his own soulful pieces on the organ, filled with complex dissonances and marvelously unexpected turns of phrase, I felt as if I were in the presence of Old Bach himself. One time I brought along a mutual friend to listen, and he—also a gifted musician—made the following unforgettable remark to Bernie: "Gee, not only is your music in the Bach style but it *sounds* good, too!" I always found this remark extremely puzzling, since to me the very *essence* of Bach style is that it "sounds good." How could something possibly sound deeply *Bach-like* and yet also sound *bad*? The tone of the remark made no sense to me—and yet I must admit that Bernie himself once made a related remark about the secrets of capturing Bach's style: "The trick is to make music not that *sounds* like him, but that also *speaks* like him."

The Nested Circles of Style

Well, of course, what is being hinted at here, though in a blurry way, is that style is a multilayered phenomenon. There are shallow aspects to style (how a piece "sounds," in Bernie's terms), and then there are deep aspects (how it "speaks"). It is quite possible that someone could be capable of capturing many of the shallower trademarks of a composer and yet miss the bull's-eye as far as essence is concerned. I always think of Schumann's short piano piece called "Chopin," which occurs in his *Carnaval*, which on one level "sounds like" a Chopin nocturne—it has the characteristic wide left-hand arpeggios and a lot of melodic embellishment—and yet on a deeper level it quite misses the mark in terms of Chopin soul (at least to my ear).

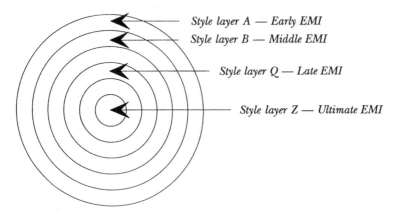

Style layer A — Early EMI

Style layer B — Middle EMI

Style layer Q — Late EMI

Style layer Z — Ultimate EMI

Figure 2.1
An extremely simple yet seemingly inevitable diagram pertaining to stylistic imitation.

This talk of different levels of style and of targets and bull's-eyes suggests the following extremely simple yet seemingly inevitable diagram pertaining to stylistic imitation (see figure 2.1).

Someone who glibly captures only the most obvious features of a composer's style—an Alberti bass, say, for Mozart—would fall in the outer ring but leave all inner rings untouched. A deeper imitator would add other outer layers of style but fail to penetrate all the way to the core, or stylistic bull's-eye. But only someone who had dedicated years to the art, and whose emotional makeup, moreover, bore a deep affinity to that of the composer in question (and this is how I see Bernie vis-à-vis Bach), could hope to come close to that elusive central core that constitutes true Chopinity or Bachitude.

And yet . . . there is something most troubling to me about this diagram, as I have drawn it—namely, the fact that the ring with the greatest area is the outermost one, not the innermost one. This disturbs me because it suggests that you will get the most effect from the simplest and shallowest tricks. The diagram suggests that as you proceed further and further in—as your mastery of the art ever deepens—the area you are adding becomes smaller and smaller. When you have acquired but one layer of style mastery, your music will surely not fool experts, but it might fool 80 percent of the general populace. Work harder, add the second ring of mastery, and now you fool 90 percent. Add the third ring, and your fooling rate goes up to, say, 95 percent, and the fourth ring gets you to 98 percent. There's still something missing, but sadly, the missing ingredient is getting subtler and subtler, tinier and tinier . . . In the end, then, with all but the innermost circle, you may wind up reliably fooling all of the world's top experts, while still lacking Bach's true soul. In short, it's a most depressing thought, if the nested-circles image is accurate, that the innermost layer, though surely the most difficult of all layers to acquire, is also the smallest and perhaps, therefore, the least significant in terms of its effect upon listeners.

There are layers of style
From the skin to the core.
The former are patterns;
The latter—something more?

If style's many layers
Are like circles that nest,
Then the ones near the crux
Grow more tiny. I'm depressed.

When Does a Beatles Song Sound like a Bach Chorale?

In an e-mail exchange with me, Bernie Greenberg was discussing his attempts to impart to others his ability to write Bach-like music, and he wrote this:

There are tricks of the trade, and you can teach chorale-writing such that anyone with a little talent can write a chorale that sounds like a Bach chorale *that you are not listening to closely.*

A little later in that same e-mail exchange, in relating an episode in which he had helped an acquaintance who wrote four-part chorales and who wanted Bernie's advice on how to get them to sound more Bach-like, Bernie amplified his remarks as follows:

There is no question that by further refinement of style, I can make them sound more like Bach chorales than many other church hymns. Perhaps the right question is:

"Do they sound more like Bach chorales than *what*?"

rather than

"Do they sound like Bach chorales?"

After all, compared to jet takeoff noise, or even Balinese gamelan music, most Beatles songs "sound like Bach chorales," right?

A Portrait That "Looks like" Its Intended Subject

Bernie's humorous point is right on the mark, and forces one to think carefully about what it means to say glibly, *X sounds like Y*. And further light is shed on the question by considering the analogous issue of what it means to say, *X looks like Y*. To make

Figure 2.2
A standard "smiley face" image.

Figure 2.3
A few strategically placed parallel vertical lines added to the bland, generic smiley face, demonstrating a tiny amount of "style."

this issue vivid, let us take a standard "smiley face" image, as shown in figure 2.2. Presumably, the bland face shown below does not remind you of any individual you know, right?

It would be surprising if it did. But if we now add to our bland, generic smiley face a tiny amount of "style"—just a few strategically placed parallel vertical lines—lo and behold figure 2.3!

All of a sudden, nearly everybody recognizes the familiar face of the *Führer* of the Third Reich. To be sure, nobody would say about this mustachioed inanity, "It looks very much like Hitler"; perhaps nobody would even say, "It looks like Hitler"; but despite that, everybody *sees* Hitler in it. They can't help it. The point of this example, invented by David Moser (who grimly subtitled his ironic image "Have a Nice Holocaust!"), is that just a minimal gesture in the direction of a known style can, if well executed, have a stunning effect, summoning up much more than is really there.

So ... how much are we being fooled when, on hearing a piece of music, we respond to some gestures that in the past we have come to associate with composer X, and then exclaim to ourselves, "This piece sounds like X?" Can we even distinguish clearly between responses at a shallow level and a deep level? Indeed, what *is* the difference, in music, between "shallow" levels and "deep" levels of style? Is it just a question of different levels of depth of syntactic pattern, or is it something more than that?

Lewis Rowell's "Bach Grammar"

Not long after I became a professor at Indiana University, I heard on the radio a very engaging piece for organ that to my ear sounded extremely Bach-like; when it was announced, however, I found out to my surprise, though not to my chagrin, that it had been composed by a music professor at IU—Lewis Rowell. I lost no time in contacting Rowell and suggested we have lunch together to talk over the idea of faking Bach. He was delighted that someone had taken an interest in his piece, and we soon met. Over lunch, I asked Rowell how he had composed such an authentic-sounding piece, and he said, "Oh, that's not hard ... Bach developed a kind of grammar that I merely picked up, as could anyone who wished to. And then, armed with this grammar, I—just like anyone with a bit of musical talent—can easily compose any number of pieces in perfect Bach style. It takes no genius, believe me. It's all straightforward stuff. The only place where genius was involved was in coming up with the grammar."

I was astounded to hear how dismissively Rowell described his acquisition of "Bach grammar," and just as astounded to hear that he thought that composing long, complex, and coherent new pieces in the full Bach style was basically merely a mechanical act, requiring no act of genius whatsoever. After all, I, a lifelong lover of Bach, had on several occasions tried composing pieces in the Bach style, and had found myself unbelievably stymied. Measures and short phrases, yes, perhaps—but a long movement? No way!

Rowell's claim, however, was that only Bach's own *creating* of his supposed "grammar" was hard, whereas *inducing* that grammar from Bach's output and then *exploiting* it was a piece of cake. A glib hack could create new works as deep and as great as any that had ever issued from the pen of the great Baroque master—or from that of any other great master. Profundity becomes a snap, emerging at the drop of a hat. By contrast, my personal feeling, based on my own experience (and, I must say, based also on long observation of Bernie Greenberg), was that *extracting* a true and deep "Bach grammar" from Bach notes was itself an act that would require extraordinary insight—perhaps even genius. And even if such a grammar could be extracted (which struck me as highly implausible, Rowell's claims notwithstanding), I felt that to *exploit* it to make new pieces as great and as engaging as those of J.S.B. himself would still be an act of enormous creativity.

Many years later, grappling mightily with the strange new world of Emmy and her algorithmically induced grammars, I remembered my stimulating lunch with Lew Rowell and wondered what Bernie Greenberg would think of our chat. So I sent

Bernie the gist of Rowell's claims through e-mail, to which he quickly responded with the following eloquent set of remarks in his own inimitable style (if I dare make such a claim!):

> I'd be very interested in such a grammar. It would have to include a "syntactic description" of the theology of Paul as expressed in Romans, the innate intellectual tension between Christ's roles as Victim and Savior, and other emotional basis vectors of the space which is "Bach."
>
> Anyone who has been moved by the *St. John Passion*, the *St. Matthew Passion*, or the Cross dialogue of Cantata 159 understands that the root of their emotional power is in the turgid psychodynamics of the Crucifixion, not in the seventh-chords, which are the mere paint that Bach has used to implement these canvases, incomparable paint though it be.

Although I sympathized with what Bernie was trying to say, I felt he had overstated the case. Does one really need to be a pious Christian to be able to compose deeply Bach-like music, or even to be powerfully moved by Bach's music? In point of fact, Bernie himself, brought up Jewish and an atheist by credo, provided a counterexample. I argued that the essence of Bach's power comes not from his deep piety but from his deep humanity—from just those human experiences discussed in my speculation (quoted from *GEB*, above) about a computational "music box" producing new Bach and Chopin pieces. Bernie, on hearing this objection, conceded that among the most important "emotional basis vectors of the space which is 'Bach'" are many that have nothing per se to do with religion but that simply follow from being born into this crazy world, growing up in it, and living a full human life. And so Bernie closed his musings by saying this:

> When the "grammar" is sufficient to cover such notions, the General AI problem will have been solved, I think.

Amen. As for myself, I was inspired by all these musings on alleged "Bach grammars" and the hidden inner fire of human creativity to write the following series of quatrains.

When music's been treated
By the likes of Dave Cope,
Is the mystery banished,
Or is there still hope?

Does true depth in music
Mean creating new styles,
So that music by mimics
Is worth just snide smiles?

Was Chopin's fourth ballade
A mere splicing of licks
From his previous three—
Or were there new tricks?

What's creative? What's rut-stuck?
What is new, and what's old?
What's derivative? What's novel?
What is weak, and what's bold?

Is a style, once devised,
A mere snap to ad lib
A bunch of new tunes in,
Provided you're glib?

Is Bach-style a grammar
A hack can acquire,
Or is there some essence—
Some deep inner fire?

Just what makes a genius
Than a mimic far better?
The former forges spirit;
The latter worships letter.

'Twixt genius and mimic,
What makes the sharp cut?
The former's unfettered,
The latter's in a rut.

Showing Up Despite Being a No-Show

When I gave my talk with Dave Cope at Santa Cruz in May of 1996, I was hoping to persuade Cope's Santa Cruz colleague Tom Lehrer, of satiric-song fame, to take part in a panel discussion on Emmy, and to that end, I called up Lehrer (whom I had known for some years and who I knew was something of a recluse) and tried to persuade him to join us. He was, however, predictably self-deprecating and in the end turned me down, although in the nicest of ways. In fact, our phone chat lasted at least ten to fifteen minutes, and I found what he said very provocative. When I hung up, I all of a sudden realized that although Lehrer had declined to come, he had actually

told me over the phone pretty much what I had most hoped he might say in front
of a live audience. Given that irony, I quickly jotted down everything that I could
remember, which was a lot, and then promptly translated it into verse. I figured that
this way I could give my audience a "virtual Lehrer" (and keep in mind that the
German word *Lehrer* means "teacher") if not the real McCoy.

I must admit that I was also secretly hoping that Lehrer would show up in person
at the back-to-back lectures Dave and I were giving, because then I could play my
little joke on him, of surprising him by delivering his own ideas, in versified form, to
the assembled group despite his having declined to participate. Unfortunately, no
such luck—Lehrer didn't attend our talks. Nonetheless, my Lehrer quatrains were
appreciated by the audience, and I feel they enrich the whole discussion, and so, for
what they're worth, here they are:

A teacher I know
Whom I asked to take part
In this meeting, said, "No,
What I do is no art . . .

"I've nothing to tell folks;
I won't take the stand.
It's true, I write songs,
But they're boring and bland . . .

"You just name me a form
Such as 'march,' and I'll play
You a piece with a march beat,
Cliché after cliché . . .

"All my songs are deriv—
They're in nobody's style.
If I try copying Kern,
It comes out sounding Weill!

"Still, old Irving Berlin
Has a style I might snag,
For his music's as patterned
As a Scott Joplin rag . . .

"Berlin plays vanilla
To Kern's chocolate mint;
So I might stamp out tunes
From that old Berlin mint . . .

"But it's truly a cause for despair
When you come to the genius of Kern.
He pulls magical chords from the air
With an ease too profound to discern ...

"Oh, I guess if I truly did yearn
To mimic the magic of Kern,
I could study and probe and might learn
Some tricks that make Kern phrases turn ...

"Then armed with this kernel of Jerome,
I might slowly begin out to churn
The patterns that once seemed so special—
The signatures of the great Kern ...

"But even at that advanced stage,
Pulling wool over Kern experts' eyes,
The flame of the novel I'd lack—
Lacking genius, I'd just plagiarize ...

"No, the greatness of Kern I can't ape;
He's a doctor, I'm merely a quack.
And that's why I wouldn't belong
On a stage with you folks with the knack!"

Ah, the irony of his remarks!
Here's a fellow who *does* have the knack
To spin songs in the styles of yore,
Yet declines, saying, "I'm just a hack!"

Yet my friend in declining said so much,
And so well that I wrote it all down,
Then converted it into this verse,
So he's here despite turning me down!

His modesty struck me as odd.
Just why, if the Kern style did yield
Its keys to his scan, would he say,
"Still I'm nought in the novelty field?"

To what higher goal could one aspire,
Than the crafting of tunes on one's forge—
Be they Kern-style, or Lerner & Loewe,
Or Bernstein, or Lehrer—or George?

Lennie Is Jealous of George

My allusion to "George" here is, specifically, a reference to George Gershwin. The reason for this is that I was deeply struck when I read, in Leonard Bernstein's *The Joy of Music* (Bernstein 1959), an article provocatively called "Why You Don't Just Run Upstairs and Write a Nice Gershwin Tune?" The article is in the form of a dialogue between L.B. himself and a character called P.M. (Professional Manager). The two of them are meeting over lunch, and we tune in on their conversation as they chat 'n' chew:

P.M.:   Learn a little from George. Your songs are simply too arty, that's all. George didn't worry about all that. He wrote tunes, dozens of them, simple tunes that the world could sing and remember and want to sing again. You just have to learn to be simple, my boy.

L.B.:   You think it's simple to be simple? Not at all. I've tried hard for years. A few weeks ago a serious composer friend and I were talking about all this, and we got boiling mad about it. Why shouldn't we be able to come up with a hit, we said? So we went to work with a will, vowing to make thousands by simply being simple-minded. We worked for an hour and then gave up in hysterical despair. Impossible. I remember that at one point we were trying like two children, one note at a time, to make a tune that didn't even require any harmony, it would be that obvious. Impossible. It was a revealing experiment, I must say, even though it left us with a slightly doomed feeling.

Let me quote from the fellow whose lyre
Gave us *West Side Story* and *Candide*—
He's a dragon whose music breathes fire,
Yet he sighed, "By George, I'm out-keyed!"

A fake luncheon chat he once penned:
"Hey, Why You Don't Just Run Upstairs,
And Write Me a Nice Gershwin Tune?"
Its point was the depth of simple airs.

Len denies, in this chat,
That new tunes he could spin
That would capture the essence
Of his idol, Gershwin.

Indeed, his whole point
Is the fact that it's tough—
Not just tough but damned tough—
To make new Gershwin-stuff.

You struggle and strive
To be Georgishly alive,
To be simple, to jive,
Yet you never arrive.

There's a spirit inside
That just won't show its face,
Though you hear it inside
Every note, graced with grace.

Lenny's right, I would say:
To dream up "I Got Rhythm"
Takes something beyond
A pure pattern algorithm.

Devilishly Infectious Rubbish Spouted by the Orwellian Versificator

While we're on the topic of famous Georges, there is another George whose ideas are highly germane to our topic. I speak of George Orwell and his frightening novel *1984* (Orwell 1949). When I read it in high school, many nightmarish images haunted me, but there was one odd passage that came flashing back to me from far across the decades when one spring morning in 1996 I caught myself humming, to my own horror, a certain mazurka in the shower . . .

And the Ministry had not only to supply the multifarious needs of the Party, but also to repeat the whole operation at a lower level for the benefit of the proletariat. There was a whole chain of separate departments dealing with proletarian literature, music, drama, and entertainment generally. Here were produced rubbishy newspapers, containing nothing except sport, crime, and astrology, sensational five-cent novelettes, films oozing with sex, and sentimental songs which were composed entirely by mechanical means on a special kind of kaleidoscope known as a versificator . . .

  Under the window somebody was singing. Winston peeped out, secure in the protection of the muslin curtain. The June sun was still high in the sky, and in the sun-filled court below, a monstrous woman, solid as a Norman pillar, with brawny red forearms and a sacking apron strapped about her middle, was stumping to and fro between a washtub and a clothesline, pegging out a series of square white things, which Winston recognized as babies' diapers. Whenever her mouth was not corked with clothes pegs, she was singing in a powerful contralto:

  It was only an 'opeless fancy,
  It passed like an Ipril dye,
  But a look an' a word an' the dreams they stirred,
  They 'ave stolen my 'eart awye!

The tune had been haunting London for weeks past. It was one of countless similar songs published for the benefit of the proles by a sub-section of the Music Department ... But the woman sang so tunefully as to turn the dreadful rubbish into an almost pleasant sound ...

She knew the whole driveling song by heart, it seemed. Her voice floated upward with the sweet summer air, very tuneful, charged with a sort of happy melancholy. One had the feeling that she would have been perfectly content if the June evening had been endless and the supply of clothes inexhaustible, to remain there for a thousand years, pegging out diapers and singing rubbish.

I didn't recall this passage word for word, but the overall image had stuck accurately in my mind for over three decades, and reading it again made me cringe just as I had back then, imagining the ragingly infectious power of the formulaic, mechanical junk-music issuing forth from the quaintly described "kaleidoscope known as a versificator." But now, having been sucked in myself by the kaleidosCope known as Emmy, I really had no choice but to write the following verses:

One mazurka by EMI
Has lodged, I confess,
In the grooves of my brain,
Causing shame and distress.

Like the proles in George Orwell's
Nineteen Eighty-Four,
I find myself humming
An emotionless score.

I feel shock and bemusement
And confusion, to boot:
Is this *rubbish* I've swallowed?
Am I that unastute?

I never did dream
I'd be mortified by
Merely humming some tune;
Now I eat humble pie.

After decades of sureness
That the pieces I hear
Are deep mirrors of passion,
Must I now reverse gear?

The Pea-Sized Creative Module Keeps on Truckin' ...

Peg Brand, a friend and colleague in Indiana's philosophy department, sent me through campus mail a remarkable article by Amei Wallach that she'd read in the *New York Times* (Wallach 1995). Its subject was the American painter Willem de Kooning, whose mental health had, in the early 1980s, suffered a sharp decline. Indeed, by the middle of that decade he was in the fullest throes of Alzheimer's disease, and yet the article was all about a series of paintings that he had executed during that period of his life, and that, rather astonishingly, had garnered high praise from not a few art critics. The curator of a large retrospective exhibit of de Kooning's last set of paintings called them "among the most beautiful, sensual, and exuberant abstract works by any modern painter." And yet one has to remember that during this period, de Kooning often would paint the same painting over and over again, unable to remember having done it before, until one day someone convinced him to keep his most recent canvases right in front of him as he worked, so he would see them and thus be able to avoid incessantly repeating himself.

Psychiatrists and neurologists interviewed in the article stressed that advanced Alzheimer's victims can no longer carry out any kind of mental activity that involves maintaining coherence—for instance, though they can play golf physically, they have to ask, on each stroke, where their ball is. Writing a sensible novel—in fact, most of the time, even uttering a sensible nonroutine sentence—is out of the question, as is sustaining a chain of reasoning beyond a few seconds. It is thus definite cause for pause to find out that paintings hailed as great art were produced by a mind whose light was day by day growing fainter, a mind whose owner no longer recognized any other human's face, no matter how long known, a mind that seemed to do nothing but wander in vague, aimless circles—when not filling blank canvases with lines and colors.

There're lots of old-timers
Who still can create;
But those with Alzheimer's—
Can *their* art be great?

De Kooning is brain-dead,
He paints as in sleep;
Yet critics acclaim him:
"Great stuff—makes you weep!"

Suppose that Old Chopin
Had lived to 89,
Losing all of his memory
As well as his mind.

Yet when he sat down
To make up a fresh tune,
His magical chords
Soon made listeners swoon.

What survived in his brain
Was the size of a pea—
A module for composing
Autonomously.

When Chopin wrote waltzes,
Did he draw on all life,
Or could some "waltz module"
Be excised with a knife?

Is composing a narrow,
Mechanical skill,
So old geezers can compose
Using minds that are nil?

Is music, like chess,
A wee, hard-edged domain,
Algorithmically handled
By a pea-sized subbrain?

Emmy Tries Her Hand at Doing Chopin

At this point in my lecture, I usually have the second musical interlude, this time involving two or three mazurkas, at least one by Chopin, at least one by Emmy. Rather than describing what happens myself, I would like to quote here what one person who was in the audience of my most recent Emmy lecture at the University of Rochester wrote to me and Dave Cope afterward.

```
From: kala pierson <kpi@ibm.net> Mon Feb 1 19:00:12 1999
To: howell@cats.ucsc.edu
Subject: EMI's big day at U. of Rochester ...
Cc: dughof@indiana.edu
```

Hi, David! I heard Douglas Hofstadter's EMI-demo at the U. of
Rochester yesterday; and though you'll probably hear an account of
it from him, I wanted to give you a report from the trenches too,
since EMI made such a dramatic impression on us.

As you know, Eastman School of Music is part of U.R.; much of the
audience was made up of theorists and composers from Eastman (I'm
a composer). DH gave us three listening tests: Bach inventions,
live; Bach arias, on video; & Chopin mazurkas, live. It was easy
for most of the audience to tell EMI from Bach; there were a lot
of knowing smirks among those around me during the not-Bach
inventions. Okay, we concluded, those imitations are pretty
remarkable on several levels but they just ain't the real thing,
and we--Those In the Know--can tell.

When the pianist played the two "Chopin" mazurkas, we were
similarly confident. The first mazurka had grace and charm, but not
"true-Chopin" degrees of invention and large-scale fluidity; there
were very local-level, "shallow"-feeling modulations--just the
type, I reasoned, that a computer program would generate based on
more sophisticated examples of the real thing. The second was
clearly the genuine Chopin, with a lyrical melody; large-scale,
graceful chromatic modulations; and a natural, balanced form.

Although DH told us that the vote on this piece looked like "about
50/50" from his point of view, there was a definite preference
among the theory/comp corner of the audience. I voted real-Chopin
for the second piece, as did most of my friends. When DH announced
that the first was Chopin and the second was EMI, there was a
collective gasp and an aftermath of what I can only describe as
delighted horror. I've never seen so many theorists and composers
shocked out of their smug complacency in one fell swoop (myself
included)! It was truly a thing of beauty.

Cheers for now,
kala

"Truly a thing of beauty!" This is an amazingly refreshing and candid statement
from someone at one of the most elite music schools in the United States. Perhaps
only a student could have written it. But no, I take that back. There are professors
who are just as honest, though certainly it is hard to swallow one's pride and admit
having been taken in. For many, it would be tempting not to admit having been
gulled, and to go around haughtily pronouncing Emmy's compositions to be cheap
forgeries of no artistic merit whatsoever. Indeed, I have run into some professional

musicians who have done just that. But I personally have heard too much of Emmy's music and been fooled too often to be haughty, even though some of it is certainly very weak (thank God!).

Suppose we discovered
A pristine Volume III
Of the "Tempered Clavier,"
With the depth of JSB.

It makes a huge splash,
And musicians galore
Compete to perform it
In grand halls the world o'er.

It meets with reviews
That are tops. All agree
These are fugues without peer:
"Ach, it's Bach—only he!"

But for some, strange to say,
If Dave Cope were to spill
Bitter beans—"It's by EMI"—
Then its worth would be nil.

They'd retract all their praise,
No more sing its great powers,
For now it's just fool's gold—
Bouquets of fake flowers.

Musicians a-plenty
There are, who, if told
In advance, "It's by EMI,"
Will find flaws. Ain't that bold?

But I fear that it's not,
For it's after the fact.
Forewarned "It's the en-EMI!",
They so "bravely" attacked.

I find it more honest
If one's judgment remains
Unswerved when one learns
It's by chips, not by brains.

When the votes were taken at my Rochester lecture, someone called out, "How'd we do compared to Indiana?" (my own university also having one of the nation's top music schools). Everyone laughed, especially when it was suggested that perhaps a new system for ranking music schools could be based on how few errors were made by faculty and students in telling pieces by Emmy from pieces by human composers.

One stunning lesson from my Rochester lecture (and indeed, from all of the times I've lectured on Emmy) is that people with deep musical gifts and decades of training can, on occasion, mistake an Emmy product for the genuine article. And remember—we are just embarking, we humans, on the pathway toward the realization of the dream of "preprogrammed mass-produced mail-order twenty-dollar desk-model music boxes"—those boxes on whose "sterile circuitry" I heaped so much scorn, back when I wrote *GEB*.

Where will we have gotten in twenty more years of hard work? In fifty? What will be the state of the art in 2084? Who, if anyone, will *still* be able to tell "the right stuff" from versificator rubbish? Who will know, who will care, who will loudly protest that the last (though tiniest) circle at the center of the style target has *still* not been reached (and may never be reached)? What will such nitpicky details matter, when new Bach and Chopin masterpieces applauded by all come gushing out of silicon circuitry at a rate faster than H_2O pours over the edge of Niagara? Will that wondrous new golden age of music not be "truly a thing of beauty"? Won't it be sweet to swoon in a sea of synthetic sublimity?

If output from EMI
Fooled all but an elite,
To protest, "Crux is missing!"
Would ring quite effete.

When the "heart" that is missing
Is unmissed by most,
Then the essence that's missing
Is a wisp of a ghost.

And this is my fear—
That what's missing will shrink
To near zero, with time.
And then—what to think?

When music's reduced
To the schemas of Cope,
Has the romance all vanished?
I would like to sing "Nope."

Scarfing Down Spastroni Down in South Delabam'

Have you ever downed a plate of delicious *spastroni* swimming in *caravinese* sauce? Or consumed *pollitucciollo* with a side order of *pomostacchi*? Ever eaten a salad with *pomodorini* and *marboli*? If you answer yes, I'd say you're a brazen bluffer, for these words were produced by a very simple computer program which had been "fed" (for want of a better word!) the names of many Italian foods, such as *spaghetti, ravioli, lasagne, vongole, rigatoni, pomodori, fettuccine, linguine, vitello, pollo, mostaccioli,* and so forth. There is no such thing as *caravinese* sauce or a side order of *pomo-stacchi*, my friend! (On the other hand, by sheer luck, there really are *pomodorini*—cherry tomatoes—for the computer-generated word just happens to be the standard diminutive of *pomodori*, "tomatoes.")

This kind of program, first shown to me in the early 1960s by my friend Charles Brenner, and which originated at Bell Labs in the late 1940s, is based on imitating the frequencies of short letter groups—in this case, *trigrams*. Given a passage of input text, the method is based on the probability of a pair of letters (*sp*, for instance) being followed by various other characters (*a*, for instance, would be a likely follower, as opposed to *q*, which would be nonexistent).

To generate a piece of output text that mimics the trigram frequencies of the input text, you begin with any digram (two-letter piece) of the input text (*sp*, let's say). Then you look at *which* characters followed that digram in the input text, and *how many times* each of them did so. Perhaps the letter *a* followed *sp* four times, *i* followed it once, *o* followed it twice, and *u* once, and that's all. That's eight *sp*'s, altogether. Now imagine rolling an eight-sided die, four of whose sides are labeled *a*, one labeled *i*, two labeled *o*, and one labeled *u*. Half the time you'll get a side labeled *a*, but half the time you'll get something else. Take that letter, whatever it is (*a*, let's say) and tack it onto your output stream, giving *spa*. Now your most recent digram is *pa*. Once again, consult the statistics telling which characters followed occurrences of *pa* in the input text, and based on these data, make an *n*-sided die and roll it, telling you which new character to append to *spa*—perhaps *s* this time. Now repeat the probabilistic process, this time with digram *as*. Each time, you will get a letter that really occurred in the input text, thus turning a digram into a trigram. And thus, left to right, letter by letter, character by character, fresh new input-imitating output text is generated in this most simple of stochastic ways.

You want some fake state names for the board game you're inventing? Well, take your pick from the following, which were generated by the trigram-frequency method from the database of the fifty real state names (and I could give you hundreds more fake state names at the drop of a hat):

Nebrado, Wessissippi, Oklawaii, New Yornia, Pentahoma, South Delabama, New Jersetts, Pennectico, Texichusetts, New Hampshington, Michigansas, Oklaware ...

Now this is recombinant language, in spades!

Using 8-grams to Ape the Great Art of the Bard

Speaking of "recombinant," back in the 1960s when DNA was quite a novelty, there was a psychologist who trained planarians (a primitive type of aquatic flatworm) on a simple food-finding task, and then ground them up and fed the resultant worm goulash to other planarians. His hope was that the learning that had taken place in the brains of the victimized worms had somehow been stored as sequences in their DNA and, as such, would hopefully survive the chopping-up process, so that the cannibals, after partaking of their worm-goulash banquet, would suddenly find themselves more skilled at finding food. This method of passing on one's learning to others was at first thought to work and made quite a splash in the press, but later was thoroughly discredited. Oh, well.

With trigrams, new state names
Can be spewed on demand.
The next stop? Why, Shakespeare!
Can his spirit be canned?

Do you remember the sixties?
Some worms were made wise,
Then chopped up and fed
To their relatives in disguise.

The wisdom, it was claimed,
Came through quite intact,
Though the poor DNA
Had been chopped up and hacked.

So let's chop up old Will
Into 7-grams, or 8—
Will's wisdom we'll distill;
Then we'll regurgitate!

This sounds like a joke—
But take text that's opaque,
And with trigrams you'll make
A respectable fake.

When *n*-grams are used,
As you jack *n* up high,
The facsimile's fakeness
Gets harder to spy.

Well, Not Quite the Bard . . .

The German philosopher Georg Wilhelm Friedrich Hegel produced text that to some folks seems buzzing with wisdom. In my experience, however, most people, at least on their first several hundred readings, find the following Hegel sample fairly unenlightening:

Further, the living substance is being which is in truth subject, or, what is the same, is in truth actual only in so far as it is the movement of positing itself, or is the mediation of its self-othering with itself. This substance is, as subject, pure, simple negativity, and is for this very reason the bifurcation of the simple; it is the doubling which sets up opposition, and then again the negation of this indifferent diversity and of its antithesis. Only this self-restoring sameness, or this reflection in otherness within itself, not an original or immediate unity as such, is the true. It is the process of its own becoming, the circle that presupposes its end as its goal, having its end also as its beginning; and only by being worked out to its end, is it actual.

What happens if you apply the *n*-gram-frequency method to this text? We can use trigrams, tetragrams, or higher. Here is what came out of a run using pentagrams:

Furtherness with itself, or immediate unity and is in truth substance is the doubling its end also as its self-restoring itself-restoring worked out to its own becoming, the mediation of position of the bifurcation of the bifurcation of this substance is, as subject, pure, simple; it actual.

Note that, even though the program knows absolutely nothing about English words, there is not a single nonword here. On the other hand, the grammar leaves something to be desired. But that gives us good reason to jack up the *n*-value to, say, $n = 6$.

Further, the movement of position, and only by being which is in truth actual only in so far as its goal, having sameness, or this reflection of its own becoming, the doubling with itself, not an original or immediation in othering which is in truth actual.

Now this time, curiously, we did wind up with two nonwords—"immediation" and "othering"—but they fit in so nicely—they seem so *Hegelian*, one might say—that few readers ever notice that they "do not compute." But let us now set *n* equal to 9 and see what happens . . .

Further, the living substance is being which is in truth actual only in so far as it is the doubling which is in truth subject, pure, simple negativity, and is for this reflection in otherness within itself, or is the mediation of the simple; it is the true. It is the doubling which is in truth ...

The grammar is surely getting better, although it is not yet perfect. But grammar aside, what about *meaning*? Well, it sounds more and more like Hegel. Of course, we must beware of that slick phrase "sounds like." To adapt Bernie Greenberg's phrase, "It not only should *sound* like Hegel, it should also *speak* like him." And yet sadly, for us philistines who can't hear the wisdom resounding in the original lines, these regurgitated lines somehow *do* seem to "speak like Hegel." And if, to your taste, $n = 9$ isn't good enough to get credible Hegelian semantics, then jack n up further. Each time you add 1 to n, your output will get a little more realistic, a little more coherent. And please note: this method for simulation of text is far simpler than Emmy, for it is *purely local*, whereas Emmy combines both local and global constraints in a far subtler manner.

Composing in Your Sleep ... or in Your Grave

Anyone who has composed a fair amount of music knows the exquisite joy of finding their own personal voice. One dreams of composing more and more, but of course time presses and one's finiteness constrains one's output. It is therefore natural to wonder what Emmy would do if fed one's own music as input. And I, given my close connection with Emmy's progenitor, could request this favor and actually find out. I submitted a diskette to Dave, containing twelve of my piano pieces (I've written around forty, all told), and he in turn fed my pieces into Emmy and started her churning. Promptly, out came pseudo-Hofstadter music!

And in the course of my Santa Cruz lecture, Mary Jane performed both a genuine Hofstadter piece and an Emmy/Hofstadter piece (called "Nope"), with me hearing myself aped for the very first time, in real time before the audience's eyes. It was delightful to listen as my own harmonies were spat back at me in new and unexpected combinations, although I have to admit that sometimes the "logic" of the flow, such as it was, sounded a bit incoherent. But then, had Hegel been listening to someone reading aloud order-9 imitations of his own text, I suspect he too would have found the flow of its logic a little wanting, here and there.

If the blatherings of George Frederick Hegel
Are captured to a quite Hei deggree
By 5-grams, shouldn't George Frederick Handel
Succumb to the same skulldugg'ree?

But why tackle just big names?
Let's climb down the ladder
To a far easier challenge:
Let's tackle Hofstadter!

Can we suck out the essence
Of Doug from his notes?
Can we psych out Hofstadter
When he hears garbled quotes?

Once his music we've caught,
That's Step 1 of our plan;
The next step's his *lectures*!
We'll make Doug-in-a-Can!

His verse, it's just patterns,
Just rhymes in a box.
There are seldom surprises
That off-knock your socks.

But even the trick rhymes
Have a formula behind;
We know that that's all
That there is to Doug's mind.

The hard part was making him
(The original Doug);
The easy part's faking him
(A canned, Doug-less Doug).

Immortality, ho!—
Thanks to Cope. How I'll rave
When I can compose
In my sleep—or my grave.

There's no one at home,
Yet the music pours out.
The lights have gone dark;
Still, my spirit soars out!

That's Prokofiev's fate.
The poor chappie expired,

Tenth Sonata half-done . . .
EMI finished it. She's hired!

A Prokofiev expert
Said she'd give a première,
So Cope sent it off,
Thinking, "She's quite a dear!"

Not too long had passed
Ere arrived her reply:
"Prokofiev would *hate* this
As much as do I!"

But why the conditional?
Why hedge, using "would"?
If he *sings* while he's dead,
Can't he *hate* just as good?

For this is my claim,
Though it sounds somewhat droll:
Total style-resurrection
Resurrects one's full soul.

Is Language Intrinsically Deeper Than Music?

You may think that that last stanza was tongue-in-cheek, but no—those precise
sentiments have been my recurrent theme, and I'm not about to abandon them now.
To delve into such matters more seriously, let me discuss more fully in prose what I
hinted at in a couple of stanzas above—the idea of a program à la Emmy producing
a spate of brand-new Hofstadter lectures or—let's go whole hog—books. (After all,
if an opera by Mahler, who never wrote one, is in the planning stages, why not a
novel by Hofstadter, who never wrote one?) What would it take? Would n-gram frequencies with a high value of n, applied to all the previously published Hofstadter
books, turn the trick?

Well, you know as well as I do that this would fail ludicrously. That kind of technique doesn't deal with *content*, with *ideas*. It just deals with sequences of letters,
and a writer does not deal with sequences of letters. And even if an Emmy-like text-
imitation program dealt with more global qualities of its input text, the problem is
that *new ideas* would not ever enter the scene. Who could have predicted, given my
first few books, that I would next write an 800-page book on poetry translation (*Le*

Ton beau de Marot)? (Hofstadter 1997). There's nothing remotely resembling the manipulation and creation of new ideas in Emmy—and yet the crazy, undeniable truth of the matter is that Emmy's music does at least a decent job of creating "new Chopin" and "new Mozart," and so on. As Dave himself speculated in the journal entry that starts out his first book, "While never as good as the originals, they will be exciting, entertaining, and interesting."

Or consider "Prokofiev's Tenth Sonata," as Dave calls it. In the liner notes to his and Emmy's first compact disk (*Bach by Design*), he wrote the following:

This computer-composed Prokofiev *Sonata* was completed in 1989. Its composition was inspired by Prokofiev's own attempt to compose his tenth piano sonata, an attempt thwarted by his death. As such it represents another of the many potential uses of programs such as Emmy (i.e., the completion of unfinished works).

To me this comes close to blasphemy—and yet let me also add the following remark, to counterbalance that reaction. The first movement of this sonata by Emmy starts out with the actual forty-four measures that Prokofiev himself had completed, and then continues with Emmy's own notes. What happens when measures 45, 46, and so on are encountered? Is it like falling off a cliff? Is there a drastic discontinuity? Well, I would put it this way. Imagine you were reading, for the first time, the genuine Hegel paragraph, and imagine furthermore that it had been extended by a high *n*-value text-imitation program. Would you instantaneously feel something was fishy when you hit the very first word of the computer's text? Of course not. It would take a line or two, possibly even a dozen, before you said to yourself, "What is going on? I'm even *more* lost here than I was at the paragraph's beginning!" In some sense that is how I hear the Emmy/Prokofiev sonata. There is no sudden drop in quality at measure 45—indeed, it is as smooth a transition as one could possibly imagine, and all the way to the movement's end it sounds quite consistent with the way it started out.

I happen not to *like* this piece by Emmy (though Dave Cope adores it!), but then I also happen not to be a fan of the last several Prokofiev piano sonatas (despite loving the first few). So to me, this "tenth sonata," though it rings fairly true, just doesn't appeal. I would never call it a work of genius, but I would credit it as being "well-crafted and Prokofievian in feel."

So what is going on? How come Emmy does a fairly passable job at resuscitating composers but couldn't conceivably resuscitate a writer—even a writer of murky and obscure philosophical verbiage? Or am I—a serious author but not a serious composer—being too vain? Are my remarks self-serving? Is my personal verbal spark every bit as susceptible to being captured via algorithmic processing as Prokofiev's musical spark is?

Falling Hard for a Pattern of Blips

For me, analogies always help to shed light on such complex disputes, and the following analogy, which I hope is provocative, came to me one day—indeed, it hit me with great emotional power, I must admit—when I haphazardly picked up a publicity brochure for books about budding new technologies to be put to use in making movies.

I suppose a good deal
Of my EMI perplexity
Can be traced back to issues
Of algorithmic complexity.

To cast all these matters
In a somewhat new light,
Let's turn to attraction,
To chemistry, to "Miss Right."

I recall, and with pain,
A few times in my past
When I fell for some actress
In a romantic film's cast.

The blips on the screen,
We all know, came from her—
A flesh-and-blood person,
Alive, sure as sure.

The image conveyed a full
Human behind the scene,
And *that's* what I fell for—
Not for blips on the screen.

But now let's imagine
A brave new film world
In which love scenes take place,
Both unboy'd and ungirl'd.

And how would this happen?
Quite simple—by CAD—
The faking of objects,
As in many an ad.

One sees things in motion
That in truth never were;
They're simply bit-patterns
Cranked out in a blur.

Of course it's one thing
To make balls bounce about;
Quite another, a person
To believe in, no doubt.

And yet we are marching
Down that very lane;
We're making CAD filmstars.
Is that not a gain?

At this point in my lectures, I generally show the cover of a book called *Synthetic Actors in Computer-Generated 3D Films* by N. Magnenat Thalmann and D. Thalmann (1990), which features a nearly believable but clearly synthesized set of images of a woman in a bathing suit, who is instantly recognizable as Marilyn Monroe, walking across a shiny floor (see figure 2.4); I then read out loud the following blurb for the book:

Figure 2.4
A nearly believable but clearly synthesized set of images of a woman in a bathing suit, who is instantly recognizable as Marilyn Monroe, walking across a shiny floor. (From Thalmann, N. Magnenat and D. Thalmann. 1990. *Synthetic Actors in Computer-Generated 3D Films*. New York: Springer-Verlag.)

Three-dimensional synthetic reincarnations [reader: note this word!] of Marilyn Monroe and Humphrey Bogart were created by the authors of this book for their award-winning feature film "Rendez-vous à Montréal." The advanced computer animation techniques developed for the film are fully described in this book. They form a technological breakthrough that can be used to produce scenes featuring any celebrity in any situation. This opens new vistas in motion pictures, television, and advertising.

To conjure up Monroe,
Just write code—40 K;
She'll then dance on your screen,
Blow a kiss, make your day.

Or morph her with Binoche—
Hey, I'd call that a coup!
But since they're just code,
It's a no-sweat morpheroo.

So now I can fall
For a screenful of blips
Behind which there's no one—
Just code caught in chips.

A human in 40 K bytes,
Now that's cheap—
And yet I might fall
For this "her." A great leap!

Or *is* it so great
To be gulled by the spiel
Of some code that's a billion
Times simpler than real?

It shakes me to think
That someday I might fall
For an "actress" who
Never existed at all.

Three Flavors of Pessimism

Yes, what worries me about computer simulations is not the idea that we ourselves might be machines; I have long been convinced of the truth of that. What troubles me is the notion that things that touch me at my deepest core—pieces of music most of all, which I have always taken as direct soul-to-soul messages—might be effectively produced by mechanisms thousands if not millions of times simpler than the intricate biological machinery that gives rise to a human soul. This prospect, rendered most vivid and perhaps even near-seeming by the development of Emmy, worries me enormously, and in my more gloomy moods, I have articulated three causes for pessimism, listed below:

1. *Chopin* (for example) is a lot shallower than I had ever thought.

2. *Music* is a lot shallower than I had ever thought.

3. The *human soul/mind* is a lot shallower than I had ever thought.

To conclude, let me briefly comment on these. Pertaining to (1), since I have been moved to the core for my entire life by pieces by Chopin, if it turns out that Emmy can churn out piece after piece that "speaks like Chopin" to me, then I would be thereby forced to retrospectively reassess all the meaning that I have been convinced of having detected in Chopin's music, because I could no longer have faith that it *could only have come from a deep human source.* I would have to accept the fact that Frédéric Chopin might have been merely a tremendously fluent artisan rather than the deeply feeling artist whose heart and soul I'd been sure I knew ever since I was a child. Indeed, I could no longer be sure of *anything* I'd felt about Frédéric Chopin, the human being, from hearing his music. That loss would be an inconceivable source of grief to me.

In a sense, the loss just described would not be worse than the loss incurred by (2), since Chopin has always symbolized the power of music as a whole to me. Nonetheless, I suppose that having to chuck *all* composers out the window is somehow a bit more troubling than having to chuck just *one* of them out.

The loss described in (3), of course, would be the ultimate affront to human dignity. It would be the realization that all of the "computing power" that resides in a human brain's 100 billion neurons and its roughly ten quadrillion synaptic connections can be bypassed with a handful of state-of-the-art chips, and that all that is needed to produce the most powerful artistic outbursts of all time (and many more of equal power, if not greater) is a nanoscopic fraction thereof—*and* that it can all be accomplished, thank you very much, by an entity that knows nothing of knowing, seeing, hearing, tasting, living, dying, struggling, suffering, aging, yearning, singing, dancing, fighting, kissing, hoping, fearing, winning, losing, crying, laughing, loving, longing, or caring.

Playing the game of pattern and pattern alone will turn the whole trick—or, as the late and witty mathematician Stanislaw Ulam once said, memorably paraphrasing

Martin Luther (and J. S. Bach), "A Mighty Fortress Is Our Math." The only difference would be that Dave Cope would proclaim, "A Mighty Fortress Is Our Mac."
And, although Kala Pierson and many others may hail its coming as "truly a thing of
beauty," the day when music is finally and irrevocably reduced to syntactic pattern
and pattern alone will be, to my old-fashioned way of looking at things, a very dark
day indeed.

If the basis for EMI
Turns out to be true,
Then all my dear notions
Will die; I'll be blue.

Upon hearing an étude,
I'd no longer conclude
That I sensed a heart's mood;
'Twas just some "pattern dude"!

Likewise Bach would be shown
To be one "pattern guy,"
Whose secrets are none—
At least not to E.M.I.

Are these two just shallower
Than ever I'd thought,
Their styles simply patterns
In EMI's net caught?

Or is music itself
Just one big formal game,
So that using brute force
You can ape any name?

Or—worst of my nightmares—
Can a full human "I"
Be stamped on a chip made
By VLSI?

Now don't get me wrong—
I maintain we're machines!
But PC's?! What a slap
In the face to our genes!

Do our millions of genes,
And our billion-celled brains,
Yield nothing but rule-bound
Algorithmic refrains?

I'd like to believe
That for music to spring
From a thing, it must strive,
It must struggle, to sing.

It must search and must seek,
Sometimes win, sometimes fail;
It must fight with the world—
If that's so, I'll not rail.

What I fear is a win by
An emotional sham—
A musical poet with
No sense of "I am."

These issues alarm me
And that's why I spoke—
Not to answer all questions,
But to prod and provoke.

And now, please excuse me
For all of my pranks;
And to Dave (and to EMI!)
I express profound thanks.

Note

1. The epigram was actually stolen from David Cope, who himself had borrowed it from Pablo Picasso.

3 Response to Hofstadter

Doug Hofstadter's highly readable and articulate accounting of how Experiments in Musical Intelligence works, while occasionally overly simplified and understandably incomplete at times, provides an accurate account of the fundamentals of the program's processes. Interestingly, however, Doug's quite vivid and even compelling terminology in describing the program's processes often does not coincide with mine. For example, Doug uses terms like "chop up" and "reassemble," where I much prefer "recombinancy." Where Doug uses terms like "voice-hooking," I prefer to use the more common "voice-leading." His definition of SPEAC, while it reveals Experiments in Musical Intelligence's overall approach, is somewhat limiting, as will be seen in chapter 6. On the other hand, Doug's coinage of the term "templagiarism" describes quite well what I call "unifications."

Some Basics

Doug occasionally admits to an understandable lack of clarity on certain issues. For example, he confesses that he doesn't

... have a clear understanding of how the very complex operation of templagiarism (or, for that matter, the somewhat simpler operation of insertion of signatures) is made to coexist harmoniously with the previously described syntactic and semantic meshing operations, because I can easily imagine them conflicting with each other.

Templagiarism and the placement of signatures occur in parallel with recombinancy rather than sequentially as some (not Doug) misunderstand. In other words, signatures are not actually inserted *after* recombination, but occur as an integral part of the recombination process. Questions about templagiarism, as well as other questions that arise in Doug's presentation, will, hopefully, be resolved in my own more detailed presentation of how Experiments in Musical Intelligence works in chapters 4 through 6.

I find Doug's description of how the program chooses new recombinations of music based on their "shapes" (local connectivity) and their "stuff" (structural considerations) wonderfully poetic and appropriate:

These could be likened to two types of constraints that a jigsaw-puzzle solver naturally exploits when putting together a jigsaw puzzle ...

In one short sentence he has captured the often complex relationships between local and global issues with a visualization that is at once apt and insightful. Unfortunately, this analogy also suggests that there is but one solution, as is the case with jigsaw puzzles. In contrast, Experiments in Musical Intelligence provides many different solutions.

Doug also comments on pattern-matching, particularly in connection with the variables that relate to pattern-matching:

Cope tended to do this adjustment of controllers himself in order to increase the effectiveness of Emmy's search for signatures, but perhaps by now he has managed to automate that aspect of the process.

I have automated this process (see Cope 1992b and 1996, particularly chapter 7) and Experiments in Musical Intelligence now routinely composes in this manner.

Doug's view of Experiments in Musical Intelligence's music, as in his description of his first brush with the program's output, often contains somewhat loaded—to me at least—terminology:

It sounded like Emmy was dealing only with the surface level of music—with patterns, not with the deep emotional substrate—and I was pretty sure that little of interest could come of such an architecture.

The words "emotional substrate" sound informational, yet I have only a vague notion of his intended meaning. Likewise,

it [an Experiments in Musical Intelligence Chopin work] was unmistakably *Chopin-like* in spirit, and it was *not emotionally empty*.

I am flattered by these comments and yet strangely confused by them as well. Alan Turing (1950) discusses emotion in his seminal article on the Turing test when he quotes from "Professor Jefferson's Lister Oration" for 1949 (the italics are mine):

"Not until a machine can write a sonnet or *compose a concerto* because of thoughts and emotions felt, and not by the chance fall of symbols, could we agree that machine equals brain—that is, not only write it but know that it had written it. No mechanism could feel (and not merely artificially signal, an easy contrivance) pleasure at its successes, grief when its valves fuse, be warmed by flattery, be made miserable by its mistakes, be charmed by sex, be angry or depressed when it cannot get what it wants." (pp. 445–6)

and

According to the most extreme form of this view the only way by which one could be sure that a machine thinks is to *be* the machine and to feel oneself thinking. One could then describe these feelings to the world, but of course no one would be justified in taking any notice. Likewise according to this view the only way to know that a *man* thinks is to be that particular man. (p. 446)

Turing claims, however, that this is "a solipsist point of view" (p. 446). He finally concludes: "I think that most of those who support the argument from consciousness could be persuaded to abandon it rather than be forced into the solipsist position" (p. 446). Of course, Doug never *actually* argues that Experiments in Musical Intelligence must be conscious to create emotionally satisfying music, just that its music does not deal with music's "deep emotional substrate." I have drawn what seems to me to be an implicit connection between emotion and consciousness.

Doug seems to retreat from this point of view somewhat when he writes

I guess I would have to say, "Emmy's compositions are precisely as deep as her capacity to listen to and understand music." Which forces us to ask, "Does Emmy listen to music, or understand music, at all?" Well, of course Emmy doesn't *hear* music, in the sense of having eardrums that vibrate in response to complex waveforms—Emmy's way of perceiving music involves just the ability to deal with *numbers* that represent pitches and times and so forth.

Doug often seems to equate deep and complex with "good" and "human." Surely simple things can also be "good" and "human." At the same time, Doug describes another view that I find compelling, one that involves The Game, which he often includes in his presentations on Experiments in Musical Intelligence. I very much like his rationale for doing so:

I don't like dishonesty, but perhaps it is best to misinform people about what they are about to hear, in order that they not listen with a preclosed mind.

These lines strike very close to the heart of what I feel occurs when audiences hear the program's output for the first time, knowing that the music they are hearing was in fact composed by a computer program. Interestingly, I have many times heard a piece of music for the first time, been moved by it, and *not known* who composed it. I typically try to discover the composer's name in order to place the music in context and, more important, so I can hear more of that composer's music. However, I have yet to change my mind about the music after discovering who—or, in the case of a computer program, what—composed it. I am more likely to change my mind about the talent of the composer than I am about the quality of the music.

I listen to the Experiments in Musical Intelligence program's output in much the same way that I listen to any music. I hear the idiosyncrasies of the performance, the mold of the music, and the logic or illogic of the musical anticipations and their consequences. I see no reason to place Experiments in Musical Intelligence's music outside of the frame of reference that I use for music composed by human beings. On the other hand, I also listen to the sound of wind through a wheat field and the sounds of distant thunder as music. While it is true that I do not listen to these sounds in quite the same way as I do human-composed sounds, they are still music to my ears.

Doug disagrees (see also chapter 16):

I think it is sloppy thinking to equate babbling brooks and birds chirping at twilight with music (at least with traditional tonal music), which is produced deliberately by a human being in order to express or communicate something to other humans.

Doug makes serious assumptions about composers here. Some of the most obvious examples of deliberate attempts at such communication classify as "program music," which I doubt Doug would include in the list of music he admires. In the tonal music that I have composed in my lifetime, I cannot say that it occurred to me to view myself as deliberately trying to "communicate something to other humans." I am much more interested in creating well-balanced structures within which I hope to weave inventive musical ideas. I view the output of Experiments in Musical Intelligence in the same light. Doug, however, points out that I am a special case, being the person who created Experiments in Musical Intelligence, and like a proud father, taking great joy in its output. I agree, to the extent that my investment in Experiments in Musical Intelligence has been significant and that I am not dispassionate about its output. At the same time I do not believe that this is the sole reason for my often finding this output musical and moving. I offer the following as possible proof of this.

In the spring of 1998 I joined composers Christopher Dobrian and George Lewis and visual artist Harold Cohen on a performance tour of University of California campuses (which included performances of the Experiments in Musical Intelligence's Bach and Schubert songs in appendix D). Harold Cohen is best known for his creation of Aaron, his computer drawing and painting program. During Harold's presentations, which were generally the same from presentation to presentation, as were Chris's, George's, and mine, I marveled at his program's creations. Aaron works quite differently from Experiments in Musical Intelligence in that Aaron does not have a database of previous artworks nor does it create using recombinative techniques. However, Aaron does produce artworks that resemble those created by humans, artworks that sometimes sell for $5000 apiece. Figure 3.1 shows a black-and-white version of one of Aaron's color paintings which I find particularly evocative—and one created especially for this book. The figure in this picture reminds me of someone I know and this figure's expression reveals many interesting contradictions. In short, my relationship to Aaron's art is precisely the same as if Harold or any other human painter had painted it. My "privileged" relationship to Experiments in Musical Intelligence does not equally connect me with Aaron so that I can say, without reservation, that for me at least, computer-created art in any form, while it must pass my own personal muster of quality, falls clearly within the same

Figure 3.1
A black-and-white version of a color painting by Harold Cohen's Aaron program.

frame of reference as does human-created art (see further discussion of these points in chapters 17 and 18).

Doug's comments on computer-generated text involves a particularly opaque quote of Hegel's which he describes thusly:

... most people, at least on their first several hundred readings, find the following Hegel sample fairly unenlightening.

He then proceeds to use the quote as a template for *n*-gram-frequency generations. After a series of attempts he writes:

Well, it sounds more and more like Hegel. Of course, we must beware of that slick phrase "sounds like." To adapt Bernie Greenberg's phrase, "It not only should *sound* like Hegel, it should also *speak* like him." And yet sadly, for us philistines who can't hear the wisdom re-sounding in the original lines, these regurgitated lines somehow *do* seem to "speak like Hegel."

This is *very* revealing. Doug seems to intimate that if it is complex enough, then it will actually sound as if it is deep, even if it isn't deep at all. As I mentioned earlier, Doug often seems to relate deep and complex to "good." I do not. Some of the most moving and profound experiences of my life have been some of the simplest and most naive.

The Source of Frustration

In all of Doug's prose and doggerel (his term), he seems fixed on three possibilities which he poses, *each* of which has to do with deepness and shallowness:

1. *Chopin* (for example) is a lot shallower than I had ever thought.
2. *Music* is a lot shallower than I had ever thought.
3. The *human soul/mind* is a lot shallower than I had ever thought.

Doug's frustration peaks when he is confronted by a work of Experiments in Musical Intelligence that seems as if it had been composed by a once-alive composer he respects. I am again, of course, delighted that the program's output seems to be of a quality that would produce such a reaction. However, it seems to me that depth of music, computer programs, or people are not the true source of Doug's frustration. The problem arises, it seems to me, from identifying the wrong source of at least part of the depth.

For example, a woman once remarked to me that she felt certain that a computer program could compose music as beautiful as that composed by humans. However, she also felt that human-composed music contains hidden messages that intrigued her to decipher. The combination of beauty and revelation from such decoding in her mind made human-composed music greater than machine-composed music. She allowed that computer-composed music could also contain hidden messages, but stated that she was not interested in decoding these messages because they were unintentional. I replied that both types of messages were of her own making and that music from both sources had intention: *her* intention. Stravinsky remarked:

... music is, by its very nature, powerless to *express* anything at all, whether a feeling, an attitude of mind, a psychological mood, a phenomenon of nature ... if, as is nearly always the case, music appears to express something, this is only an illusion and not a reality. It is simply an additional attribute which, by tacit and inveterate agreement, we have lent it, thrust upon it, as a label, a convention—in short, an aspect unconsciously or by force of habit, we have come to confuse with its essential being. (Stravinsky 1975, pp. 53–4)

John Cage echoes these thoughts when he observes that

Most people think that when they hear a piece of music, they're not doing anything but that something is being done to them. Now this is not true, and we must arrange our music, we must arrange our art, we must arrange everything, I believe, so that people realize that they themselves are doing it, and not that something is being done to them. (Nyman 1974, p. 21)

Listeners obviously play a significant role in the musical experience. More than that, however, listeners play a *primary* role in this experience. We love or hate music not because the music itself is lovable or hatable but because we, through a complex and probably impossible-to-define set of aesthetic processes, decide to love it or hate it.

However, I don't mean to imply that music itself does not contain meaning. Consciously *and* subconsciously, composers invest in music aspects of everything they have heard and understand about music. After all, composers compose *recombinantly*. I use this term deliberately, since I believe Experiments in Musical Intelligence uses processes of recombinance similar to those that human composers use to compose. I believe as well that these same processes create the meaning we hear in music (more on this later).

Doug once confided in me that he had dreamed that I had confessed to composing Experiments in Musical Intelligence's entire output myself. This dream apparently produced a great feeling of relief in him. Since Experiments in Musical Intelligence has now composed over six thousand works, I doubt that his dream has recurred. This dream, along with Doug's three possibilities of deepness in music, suggests to me that he feels the quality of Experiments in Musical Intelligence's works somehow *cheapens* the works of his favored composers. To me, however, the flaws in the program's output help me *appreciate* the human-composed works I love more than ever. Remember that no Experiments in Musical Intelligence music would exist without the originals in the database—a fact that in itself should dilute any imaginings that these works supersede their predecessors in quality.

Doug's final assertion—"The *human soul/mind* is a lot shallower than I had ever thought"—is wrong. I think that we are all a lot *deeper* than even he imagines us to be. And I, for one, am not at all convinced that this is necessarily such a good thing.

Doug's idea of musical depth (see also chapter 16) seems intertwined with our Western tradition of ascribing "greatness" to some composers while others are of lesser quality:

... to claim that the active involvement of our recipient brains transfers all credit for greatness and depth from the creator to the recipient is nonsense. Such a viewpoint would imply that we can find greatness in anything at all, simply by using our receiving brains' power.

This quote raises some very important issues, one of which, the role of the listener, I address extensively in chapter 18. Here I wish to address the notion of "greatness." I do not believe that any work of art is intrinsically better than any other work of art. Greatness is something we impose on certain favored composers or works, not something that resides implicitly within them. Greatness arises and passes only by the whims of social, cultural, and historical fashion, not because works of art are *actually* great. Greatness is an opinion, not a fact. Unfortunately, in our rush to lionize certain composers we forget the extraordinary achievements of many less fortunate but nonetheless highly gifted lesser-known composers. This seems so self-evident to me that I find it difficult to articulate, and fear that by saying it I will insult my reader's intelligence. It is because I find many of my professional colleagues in disagreement that I risk raising the point here.

A friend of mine often asks the question: "Why are squirrels so damned cute and rats so damned ugly? They are both rodents. They both carry disease. Is it just because the squirrel's tail is so damned cute and the rat's tail so ugly?" The answer, he claims, is simple: "The squirrel's tail *is* damned cute." I do not yet know of anyone who favors the rat in such a comparison, nor anyone who, when asked to truly evaluate their answer to this question, actually believes that there is something intrinsically better about squirrels than rats.

Soul

Doug often grieves of his being "moved by 20,000 lines of code" (his way of describing Experiments in Musical Intelligence). By abstracting the program in this way, Doug focuses our attention on the inspiration-less, imagination-less, and soul-less form that he perceives the program to be. What this image (not Doug) fails to take into account is the thousands of hours of human labor that went into the program's creation. The fact is, any words or musical notes spread out on a sheet of paper look as cold and lifeless as do 20,000 lines of code. It is only our imaginations that breathe life into those markings. My 20,000 lines of code are, after all, simply *instructions*. Hemingway's instructions involve words to read. My instructions relate to how I want my computer to act. While my instructions may seem once removed from the actual creation of a new work of art, they are just as real and just as filled with my hopes for success as are Hemingway's instructions.

As Doug notes (see his comments in chapter 16), I dedicated a mazurka in the style of Chopin by Experiments in Musical Intelligence to him. My hope was twofold: to thank him for his continued efforts to make this body of work visible and audible in his concert-lectures and to personalize for him what was obviously an impersonal process. This mazurka appears, along with its dedication, in appendix D. My emphasis over the years with Experiments in Musical Intelligence has been to focus on its output—the music—rather than the source, the computer program. In so doing, I hope to underscore what I feel, as a composer, is the program's most important contribution: interesting and, to me at least, occasionally deeply moving music.

The essence of Doug's frustration appears in his own words, and again seems intimately connected with his notions about depth:

What troubles me is the notion that things that touch me at my deepest core—pieces of music most of all, which I have always taken as direct soul-to-soul messages—might be effectively produced by mechanisms thousands if not millions of times simpler than the intricate biological machinery that gives rise to a human soul.

The question of "soul" surfaces almost every time someone hears and then responds to a work by Experiments in Musical Intelligence. To begin with, I always try to start with a good definition of *soul*. *Webster's Dictionary* (1991, p. 1278) defines *soul* as "The principle of life, feeling, thought, and action in humans, regarded as a distinct entity separate from the body." There are three particular aspects of this definition that clearly exclude computers and hence computer creations from having soul. First, computers do not have life, by any current biological definition of that word. Second, computers are not human. Third, by inference at least, computers do not contain anything separate from their bodies, nor do I imagine that they will have any such separate "thing" in the near future. Therefore, computers do not have soul by definition. Nor can they ever have soul by such an exclusionary definition.

The bigger question for me, however, is not whether Experiments in Musical Intelligence compositions have soul but whether *human* compositions have soul (note that I deliberately avoid the question of whether humans themselves have soul). With such a vague definition of soul, I cannot see anyone arguing convincingly that the notes gathered on a page of music contain in them a "principle of life, feeling, thought, and action." No, the soul we perceive when we hear a deeply moving musical work, if "soul" is even the right word, is *our own soul*.

I believe the fact that we cannot, in general, recognize the difference between a machine-created and human-created work of art means that the program uses processes that in some ways mirror those used by human composers. In fact, I make the case for this in Cope 1996. Doug argues (see also chapter 16):

I would take issue ... that a composer starts out spending a good deal of time devising a grammar, and then, that having been done, just turns into a drone who spins off piece after piece using the rules of the grammar.

Doug is a master of language and here he wields "drone" and "spins off" as natural consequences of what he describes. I would argue that Experiments in Musical Intelligence is *not* a drone and that it *composes* rather than spins off new works.

However, Doug's commentary often proves quite insightful, pointing out aspects of the program that I rarely if ever mention, but should. First, he comments on how the program is not singular but plural:

It is indeed true that Emmy is evolving—it is a moving target.

This is a very important point. Many lovers and critics of Experiments in Musical Intelligence works seem to feel that there exists one single stable version of the program, when in fact there have been many (perhaps dozens of) versions of the program. Were it not for the fact that I keep rigorous documentation, it would be difficult for me to account for the differences between various Experiments in Musical Intelligence outputs.

Doug also notes (in reference to the creation of an Experiments in Musical Intelligence work in his own style in chapter 16) that

if you have such a sparse database on which to draw, your output is going to reek of its sources in a conspicuous manner. If Dave had been able to use all twelve of the pieces I sent him (or better yet, all forty of the pieces I've composed), then of course the mixture would have been far, far subtler.

I agree. A composer I know went to one of Doug's presentations on Experiments in Musical Intelligence. During the question period following the presentation he commented to Doug: "You should spend your time speaking about the possibilities of computers being used to compose *contemporary* music rather than all of these style imitations." For me, this anecdote accentuates the controversy created by Experiments in Musical Intelligence. There doesn't seem to be a single group of people that the program doesn't annoy in some way.

Interestingly, Doug's experiences with audiences is inversely proportional to my own experience.

Hardly anyone seemed upset at Cope's coup in the modeling of artistic creativity; hardly anyone seemed threatened or worried at all.

Doug's presentations, at least the ones that I have attended, range from delightfully humorous to almost painfully emotional. My presentations, on the other hand, cover the nuts and bolts of how the program works, usually without any references to emotion or to the program's philosophic implications. I suppose that audiences tend to pale when faced with his angst while they anger at my apparent detachment.

When Doug says (see chapter 16) that

Emmy's power of course comes, in *some* sense, from borrowing, for by definition and by intention, that is all that Emmy is—a borrower.

I must remind him of the quote he uses at the beginning of his commentary:

Good artists borrow; great artists steal.

While on this topic, I note that Doug's endnote is mistaken:

The epigram was actually stolen from David Cope, who himself had borrowed it from Pablo Picasso.

I did not *borrow* this line from Picasso, I *stole* it from Picasso, who actually *borrowed* it from Stravinsky.

4 Composing Style-Specific Music

I began Experiments in Musical Intelligence in 1981 as an attempt to create new music in my style. I soon realized, however, that I was too close to my own music to define its style in meaningful ways, or at least in ways which could be easily coded into a computer program. I opted therefore to create a program to compose music in the style(s) of composers whose works I had studied since my early youth—the classical composers of Western Europe.

Coding the Rules of Basic Part-Writing

My initial idea for Experiments in Musical Intelligence was to code the rules of basic part-writing (how chords smoothly connect to one another) as I understood them since such processes were common practice for many classical composers. These rules resemble those typically taught to undergraduate college music students and derive from generalizations made about music of the late Baroque to the middle Romantic periods of music history—roughly 1700 to 1860. After much experimentation, I created a program which produced a kind of styleless music which basically adhered to these rules. Figure 4.1 shows an example of music composed by this program. As can be seen and heard, the results are fairly sterile and while generally correct, convey little of the vibrancy of the music from which the rules derive. The statistical abstractions of the rule-making and rule-applying processes have neutralized any real musical interest.

While some of the output from this version of the program proved relatively successful, most of the music was uninteresting and unsatisfying. As well, having an intermediary—myself—form abstract sets of rules for composition seemed artificial and unnecessarily premeditative. Coding rules for a specific composer's style also meant that I had to create new versions of the program each time I wanted it to produce music in a different style. I therefore created a new program to derive rules from music coded in a database.

Recombinancy

I began by having this new program segment Bach (1685–1750) chorales into beats and saving these beats separately in objects using object-oriented programming (OOP) techniques. Object-orientation allows storage of data and analyses of those data in ways analogous to the real world, thus making access and manipulation of those data easier and more logical. Along with each beat I had this new version of the

Figure 4.1
An example of music composed by an early rules-based version of Experiments in Musical Intelligence.

program retain the name of the destination pitch to which each voice moved in the next beat. I further had the program collect these beat objects in various groups called lexicons named according to the pitches and register of their entering voices (e.g., C1–G1–C2–E3, where the number suffixes reflect the octave of the note name). To compose, then, the program chooses the first beat of any chorale in its database and examines this beat's destination notes. The program then selects one of the stored beats in the lexicon whose name matches the current beat's destination notes. New choices then create the potential for different offbeat motions and different following chords while maintaining the integrity of Bach's voice-leading.

Seeing—and hearing—is believing, and following the creation of an actual new phrase of music, while to some extent repeating the process just described, can usefully establish a modus operandi for later chapters.

Figure 4.2 shows the first phrase of Bach's Chorale no. 26 (Bach 1941). Note how this music can be grouped by quarter-note beat with each voice in the groupings having a distinct destination, as just described. Figure 4.3 shows each beat of figure 4.2 boxed to show this grouping process. Figure 4.4 then provides an exploded view of the first three beats of Chorale no. 26 with lines connecting the last heard notes of one beat to the first heard notes of the next beat (destinations). These lines also follow the voice-leading rules of four-part writing, the rules which the program will attempt to emulate in creating a new chorale.

Given that databases can have thousands of chords stored in objects, many will appear more than once. Often these duplications will move in different directions, a fact that contributes to the program's ability to create new chorales. To increase the number of possibilities, Experiments in Musical Intelligence transposes all of the

Figure 4.2
Bach Chorale no. 26, phrase 1.

Figure 4.3
Bach Chorale no. 26, phrase 1, with beats separated.

Figure 4.4
An exploded view of the first three beats of Bach Chorale no. 26, phrase 1, with destination notes high-lighted by connecting lines.

music in its database by phrase to a single key before analysis. Any key will do as long as the key choice is applied equally to all phrases.

Figure 4.5 shows how the third beat of the third full measure of Bach Chorale no. 6 has the identical notes as those of the second beat of Bach Chorale no. 26. Measure numbers include pickup measures. Experiments in Musical Intelligence substitutes this new beat in place of the actual second beat of Bach Chorale no. 26, producing the beginning of a new phrase. Since the destination notes remain the same as those in the original chorale, the integrity of Bach's voice-leading remains intact while the music continues in a different way than Bach originally intended (refer to figure 4.2).

Figure 4.6 continues this process by replacing the next beat of Bach Chorale no. 6 with music from measure 14 of Bach Chorale no. 323. This choice takes the newly created music further yet from the original music of Bach Chorale no. 26. Figure 4.7 then links Bach Chorale no. 224 with Bach Chorale no. 323. The program's failure to discover substitutes for these few beats of the new chorale is due to a lack of logical substitutes in the database. The resultant phrase, however, is new and substantially different from that shown in figure 4.2. In this manner, this simple version of Experiments in Musical Intelligence creates interesting new chorales, all correct in terms of chord-to-chord rules for voice-leading, but without the program having to apply any user-supplied rules. I use the term *recombinancy* to describe this approach. The music, in effect, inherits the voice-leading rules of the works upon which it bases its replications.

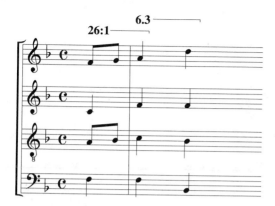

Figure 4.5
Music from Bach Chorale no. 6, m. 3 grafted to the first beat of Bach Chorale no. 26.

Figure 4.6
Figure 4.5 continued with music from Chorale no. 323.

Structural Logic

The problems with this approach, however, are many. First and foremost, the resulting music wanders with very unbalanced and uncharacteristic phrase lengths. This
occurs because phrases cadence only when the program randomly encounters a
cadence in the original music. In essence, the program has no real logic beyond the
chord-to-chord syntax. Further, the program has no large-scale structure and phrases
simply string together randomly, usually in a single key, and without any sense of the
kinds of repetition and development necessary for intelligent composition.

Figure 4.7
Figure 4.6 continued with music from Chorale no. 224.

In order to provide some sense of structural logic, and wanting to avoid directly programming the various constraints of musical form myself, I rewrote the program to inherit more of the structural aspects of the music in its database. This inheritance involved coding an analysis subprogram that stores other information with each beat along with its immediate destination notes. Storing references pertaining to general temporal location of cadences, for example, helped the program create effective phrase and section endings without duplicating entire phrases.

Figure 4.8 provides a visual example of how Experiments in Musical Intelligence produces music with proper phrase lengths. The program first chooses a chorale upon which to model its new composition. The program stores this single-chorale data in a separate location for consultation during the composing process. As new phrases are composed using the previously described recombination, the program maintains a connection with the structural model in regard to overall form, basing choices for new beats on how well their original position in relation to cadence relates to the current in-progress phrase's relation to cadence. The model also provides general information such as number of phrases, cadence types, and so on. The model, however, does not dictate the absolute length of phrases (determined within reasonable limits) since doing so could force dead-ends, and retaining too much information can cause the program to simply reiterate one of the chorales in its database.

Figures 4.9 through 4.13 show successive phrases completed in the same manner as the phrase shown in figure 4.7. Each of the source chorale numbers appears above the associated music. Figure 4.14 then shows how the new chorale matches its particular model, Bach Chorale no. 299. While the notes differ between the new music and the actual Bach, the functional relationships between the successions of cadences do not.

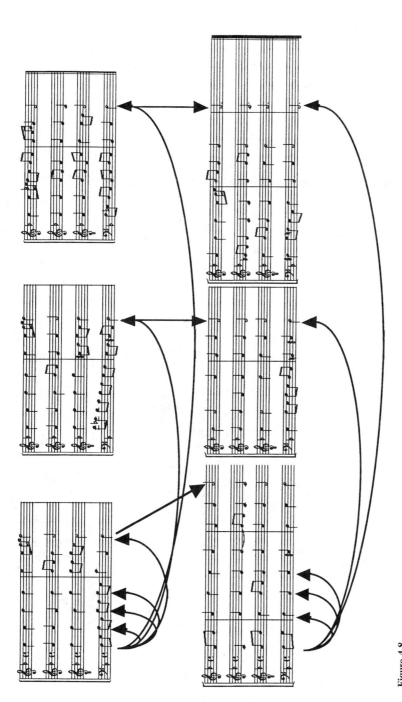

Figure 4.8
A Bach chorale (top) used as a model for a new Experiments in Musical Intelligence chorale (bottom).

Figure 4.9
A second phrase of a new chorale.

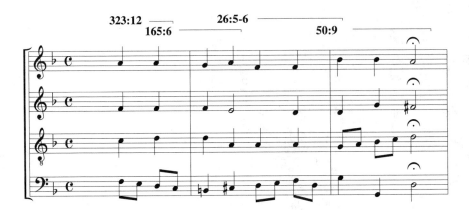

Figure 4.10
A third phrase of a new chorale.

Figure 4.11
A fourth phrase of a new chorale.

Figure 4.12
A fifth phrase of a new chorale.

Thus, while the phrases themselves accrue by successively adding material at the local level, larger structures proceed by developing a logical succession of cadences. Viewed closely, this process projects what music theorists refer to as complete authentic cadences from incomplete authentic cadences, full cadences from half-cadences, and so on (see chapter 2 of Cope 1991a for further information). The creation of movements and works follows much this same process.

Modulation presents a special case for Experiments in Musical Intelligence. When the program encounters music that modulates, it allows a new phrase to modulate as well and then transposes the ensuing phrase to the new key so that new music estab-

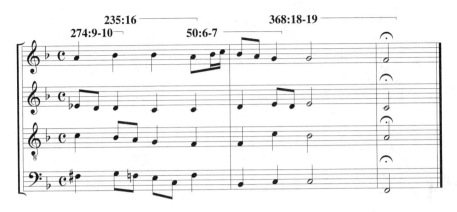

Figure 4.13
A final phrase of a new chorale.

lishes this key appropriately. Passages that modulate are then coerced back to the original keys or to new keys following the chosen structural model, as demonstrated in figure 4.14.

Since the database music has all been transposed to the same key prior to composing, the program's initial key of a newly composed chorale is that same key. However, to add variety to output, I determine the final overall key based on the range limitations of the performing voices or instruments and, as possible, other factors contributing to ease of performance.

Variations

Even with hundreds of examples of original music in a database, however, Experiments in Musical Intelligence will occasionally produce music with recognizable parts (see particularly the Mendelssohn example in appendix D). The strange juxtaposition of known materials can cause even well-formed output to be unacceptable. To alleviate these problems, the program incorporates numerous variations of the recombinant processes thus far discussed.

For example, Experiments in Musical Intelligence diatonically transposes measures to other scale degrees. Diatonic transposition differs from exact transposition because diatonic transposition produces music with altered intervals. Figure 4.15 demonstrates this process. Note that many of the actual intervals change from transposition to transposition because the notes must conform to a single key. With these added

Figure 4.14
Transposed version of Bach Chorale no. 299 (the model, to the left) aligned with the newly composed Experiments in Musical Intelligence chorale (to the right).

(a)

(b)

(c)

Figure 4.15
Diatonic transpositions of the first full measure of Bach Chorale no. 26.

transpositions, the program increases database size sevenfold, thus often creating new-sounding music even when it has very little data present in its database.

Experiments in Musical Intelligence also includes an elaborate subprogram capable of combinatorially reorganizing music by voice as well as by beat. I term this reorganization *transformational* recombination, since the music being recombined is transformed (Cope 1996 discusses a subset of transformative recombination called MATN). This transformation may take place between the various voices of a single beat or between voices of different beats which have the same function and entering notes. Figure 4.16 demonstrates how various recombinations—including octave transpositions—succeed in transforming beats of Bach chorales into new music.

Figure 4.16a shows vertical voice interchange. Here the voices of the same beat (the beginning of the last phrase of Chorale no. 235) are interchanged, effectively transforming the beat of music. This process poses a risk for the program in that some of the voices now have different ending notes which may not as easily connect with appropriate configurations in the database. Figure 4.16b shows examples of voice interchange between the second measures of Bach chorales nos. 6 and 26. These two chorale measures have identical initial notes. When recombined as in the three examples which follow Bach's originals, rules of counterpoint have been maintained though the resultant music differs from the original music in many ways.

Another form of transformational composition involves retaining voice order but transposing one or more voices by an octave or other interval. Such transformation requires that the transposing voice not cross other voices. As will be seen in chapters 7 through 9, this form of transformation allows some measures, otherwise not available for recombinancy, to connect properly. However, such transformational composition can be risky in that transposing by any other interval than an octave can cause serious stylistic discontinuities such as inappropriate harmonic dissonances.

Texture

All music does not follow such consistent textures as do Bach chorales. Most music in fact varies significantly in terms of numbers of voices. This texture shifting can cause numerous problems for a recombinant program like Experiments in Musical Intelligence. Likewise, beats having the same function and destination notes can have very different characters producing sudden shifts in output music. No matter how carefully works are chosen for the database, almost anything besides Bach chorales will create incongruities between individual beats during recombinancy—combining music with the proper connectivity and structural order with music of completely

Figure 4.16
Examples of transformation: (a) vertical voice interchange of the beginning of the last phrase of Chorale no. 235; (b) examples of voice interchange between the first three beats of the second measures of Bach Chorale no. 6 and no. 26 (shown first).

(a)

(b)

(c)

Figure 4.17
Transposed and clarified (see chapter 8) versions of (a) mm. 1–2 of Mozart's K. 284, mvt. 2; (b) juxtaposition of m. 1 of K. 284, mvt. 2 and m. 62 of K. 310, mvt. 2, which does not work; and (c) juxtaposition of m. 1 of K. 284, mvt. 2 and a slightly transformed version of m. 61 of K. 330, mvt. 2, which works effectively.

different character (see figures 4.17 and 8.1 for examples of this kind of juxtaposition). One way to avoid this problem involves storing representations of the musical texture and character of each segment so that continuity can be maintained during composition. In fact, Experiments in Musical Intelligence analyzes such continuities in the original music before it breaks the music into segments to ensure that changes of continuity take place at musically reasonable locations in the output.

To accomplish this continuity analysis I use a variety of techniques borrowed from various fields, including artificial intelligence (AI) and natural language processing (NLP) which I discuss in detail elsewhere (Cope 1991a, 1996). These techniques provide the basic logic required for the assembly of segments of music from different works by the same composer. In brief, this means that only segments of compatible music are chosen from the available segments with identical initial notes. This compatibility results from storing abstractions of each segment's musical texture and character and from mapping these to the model composition in the database.

Figure 4.17 provides a simple demonstration of how correct connections in terms of destination notes can still produce disjunct music in varying textures. Note here that only the melodic destination is considered important—harmonic connectivity in most styles need not be so carefully monitored as in Bach chorales. Likewise, recombinancy by measure, rather than by beat, works effectively in this music. Figure 4.17a shows two original measures by Mozart, the first measure of which will become the first measure of a hypothetical new computer-composed sonata movement. Figure 4.17b provides an example of how, even when the destination note of the melody matches, the characters of the two groupings can conflict and create contrast where none exists in the original. The sudden sixteenth-note motion in the second measure here dramatically shifts the character of the music. Figure 4.17c, on the other hand, demonstrates how, when the program considers the contextual continuity of the characters of the first and subsequent measures, a more logical second measure results.

5 The Importance of Patterns

Recombining segments of music from a database to create new music ignores the possibility that important indicators of musical style may be disassembled in the process. For example, certain musical patterns, which I believe are critical to the recognition of musical style, extend beyond the size of segments. I call these patterns *signatures*.

Signatures

Signatures are contiguous note patterns which recur in two or more works of a single composer and therefore indicate aspects of that composer's musical style. Signatures are typically two to five beats (four to ten melodic notes) in length and usually consist of composites of melody, harmony, and rhythm. Signatures typically occur between four and ten times in any given work. Variations often include pitch transposition, interval alteration, rhythmic refiguring, and voice exchange. With few exceptions, however, such variations do not deter aural recognition. Signatures are typically revealed by using pattern-matching processes (see Cope 1991b, 1996, 2000). Signatures can tell us what period of music history a work comes from, the probable composer of that work, and so on.

Signatures and recombinancy are fundamentally opposite in nature. That is, while recombinancy seeks to break music into small parts in order to recombine these parts into newly organized music during composition, signatures must resist such fragmentation which would ultimately detract from accurate style replication. Therefore, the Experiments in Musical Intelligence program protects signatures from being broken into smaller groupings for recombination.

Experiments in Musical Intelligence uses pattern-matching, a standard artificial intelligence technique, to discover signatures. In music, matching patterns exactly yields little of consequence because precisely repeating sequences are the exception rather than the norm. Therefore, the program seeks patterns which resemble one another enough to have musical consequence but do not differ so much as to sound unrelated.

Figure 5.1 presents various incarnations of a signature found in different movements of Mozart's piano sonatas. This signature is characterized by an upward-leading scale passage followed by a downward leap which ultimately resolves by stepwise motion. The harmonic underpinnings vary somewhat depending on the example. However, the basic structure follows a cadential tonic six-four chord followed by a dominant-tonic cadence (see Cope 1991a). The number of notes in the rising scale, the actual interval of the falling leap, and the concluding notes all vary from example to example. An intervallic pattern-matcher which allows appropriate variances will identify all of these results as variants of the same basic pattern. Our

Figure 5.1
Clarified (see chapter 8) Mozart signatures from: (a) K. 279 (1774), mvt. 2, m. 17; (b) K. 280 (1774), mvt. 2, mm. 56–7; (c) K. 311 (1777), mvt. 3, mm. 158–9; (d) K. 330 (1778), mvt. 2, mm. 48–9; (e) k. 331 (1778), mvt. 1, mm. 17–8; (f) K. 331 (1778), mvt. 2, mm. 47–8; (g) K. 332 (1778), mvt. 3, mm. 220–1; (h) K. 333 (1778), mvt. 2, mm. 42–3; (i) K. 533 (1788), mvt. 1, mm. 172–3; (j) K. 494 (1786), mvt. 1, mm. 17–8; (k) K. 570 (1789), mvt. 3, mm. 22–3.

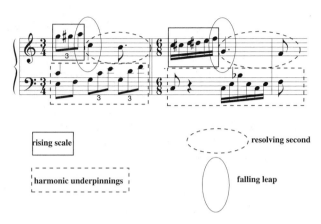

Figure 5.2
How a pattern matcher discovers signature variants.

ears likewise forgive the differences and, consciously or subconsciously, most experienced listeners will recognize these figures as characteristically Classical in nature and Mozartean in these specific uses. For further examples of this Viennese signature, see figure 3.8 in Cope 1996 and related text.

Figure 5.2 shows how the first two variants of figure 5.1 can match when compared by a pattern-matcher. Both rising scales contain half-steps which the matcher assumes carry more weight than their difference in number (two intervals compared to five intervals). The leap downward exceeds a fifth in both cases which this particular matcher counts as more significant than their half-step differences (one is a major sixth and the other a minor seventh). The final motion is stepwise in both cases even though one resolves by half-step and the other by whole-step. The harmony in both cases outlines a basic cadential motion, which is all that this matcher requires to favorably compare the two patterns. The fact that the patterns differ in key (the first in C major and the second in F major) and notes (the melodies have but two notes in common—C and G) are inconsequential since the matcher compares intervals.

Variables I call "controllers" allow variations of patterns to count as matches. Pattern-matching controllers for these types of variations must not be set too freely or many matches will occur which do not represent variances of the same pattern. In contrast, controllers must not be set so narrowly as to not allow patterns that should match to match. Controllers may be set by users or by Experiments in Musical Intelligence itself using typical numbers of matches to guide it to appropriate controller levels (see Cope 1992b).

Figure 5.3 presents another signature in varying guises. This Chopin mazurka signature is characterized by a triplet turn followed by downward-moving motion using small intervals. Most often the triplet occurs on beat 2 of the triple-metered mazurka though three times here it occurs on the first beat. The triplet rarely occurs on the third beat in mazurkas, the weakest beat in mazurka style (the second beat usually receives the accent). The accompanying harmony in figure 5.3 is less predictable than the Mozart examples in figure 5.1, though the Chopin signature does follow a measure-by-measure harmonic rhythm relevant to the mazurka style. I discuss a different version of this signature *The Algorithmic Composer* (Cope 2000, pp. 148–50).

As with figure 5.1, few of the examples shown in figure 5.3 contain precisely the same notes, intervals, and harmonies. Matching subtle differences can be quite difficult even for a sophisticated pattern-matcher because the controller levels necessary to recognize these variants may also produce numerous nonvariants. Figure 3.7 of *Experiments in Musical Intelligence* (Cope 1996, p. 89) shows further how Chopin can bury repetitions of his themes and signatures in extremely ornamented variations. In such cases, high controller levels designed to permit several interpolated notes will produce false matches elsewhere in the music. To reduce this noise in the output, the program must factor elements such as the precise location and context of variations. This kind of precision allows the Experiments in Musical Intelligence pattern-matcher to discover signatures which are aurally recognizable but numerically appear very different.

Experiments in Musical Intelligence uses signatures in many ways. Some signatures, particularly signatures at cadence points, can be used in generally the same form as they originally appeared. Other signatures, either because they have unique-sounding material or because they consist of a character quite different from the material surrounding them in their new environs, must be revised. Such revisions usually involve a refiguring of accompaniments to provide musical continuity. This continuity is typically created by using previously described transformational techniques (i.e., borrowing individual lines with equivalent destination notes).

Earmarks

There are other important patterns in music besides signatures (Agawu 1991, Gherdingen 1988). As an example, pattern-matching has revealed certain gestures in music which seem to foreshadow important structural events. For instance, the two principal cadential trills near the ends of the second exposition and precadenza sections in the first movements of the last twenty-two of Mozart's piano concerti prepare

Figure 5.3

Clarified (see chapter 8) variations of a signature in Chopin's mazurkas: (a) op. 7 (1830–1), no. 3, m. 96; (b) op. 24 (1834–5), no. 2, mm. 91–2; (c) op. 24 (1834–5), no. 3, mm. 6–7; (d) op. 30 (1836–7), no. 2, mm. 14–5; (e) op. 33 (1837–8), no. 2, mm. 4–5; (f) op. 33 (1837–8), no. 4, mm. 18–9; (g) op. 41 (1839), no. 3, mm. 35–6; (h) op. 50 (1841–2), no. 1, mm. 24–5; (i) op. 50 (1841–2), no. 3, mm. 88–9; (j) op. 67 (1835), no. 1, mm. 27–8; (k) op. 67 (1849), no. 2, m. 24.

listeners for the music that follows. These location-specific gestures provide us with a deeper understanding of musical structure and ultimately reveal why some works possess a sense of inevitability. I call such patterns *earmarks*.

Earmarks provide structural guides beyond thematic repetition, key changes, and so on. Earmarks indicate important attributes, at least to the relatively experienced listener, about one's place in a work by foreshadowing important structural events. Earmarks can also contribute to expectations of when a movement or work should reach a point of arrival or end. Interestingly, unlike signatures, earmarks are icons which typically hold little interest in themselves but great interest for what they tell us about structure and what they can foretell about ensuing events.

Figure 5.4 shows twelve examples of the aforementioned Mozart piano concerto earmark. Note how the first few measures of most examples abruptly shift to music of a different character as the final chord of the precadenza approaches. The music which precedes these examples resembles the initial measures of music shown here. The exact nature of the suddenly different music is not important (though note here how often these earmarks have a syncopated rhythm). The fact that sudden interruptive music occurs *is* important and announces the oncoming cadenza.

These examples are simple, possibly obvious, and with even limited experience listeners can become accustomed to the introduction of new material late in a movement and anticipate the eventual appearance of cadenzas. Earmarks such as these produce structural anticipations requiring fulfillment to convince us of the movement's formal integrity. Experiments in Musical Intelligence therefore analyzes the music in its database for earmarks and ensures that once found, these structural patterns are not shifted to other, inappropriate locations or omitted from the music the program composes.

Discovering earmarks requires a substantially different kind of pattern-matcher than does the finding of signatures. To locate earmarks, a pattern-matcher must report only those patterns which *fail* to match any other pattern in a movement of music. These patterns are then considered unique and regardless of their makeup constitute earmarks. In effect, an earmark pattern-matcher eliminates all of the more numerous matches relevant to signatures and thematic development. Typically, earmarks occur only once or twice in a movement or work and appear as lone survivors after all other matched patterns have been discarded. The distinguishing characteristic of earmarks is that they appear at particular locations in compositions, just before or just after important events. Earmarks have global position sensitivity, usually to the ending or beginning of a major section of a movement or work, as opposed to signatures which have local position sensitivity.

(a)

(b)

Figure 5.4

Clarified (see chapter 8) reductions of precadenza measures from Mozart's (a) K. 238 (1776), mvt. 1, mm. 187–91; (b) K. 238 (1776), mvt. 3, mm. 257–61; (c) K. 365 (1779), mvt. 1, mm. 288–91; (d) K. 365 (1779), mvt. 3, mm. 456–65; (e) K. 415 (1782–3), mvt. 1, mm. 295–300; (f) K. 415 (1782–3), mvt. 3, mm. 229–32; (g) K. 450 (1784), mvt. 1, mm. 290–5; (h) K. 450 (1784), mvt. 3, mm. 277–85; (i) K. 456 (1784), mvt. 1, mm. 346–8; (j) K. 456 (1784), mvt. 3, mm. 289–91; (k) K. 491 (1786), mvt. 1, mm. 480–6; (l) K. 491 (1786), mvt. 3, mm. 217–20.

(c)

(d)

Figure 5.4 (continued)

(e)

(f)

Figure 5.4 (continued)

(g)

Figure 5.4 (continued)

(h)

Figure 5.4 (continued)

Figure 5.4 (continued)

(l)

Figure 5.4 (continued)

Earmarks are *principles rather than data* and hence the earmark pattern-matcher returns an abstraction representing the type of material used rather than actual musical events as required of recombinative composition. Experiments in Musical Intelligence then seeks material that exemplifies the nature of this abstraction. Figure 5.5 shows how the program integrated an earmark into its piano concerto in the style of Mozart. Unfortunately, this earmark somewhat resembles the material preceding it and does not create the contrast necessary to clearly announce the oncoming cadenza. This less-than-satisfactory earmark results from the fact that composing completely different music than found anywhere else in a composition requires significant analytical processes somewhat beyond the scope of the version of Experiments in Musical Intelligence which composed this music. More recent implementations of the program create more satisfactory earmarks for insertion at the appropriate locations.

Figure 5.5
A piano reduction of an earmark used in mm. 322–6 in the first movement of the Experiments in Musical
Intelligence Mozart Piano Concerto.

Earmarks play a critical role in Experiments in Musical Intelligence's ability to
generate logical musical structures. Using earmarks appropriately in algorithmic
composition enhances stylistic integrity, formal and structural balance, cohesion,
and ultimately, I feel, aesthetic value. Misplaced earmarks can disrupt an educated
listener's perception of musical structure. For example, earmarks that do not precede
anticipated events, that occur out of sequence, or are otherwise ill-timed can cause
otherwise substantial works to lack musical coherence.

Figure 5.6 shows a fourth-movement earmark found in an Experiments in Musical
Intelligence symphony in the style of Mozart. This earmark can be found in type if
not character in many of Mozart's symphonies. Three fourth movements of Mozart's
symphonies were used in the pattern-matching which found earmarks near this location. Again, as with the earmark found in the concerti, the music here is not particularly distinguished. This earmark differs from the surrounding material enough,
however, to make its structural importance clear to the ear. In this case, the earmark
announces the recapitulation of the first theme in the movement's original key.

Unifications

Experiments in Musical Intelligence also seeks patterns which help to unify the music
it creates. I call such patterns *unifications*. While signatures contribute to the recognition of the *style* of the composer whose music the program is attempting to emulate, unifications have greater local importance and relate to harmonic, thematic, and

Figure 5.6
An earmark from the fourth movement of the Experiments in Musical Intelligence Program's Mozart's Symphony (mm. 82–5). The earmark begins on the fourth beat of m. 82 and ends on the downbeat of m. 85.

rhythmic elements only in a single work. Discovering and using such patterns can be quite important to programs creating virtual music. Otherwise, the new music that the program composes, no matter how relevant it might be to the general style of the music in the database, would poorly reflect the compositional techniques of the composer being replicated.

Experiments in Musical Intelligence initially ascertains the numbers, locations, and variation types of unifications in the music of its database. For example, knowing that a certain pattern has repeated during a passage is of little use if the program doesn't also know that this pattern repeats few or many times, repeats only in certain circumstances, repeats only after predictable delays, or repeats only with certain vari-

Figure 5.7
Examples of clarified (see chapter 8) and transposed unifications in Mozart's K. 284, mvt. 2: (a) mm. 2–4;
(b) mm. 32–4; (c) mm. 40–2.

ations. The program then takes a naturally recurring motive in the work that it is creating and attempts to coerce the new music toward like numbers of motives and their variations to help create unity.

Experiments in Musical Intelligence uses three basic techniques to find unifications and replicate them in its musical output. First, and foremost, actual patterns are collected only from the music of the work being composed once a substantial portion of a theme or idea has been created. In effect, for this process at least, the program ignores the music in the database. Second, the program only matches patterns in defined regions. Last, the program looks for patterns *within* individual phrases rather than *between* phrases. In effect, the program seeks patterns integral to the basic continuity of the music of the work being composed in order to extend that music in logical and musical ways.

As with signatures, Experiments in Musical Intelligence keeps unifications generically intact during the composing process so that they retain their recognizability.

Unlike signatures, however, unifications may be quite numerous and, rather than spread their use over entire sections of compositions, the program often uses unifications in close quarters, even in combination by overlapping them or using them contiguously in sequence.

Unifications also help Experiments in Musical Intelligence devise contrasting music for new sections during composition. The program accomplishes this by carefully contrasting already-composed unifications and then representing these new unifications in numbers of occurrences and types of variations as represented by the music found in the database. Presuming that the order of contrast necessary may require a different unifying factor, the program may use a contrasting set of unification numbers for contrasting machine-based composition.

Using unifications does not presuppose that all music consists of repetitions and variations of motives. Using unifications does, however, assume that music itself constitutes patterns and that all music can be analyzed as patterns, even if repeats of these patterns occur rarely. Relying on a database as a model for newly composed music ensures like numbers of unifications in output even if these numbers are very small. In this way, music which does not utilize obvious pattern replication does not suffer from the program's mode of composition.

Figure 5.7 shows variations of a unification in Mozart. This simple chromatic scalelike motive, typical of unifications, helps to meld the more important thematically related material. Whenever this unification appears in this movement, it helps to provide the unity required to coalesce music into a consistent whole. As will be seen in chapter 9, Experiments in Musical Intelligence creates the same type of unity in its own musical composition through this use of unifications.

6 Structure

Musical form has been handled differently by various incarnations of Experiments in Musical Intelligence. Early versions of the program, for example, depended on users for all but motivic composition. By this I do not mean that users composed phrase and section variations and so on, but that they dictated the levels at which variation took place in machine composition. Later versions of the program require significantly less user input and rely more heavily on the analysis of music in the database. This structural analysis exceeds that of simply finding signatures, earmarks, and unifications. The program utilizes a multifaceted approach to structural analysis. Initially the program seeks out major thematic areas, a technique which usually succeeds with classical music. If that analytical process fails, the program analyzes for contrast, changes in density, and shifts of composite rhythm. Each of these processes deserves further explanation.

Detecting Thematic Boundaries

In many musical styles, form follows the initiation of repeating or contrasting thematic ideas and their repetitions which delineate sectional boundaries. Experiments in Musical Intelligence uses a variation of its conventional pattern-matcher to detect such thematic boundaries. Since this thematic pattern-matcher seeks *differences* between patterns rather than similarities, new sections are detected when the program encounters no matches between ongoing and newly found patterns.

If thematic pattern analysis fails to determine sectional boundaries, the program attempts to define other areas of contrast for such determination. Analyzing continuities of textures, rhythms, and dynamics helps the program to discover contrasting music. Timbre choices and phrase lengths can also distinguish new material from previous ideas.

If these processes of differentiating contrast also fail in detecting form, Experiments in Musical Intelligence uses density as a primary factor in determining when sections end and new sections begin. The program calculates density by first breaking music into contiguous groupings the size of the shortest durational element. Hence, music with a sixteenth-note as its shortest member will be grouped into continuous sixteenth-note–length groups. The program then averages the number of voices over a span of time, stopping when it encounters a significant change in that average.

While thematic separation and density are excellent techniques for discovering contrast in music, even these processes in combination are not often sufficient enough to distinguish all of the various elements of form. This deficiency can be especially noticeable when analyzing works with transitions between sections rather than having abruptly contrasting ideas. For such works, and other works in which structure evolves smoothly rather than suddenly, texture and other formal analyses must be combined with cadence mapping to produce a useful formal analysis. Such mapping indicates more precisely where the ideas of one section end and another section begins.

Harmonic cadences represent the hierarchical linchpins of most musical styles. Discovering the precise locations of harmonic cadences, however, can pose problems in certain styles of music. Bach, in his fugues, for example, provides few clues as to when cadences occur. Harmonic analysis can suggest cadences where none actually exist. The aforementioned texture analysis may occasionally help but can often actually disguise the true position of cadences.

Experiments in Musical Intelligence accounts for these difficulties by using proportions in its analysis. Believing that composers, no matter what their approach to cadences may be, establish phrase and section lengths according to certain basic principles of balance, I have the program use phrase lengths discovered previously in other works by the same composer to project new phrase lengths, and hence cadences, where otherwise none tend to easily surface. The program then verifies these cadences by using one or more of the previously discussed techniques.

Creating Musical Forms

Creating musical forms, of course, involves more than the coordination of a work's cadences. Form implies the degree of repetition, variation, or contrast that takes place at many different levels in a work's hierarchy. In Experiments in Musical Intelligence, these hierarchical levels refer to motive, phrase, and section. Motives are small eight- to twelve-note melodic ideas which repeat, sequence, or vary in ways that can contribute to the recognition of a musical style. Phrases are larger than motives, culminate in cadences, and repeat, vary, or contrast according to structural concerns. Sections consist of phrases which repeat, vary, or contrast to create large-scale forms.

In order to demonstrate how Experiments in Musical Intelligence produces motivic repetition, variation, and contrast, I will use the program's Prokofiev sonata second movement from appendix D. This movement has a double binary form of ABAB, where the second B is an extended version of the first B section. The A section (beginning in m. 1 and again in m. 22) has a distinct texture of three to four voices primarily in the left hand while the B section (beginning in m. 10 and again in m. 27) often inverts this arrangement.

The overall binary plan of this movement, not atypical of Prokofiev slow movements, contains a number of imitative and sequential subsections, particularly noticeable in section B. The most pronounced motive begins with thirty-second-notes as shown in consecutive measures beginning in measure 10 in the left hand. This motive would not repeat or vary with recombinative compositional approaches. Unifications will occasionally support such motivic imitations but not typically with a motive of this length. Therefore, Experiments in Musical Intelligence, after locating such imitative material in the database, attempts to replicate it in its output. The program accomplishes this by creating a characteristic motive, usually of shorter length than themes in music, and then broadcasting this motive throughout the current section of music at a rate consistent with that found in the music in the database.

Doug Hofstadter calls this *templagiarism*. In chapter 2, he points out that

It would have been pleasing if at that point we had scoured Prokofiev's scores until we found exactly such an episode, but we didn't take the trouble to do so. I'll take Dave's word for it that we would find it somewhere or other.

Figure 6.1 provides a number of examples of such imitating figures as drawn from Prokofiev's piano sonatas. In each of these cases, the unifications provide a continuity to their themes and phrases and vary by (at least) transposition and metric placement as well as less often by additive and subtractive processes.

It should be noted that fugues, canons, and other strict contrapuntal forms pose special problems for Experiments in Musical Intelligence. Because these formalisms adhere to structural constraints that affect every level of the compositional process, I have built special subprograms for the creation of these types of works. As documented in my previous books (see particularly Cope 1996, pp. 213–4), fugues, in particular, are first created as full-textured compositions using recombinancy and then unwound into their eventual forms (see the machine-composed Bach fugue in appendix D as an example output from this process).

SPEAC

The Experiments in Musical Intelligence program often arrives at decision points where more than possible correct possibility exists. This occurs most often when choosing new groupings for recombination. Leaving such decisions to random selection often introduces uncharacteristic anomalies into recombinant music. Early on in the process of creating the program I opted to use a different approach to making such choices. As with many other basic elements of the composing process, I based this approach on the analysis of music in the database.

There are many methods for analyzing musical groupings. These methods range from tonal functional analysis to pitch-class set theory (see Cope 2000) and so on.

Figure 6.1
Clarified (see chapter 8) unifications from (a) Prokofiev Sonata no. 4 (1917), mm. 118, 124, 126; (b) Prokofiev Sonata no. 6 (1939–40), mvt. 4, mm. 185, 210–3; (c) Prokofiev Sonata no. 8 (1939–44), mm. 151,
155–6, 161, 165.

While each of these approaches can produce revealing results, few relate to other
parameters besides pitch or define significant hierarchical or structural relationships.
Furthermore, while many contemporary analytical techniques provide information
on how one grouping compares to another grouping, they yield little useful information about actual musical function. In short, no single method seems appropriate
as the ideal choice for analysis.

SPEAC analysis (discussed at length in Cope 1991b and 1996), in contrast, uses the
context provided by parameters such as metric placement, duration, location within a
phrase, and vertical tension to differentiate between groupings which may appear
identical or similar but which sound different due to context. A grouping used as a

Figure 6.1 (continued)

pickup to the first measure of a work, for example, can play a significantly different role than the identically appearing penultimate chord in the final cadence of the same work. SPEAC analysis clarifies such differences.

The SPEAC approach abstracts musical notes and harmonies on the basis of ideas derived from the work of Heinrich Schenker (1935). SPEAC is an acronym for *s*tatement, *p*reparation, *e*xtension, *a*ntecedent, and *c*onsequent. SPEAC analysis allows notes and chords to vary in meaning depending on their context. Therefore, the analysis of a C–E–G grouping in C major can change depending on its use. For example, at the beginning of a phrase in C major, C–E–G may be a statement, S, whereas in a cadence it may be a consequent, C. Thus, whereas traditional functions provide analysis of surface detail, the SPEAC system reveals a deeper context in music.

SPEAC abstraction does not replace other types of analysis. Rather, SPEAC enhances these analyses since SPEAC differentiates between otherwise identical results. SPEAC can also be used in parallel with any other analytical approach.

As a simple example, figure 6.2 shows the first two phrases of Bach Chorale no. 1 (Bach 1941). Standard Roman numeral analysis shows the presence of seven tonic (I) chords. With the exception of the first inversion tonic chord on the downbeat of measure 7, the analysis of these chords does not indicate that they have different musical meanings. Even the two chords which repeat in precisely the same voicings,

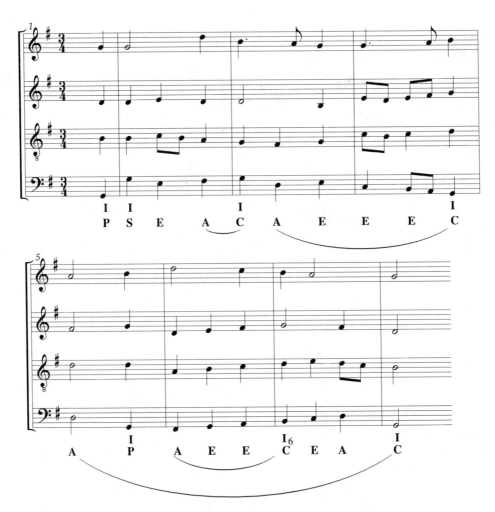

Figure 6.2
First two phrases of Bach's Chorale no. 1 with tonic chords marked in function and SPEAC analysis showing how SPEAC provides extended meanings.

tonic chords 4 and 5, and tonic chords 1 and 7, for example, have somewhat different implications if not meanings. Each tonic chord here has different preceding and following chords, different metric placement, different durations, and/or different location in regard to phrase and section context. The SPEAC identifiers shown below each chord in figure 6.2 demonstrate how SPEAC differentiates meanings of chords which otherwise have similar or equivalent functional analyses.

SPEAC identifiers have the following definitions:

S = *statement*; stable—a declaration of material. Statements can precede or follow any SPEAC function.

P = *preparation*; active—an introductory gesture. Preparations precede any SPEAC function though more typically occur prior to statements (S) and antecedents (A).

E = *extension*; stable—a continuance of material or ideas. Extensions usually follow statements (S) but can follow any SPEAC function.

A = *antecedent*; very active—requires a subsequent consequent (C) function.

C = *consequent*; conclusive—must be preceded directly or indirectly (with intervening extensions) by antecedents (A).

Thus, progressions of identifiers such as P–S–E–A–C and S–E–A seem logical, while progressions of identifiers such as A–E–P–S and S–A–P–C, while still possible, are less plausible. SPEAC identifiers follow an A–P–E–S–C kinetic order with the most unstable function to the left and the most stable function to the right. Therefore, A and P require resolution while E, S, and C do not. SPEAC is multidimensional as well: no two groupings labeled A, for example, have precisely the same amount of A-ness. Typically, this multidimensionality appears when producing structural levels of SPEAC analyses. Labeling groupings with SPEAC functions is also *personal* rather than universal.

One of the most direct ways Experiments in Musical Intelligence uses SPEAC involves analyzing dissonance or tension relationships. To accomplish this analysis, the program calculates a tension weighting for each grouping of intervals. The interval values governing this weighting are independently defined by users and take into consideration variations due to octave displacements. Each grouping receives an identifier based on its tension within its local and global context. Basically this identifier assignment depends on the values and identifiers of the preceding and following groups. Therefore, a given grouping may have any SPEAC identifier attached to it depending on its context. Hierarchical groupings of identifiers show tension at larger and larger levels using the same procedures. SPEAC hierarchical analyses are not necessarily based on succession orders but on contextual analysis.

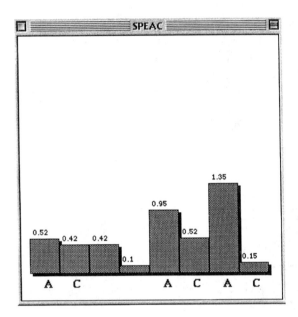

Figure 6.3
SPEAC column chart (columns without identifiers assume continuance of the last named identifier).

I have programmed the Experiments in Musical Intelligence SPEAC subprogram in this way because tension is one of the ways in which I listen to music, and few existing methods of analysis view tension as a significant factor. I am also partial to analytical approaches which incorporate personal interpretation. Different weightings for intervals in the program will lead to distinctly different analyses.

Figure 6.3 shows an example of SPEAC used as a phrase analysis tool. Experiments in Musical Intelligence uses a column chart to visually present users with a SPEAC phrase analysis. Tension levels are listed above and SPEAC identifiers presented below the columns. The program uses SPEAC analysis in many different ways when composing. For example, the program uses SPEAC whenever it encounters more than one correct possibility when choosing new groups for recombination. Using SPEAC to make best choices based on a complete grouping and not just its destination notes allows the program to continually attempt to create music of logical ordering rather than simply recombining related but otherwise random collections of groupings. Since SPEAC also takes metric placement into account, the program chooses groupings more likely to fall on appropriate beats. Metric sensitivity therefore plays an important role in the stylistic application of recombinancy.

Figure 6.4
Clarified (see chapter 8) and transposed versions of (a) Mozart K. 333, mvt. 2 beginning and SPEAC analysis; (b) new phrase (K. 333, mvt. 2, m. 1 and m. 5) with different SPEAC analysis; (c) new phrase (K. 333, mvt. 2, m. 1 and m. 6) with complementary SPEAC analysis.

Figure 6.4 shows an example from Mozart with SPEAC labels (figure 6.4a). Figure 6.4b shows a newly composed phrase intended to be in the style of Mozart. Voice-leading follows that of the original. As can be seen, however, a SPEAC analysis indicates that the two phrases in figure 6.4a and b move in quite different directions. The original Mozart extends the opening measure and moves toward an inner cadence with incrementally increasing levels of tension. The newly composed phrase in figure 6.4b, on the other hand, develops significant anticipatory motion. Figure 6.4c shows a newly composed phrase which takes into account the original SPEAC analysis of figure 6.4a. This new music has no less attention paid to voice-leading.

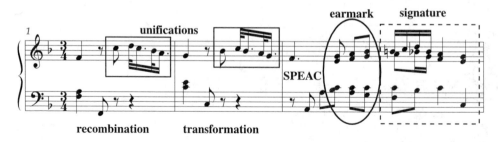

Figure 6.5
An overview of how the various analysis, composing, and pattern-matching programs work together.

However, as the SPEAC analysis shows, the phrase in figure 6.4c follows the same directions in terms of tension as does the original music by Mozart.

The machine-created music in figure 6.4c results from SPEAC-coerced choices where many correct possibilities exist at decision-making points during composition. Hence, SPEAC is most effective when using a rich and deep database. With smaller databases often only one possible choice exists and even when using SPEAC the program cannot compose new music very effectively.

As previously mentioned, SPEAC may be used in conjunction with virtually any type of analysis. Using SPEAC with functional tonal analysis, for example, can help differentiate between various uses of similar functions which otherwise might remain hidden (see Cope 1991b, chapter 2 for more information regarding this use of SPEAC). SPEAC can also be applied to every level of structural analysis—from measures to sectional relationships—in ways other than using tension. In each of these cases, productive analysis occurs only with proper assignment of SPEAC identifiers. While such assignments may initially seem vague to some, especially when compared to, say, assignment of traditional tonal functions, experience with this process helps produce useful musical results and insights.

As mentioned earlier, metric placement can also contribute to successful choices of new material for composition. Looking back to the Bach chorale examples in chapter 4 indicates that new beat choices often appear without regard to their original metric context. Common sense suggests that Bach was not unaware of the meter of the music that he composed. Unfortunately, allowing only those beats with exactly the same metric relations during recombination would greatly limit the program. Using SPEAC to translate metrically equivalent beats increases the range of possible choices and the probability of logical selection.

At this point, some readers may be overwhelmed by the various methods Experiments in Musical Intelligence uses to analyze music, as well as the processes it uses

for composing works based on the music in its database. Figure 6.5 hopefully provides some clarity on how these various methods operate in tandem. Here we see
signatures, earmarks, unifications, SPEAC, and so on interlocking to create new music.
Signatures help produce stylistic continuity. Unifications ensure that in-progress
compositions continue developing similar materials. Earmarks provide clues for important structural events. SPEAC contributes to the contextual selection of logical
choices during recombinancy.

II PROCESSES AND OUTPUT

Since the early days of Experiments in Musical Intelligence, many audiences have heard its output in the styles of classical composers. The works have delighted, angered, and provoked those who have heard them. These reactions result no doubt from the computational source of these works. I do not believe that the composers and audiences of the future will have the same reactions. Computers represent only tools with which we extend our minds and bodies. We invented computers, the programs, and the data used to create their output. The music our algorithms compose is just as much ours as the music created by the greatest of our personal inspirations. Hopefully, the following step-by-step creation of a new computer-composed work by Experiments in Musical Intelligence will help to clarify this view.

7 Databases

Databases can be created in a variety of ways. Prior to MIDI (musical instrument digital interface), I typed numbers representing pitch, on-times, and durations for each note of a work into text files which I then loaded into the Experiments in Musical Intelligence program. MIDI offers the advantage of downloading files from the World Wide Web (for example), converting these files to notation using standard commercial applications, correcting the resulting file as necessary using both eye and ear, and then loading and automatically translating the file into the program's database format. Unfortunately, quantizing—the filtering of MIDI as to what constitutes correct translations of channels, tracks, on-times, durations, and so on—often produces errors, and such transferred MIDI files typically require extensive editing before they can be used as databases. Ultimately, creating a database of correctly represented music is a time-consuming and difficult task.

Optimally, databases should not require unnecessary translation to different formats and, at the least, should respond reasonably quickly to analysis, pattern-matching, and MIDI performance. I use what I call *events* for this purpose. Events describe many of the attributes of musical notes with a single list of five separate but related parameters. Figure 7.1 shows an example event as it would appear in an Experiments in Musical Intelligence database.

Events

The first element of an event (or 0 in figure 7.1) represents its on-time. On-times appear first because they are the most often referenced data in an event. On-times are computed at 1000 ticks per second. However, for easier correlation to printed music notation, Experiments in Musical Intelligence relates these 1000 ticks to quarter-notes. The Play function of the program calculates real on-times by dividing the on-time in the event by the current tempo divided by 60 (the metronome marking for quarter-notes equaling 1 second). In actuality then, an on-time of 1000 begins 1 second after zero with a tempo of metronome marking 60, 2 seconds after zero with a tempo of metronome marking 30, half a second after zero with a tempo of metro-nome marking 120, and so on. This tempo calculation is hidden from users, however, just as the actual calculation of the duration of a quarter-note is hidden from performers in notated scores. The relative values of half-notes (2000 ticks), eighth-notes (500 ticks), and so on relate appropriately to the standard of 1000 ticks per quarter-note. Triplet eighth-notes receive 333 ticks with one of the three notes listed at 334 ticks for a total of 1000. On-times of notes must constantly be refigured since recombinancy requires that measures be reordered and the resulting on-times recalculated for performance.

(0 60 1000 1 64)

Figure 7.1
An Experiments in Musical Intelligence event.

The second entry of an event (or 60 in figure 7.1) represents pitch. Pitches are figured with middle C (560 cycles per second) equal to MIDI note number 60. Additions and subtractions of twelve produce Cs in various octaves, and additions and
subtractions of one create half-steps. Thus, 60–62–64–65–67–69–71–72 represents a
C-major scale with intervening numbers producing chromaticism to that key. Events
describe only note-ons (and by inference note-offs) and not rests, relieving databases
of vast amounts of unnecessary data. In essence, rests occur naturally as the result of
a lack of events. Not all systems function in this manner. Systems that relate to
standard musical notation, for example, need to signify rests because all measures
must be complete. Other systems require rests to signal channel presence for internal
clocks or other timing devices.

The third entry of an event (or 1000 in figure 7.1) represents duration. Duration, as
with on-time, receives 1000 ticks per quarter-note with relative durations figured
accordingly. MIDI note off-times can be independently calculated by the addition of
the on-time plus the duration. Thus, an event with an on-time of 6000 and a duration
of 1000 has an off-time of 7000. Such information can be important, particularly
when events straddle groupings which then require ties to maintain stylistic integrity.
Note that durations can be contradicted by choice of timbre in MIDI output devices.
For example, performing a pitch of long duration with a synthesizer sound of short
duration (or vice versa) can nullify much of the durational aspects of the program's
output.

The fourth entry of an event (or 1 in figure 7.1) represents the channel number—
1 to 16. Channel numbers indicate the MIDI channel on which events are scheduled
for performance. Ultimately, channels control synthesizer or sampler timbre selections via MIDI interfaces. Channel numbers in Experiments in Musical Intelligence
follow the original channel assignments of the music in the database except during
transformational composition.

The fifth entry of an event (or 64 in figure 7.1) represents dynamics. Dynamics
have the extremes of 0 for silence and 127 as fortissimo, with intervening numbers
relative to these levels. Dynamics in Experiments in Musical Intelligence can be contradicted by loudness controls in various playback hardware connected to the MIDI
interface. Aftertouch, tremolo, filter shaping, and so on are considered post-MIDI
controls and left to the output stage of performance.

Events are open-ended; that is, any desired parameter can be added to the end of events with no ill effects on the first five elements. For example, a sixth position in some events may be occupied by representations for effects, articulations, and so on. Though these additions will not translate into MIDI performance, they can be useful for converting events to other musical representations such as standard notation or graphs.

Events occur in work lists and not independently. Because works can often be quite long, finding a given event can be difficult. The best method for tracking events is by locating on-times. Events thus appear sequentially by on-time, making event finding easier.

Appendix A presents the music that will be used as a database for the creation of an Experiments in Musical Intelligence Mozart replication. This music appears in music notation since the just-discussed event notation would be very difficult to read. These five Mozart sonata second movements exemplify many of the important attributes which music should possess in order to serve effectively as a database. First, and at a minimum, databases must contain at least two complete examples of music of the composer whose musical style is being replicated. The more examples included, the more the output will sound different from any individual work or movement in the database. I include five examples here as a good model and one that typifies the database sizes used to create the music presented in appendix D.

Choosing Works for a Database

While it may seem obvious, works chosen for a database must demonstrate stylistic similarity. Otherwise, it will be difficult to perceive style inheritance in the output music. I discuss some of the elements of style in chapters 4 and 5 and cover further aspects of signatures, earmarks, and so on in later chapters. Ultimately, however, style is discovered by user sensitivity and experience with a particular composer's music.

It is also important that style in music in a database be evident primarily in its pitches, timings, and durations. For example, while orchestration, lyrics, articulations, timbres, and so on can play important roles in determining musical styles, music in a database will not transfer style for these attributes to output music since these parameters are not represented in the events of the Experiments in Musical Intelligence program.

The music used in databases must also share other general characteristics. For example, all of the works shown in appendix A represent slow movements of piano sonatas by Mozart. Including fast movements or movements of works other than piano sonatas in this database would risk serious dislocative passages in the output music. Each of the movements in appendix A is also in triple meter, an important feature to keep consistent in databases. Introducing music of diverse meters into databases, when such mixing of meters does not represent a composer's style, risks stylistic discontinuity.

Aside from their common source (Mozart), instrumentation (piano), tempo (slow), and meter (triple), I chose the particular movements of appendix A because of their apparent similarities in terms of register, texture, general accompaniment types, and shared mode (major). Mode choice in Experiments in Musical Intelligence is considered integral to the composing process. The program invokes special code for mode differences and allows for storage and reapplication of such information during composition. Using major-mode music in the database will produce major-mode output and vice versa. Therefore, all of the movements in appendix A begin in major keys. Mixing major with minor examples can cause serious breaches of stylistic integrity in musical replications. The original keys of database music, however, do not have to agree. In fact, Experiments in Musical Intelligence transposes all entered pieces automatically to the same key.

Character also plays an important role in choosing works for a database. Clearly, the fact that two pieces have the same mode, meter, tempo, and so on in no way guarantees that these works have the same character. Accompaniment figures represent an obvious example of character. A work using exclusively Alberti bass, for example, paired with a work with primarily chordal accompaniment, will produce music dramatically different from a database consisting of music primarily of the same or similar accompaniments.

Ornamentation represents another consideration in choosing works for a database. Including highly ornamented music along with music using relatively few ornaments will likely produce output which shifts radically between the two extremes. As with accompaniment figures, ornaments (if used) should generally be consistent across different works in a database rather than unique to one or a few works. Ornaments such as trills, mordents, grace-notes, and turns provide immediate indicators of certain musical styles and, as such, seem critical to the composing process. Unfortunately, leaving such details in coded music can often cause more problems than the retention of these same details enhance. The areas where ornaments cause problems include (1) pattern-matching, where the multitude of often extraneous notes can cause serious misinterpretations; (2) recognition of the database in the output, where such distinguishing figures directly indicate their origins; and (3) SPEAC misanalysis. In some cases, such as pattern-matching and SPEAC analysis, special software filters can be used to restrict program recognition to notes at or larger than certain durations. Most of the early databases coded for Experiments in Musical Intelligence, however, do not contain ornaments. When output requires such figures, I add them according to the performance practice of the period in which the replicated composer lived. Some view this as tampering or insist that the original ornaments provide grist for interesting musicological and theoretical study. More recently, I have included ornaments in databases with durations stolen from previous or following notes, as shown in figure 1.13.

Ornaments such as trills, turns, grace-notes, and so on must be explicitly entered for the program to reuse them logically in the output. The ornament realizations in the database in appendix A are my own, based on comparisons of several editions of the Mozart sonatas (see Mozart 1956, 1968, 1986). Ornaments included in these editions that do not appear in the database were removed to avoid the aforementioned problems with pattern matching, misanalysis, and so on. Most articulations do not appear in databases. Slurs, for example, have no clear method of MIDI representation and may be added to output music notation by hand as logically as possible after replication if desired. Staccato, on the other hand, can be represented as abbreviated note-values, although these altered note-values will appear in the output and should be retranslated to staccato marks with the original note-values.

It is important to note that, for me at least, the foremost goal when coding and preparing data for the Experiments in Musical Intelligence program is to increase the potential for creating aesthetically pleasing and meaningful output, not the accurate rendering of composer intent. Though I am concerned about the continuity of musical style (and certainly altering data can obscure style when applied inappropriately), I am also determined that the origins of the program's output not be detectable. When one can accurately perceive the music of derivation, the output can become a superficial pastiche.

Experiments in Musical Intelligence relies almost completely on its database for creating new compositions. This means that a single error in the database can have serious consequences in the output music. Therefore, data must be proofread and proofheard repeatedly to ensure that it accurately represents the music of the composer being replicated. Thus, creating worthwhile databases can take enormous amounts of time and require considerable user expertise for even routinely acceptable output, no less excellent results. Those individuals fearing that programs such as Experiments in Musical Intelligence may replace human composers should be placated knowing that in many ways it is often harder to use such programs to compose replications than it is for humans to compose such replications themselves.

Once a good database has been created, however, it will produce numerous works of roughly the same quality. These works will differ from one another in direct proportion to the number of works in the database. Such variations result in part from beginning with different initial musical choices. One can also vary output by removing one or more works in a database or using different combinations of works in lesser numbers. For example, using only the first, second, and third examples in appendix A will produce significantly different output than using only the third, fourth, and fifth examples. In general, using only one work as a database will produce a predictably similar-sounding work. In contrast, using ten or more different-sounding works, each having the aforementioned musical similarities of key, meter, and so on, will produce quite unpredictable results. There are, of course, many gradations between these two extremes.

Honing choices of music for a database can also include factors such as register, harmonic rhythm, texture, phrase lengths, use of rests, articulation, and so on with similarity of use producing more predictable output and dissimilarity creating less predictable and often unstylistic results. I term such database construction *sculpting*. Databases can be so carefully sculpted that users can almost be said to *compose* the output themselves. Such sculpting usually involves finding and utilizing music with not only similarities in all of the areas thus far mentioned but music with similar themes and thematic development as well.

Sculpting databases also provides the opportunity to create larger works such as operas where the program otherwise cannot produce music of such diverse extremes of form. Sculpting databases to produce an aria, for example, involves very different choices than sculpting databases for recitatives, and so on. As currently constituted, Experiments in Musical Intelligence does not otherwise create such multiple movement forms in a single operation. Until such time as the program can overcome these limitations, sculpting databases seems a reasonable and proper approach to creating multiple-movement forms.

The movement Experiments in Musical Intelligence chose as a model for its replication, K. 284, follows a rather complex formal structure—a kind of rondo variations (A mm. 1–16; B mm. 17–30; A' mm. 31–46; [c] mm. 47–52; B mm. 53–69; A" mm. 70–89; coda-cadence mm. 90–2) where letters denote different themes and single quotes indicate variations of those themes. Such forms pose far greater problems for machine replication than more standard forms which have literal or near-literal repetitions. Not only do the materials in K. 284 not repeat verbatim, but Mozart invests in the work a subtle approach to varying material which might elude even human analysis, no less, as we shall see, computer analysis. However, I have permitted the model so that readers can view the program performing complex analysis and replication. Such intricate forms also provide more interesting reverse engineering as will take place in later chapters.

8 Analysis

Clarifying Data

Databases must often be rhythmically analyzed and revised or the output will be otherwise rendered haphazard by the vagaries of musical representation. This is a first step in what I call *clarifying* the data. An example of this clarification involves the basic agreement of composite rhythms. In figure 8.1a, the music moves by eighth-note. In figure 8.1b, the music moves by sixteenth-note. It is imperative that one of the two examples be rhythmically altered to account for this difference; otherwise, the output will exaggerate the discrepancies between the two examples. Figure 8.2 demonstrates how the different rhythms of the left-hand figurations of figure 8.1a and b can conflict if the music were recombined without such alterations. The examples here have been transposed to a common key and follow a typical implied harmonic progression. Note, however, how the speed of the Alberti-style bass shifts dramatically and without regard to style. In fact, such a simple conflict will cause immediate style contradictions even when, as in this case, only one voice (left-hand accompaniment) is involved. Without care taken by both users when inputting music and the program when analyzing music, compositional output can become trivial. Finding a common rhythmic equivalency for databases containing music from different movements and works is therefore a critical element in creating successful new compositions.

Figure 8.3 shows two ways in which equivalency can be obtained. In figure 8.3a, the durations of figure 8.1a halve to match the durations of figure 8.1b. Figure 8.3b shows the reverse. Either case can effectively accomplish rhythmic equivalency. This kind of alteration must be consistently maintained for all the music of a given database.

Databases must also be properly channelized; that is, data destined for separate voices or timbres must be assigned separate channels for correct playback and pattern-matching. Often several channels must be assigned per staff in a visually represented musical score to account for the various lines present in the music.

Clarifying the data enhances the program's ability to compose effectively by ensuring that deconstructed musical fragments will have a multitude of choices for musical recombinancy. Data left unclarified will often have such unique characteristics as to almost guarantee that only the music that previously preceded or followed it will do so again during recombination. Thus, unclarified databases often create instances of their former selves rather than new examples of music in their former styles.

Figure 8.4 shows the opening measure of a Mozart piano sonata. This example, in the key of F major, has a pickup gesture, grace-notes, and articulations. Transposing this music to a database-established key, removing the articulation, and utilizing four separate channels (one for the upper line, one for the second line in the treble staff

(a)

(b)

Figure 8.1
Mozart's sonatas, (a) K. 284, mvt. 3, transposed m. 1; and (b) K. 279, mvt. 1, m. 5.

Figure 8.2
Conflicting rhythmic notations of figure 8.1 during recombinancy.

beginning on the second half of the second beat of the first full measure, and one each for the two bass-lines) will allow for proper pattern matching, SPEAC analysis, and flexibility of the grouping(s) during recombinancy.

Ties and long-duration notes, especially when they cross grouping boundaries and thus fall out of the data of a single object in the database, must also be clarified. Ties become repeated notes in these circumstances, as do long-duration notes. However, information about ties is collected at the time grouping occurs and then stored with the affected voice so that ties may be returned appropriately in the final output. Ties internal to defined groupings remain intact and continue to contribute to style fidelity. In general, users of Experiments in Musical Intelligence clarify music during input. However, the program translates ties and long-duration notes at the time analysis takes place.

Figure 8.5a shows the Mozart phrase of figure 8.4 after clarification. Note how the grace-note has been converted into an actual duration (factored into the beat). The

Figure 8.3
The music of figure 8.1 clarified rhythmically in two different ways: (a) as sixteenths; (b) as eighths.

Figure 8.4
The first measures of the second movement of Mozart's K. 310.

(a)

(b)

((2000 65 250 1 64) (2250 69 250 1 64) (2500 72 250 1 64) (2750 77 250 1 64)
(3000 72 125 1 64) (3000 53 1000 3 64) (3000 41 1000 4 64) (3125 81 625 1 64)
(3750 77 250 1 64) (4000 72 500 1 64) (4000 57 1000 3 64) (4000 45 1000 4 64)
(4500 72 750 1 64) (4500 69 750 2 64) (5000 60 1000 3 64) (5000 48 1000 4 64)
(5250 70 250 1 64) (5250 67 250 2 64) (5500 69 250 1 64) (5500 65 250 2 64)
(5750 70 250 1 64) (5750 67 250 2 64))

Figure 8.5
Clarified version of Mozart's K. 310 from Figure 8.4 (a) in music notation; (b) in event notation.

pickup gesture now fits into a full measure. The voices have been channelized and the articulations and dynamics removed. The key in this case remains the same since the original key of the music happens to fit the common key of the database. The resulting event notation in figure 8.5b demonstrates the effectiveness of the clarification process. These events represent all of the music in figure 8.5a and the potential for logical recombination has increased significantly.

Incipient (pickup) gestures are considered special cases in Experiments in Musical Intelligence and are placed in separate lexicons designed for appropriate reuse. Typically a measure in length but containing mostly silence, incipient gestures are endemic to certain types of musical forms, optional in other forms, and a rarity in still others. Such initial figures, because they often constitute single notes, gestures, or chords, would prove disruptive if used in normal recombinant composition by causing sudden silences and texture fallout. Therefore, the program labels these measures as special. The program then uses these incipient gestures when appropriate in output.

Basic Analysis

The Experiments in Musical Intelligence program analyzes the basic voice-leading and character of the music in the database as described in chapter 4. The program analyzes voice-leading by organizing the music into groupings. Users may establish grouping size or the program may determine size—as is the case here—based on principles inherent in the music itself, including rate of texture change, meter, and other less important factors such as composite and harmonic rhythms. The program makes many mistakes, of course, which can be fixed by changing code or by altering the music in the database. I make such changes between generations of replications, rather than repair replications themselves. Such coding and debugging makes Experiments in Musical Intelligence unfit for general use since few people have either the expertise in Lisp or the knowledge of music and the program itself to make any useful corrections in code.

As mentioned in chapter 4, and unlike the creation of the previously described Bach chorale replications, Experiments in Musical Intelligence's keyboard music often uses only one voice (typically the top voice) for connecting groupings. The remaining voices do not need to follow their original destination points but should retain their basic character. This character continuity must adhere to an interplay between the character of the destination material of the currently chosen segment and the character template of the music being used as a model. This process avoids a random approach to character, which can occur when using destination choices alone, or a simplistic mirror of the model, which can occur with a simple rehashing of the model itself. In general, the program compares the destination possibilities with the model and reduces its recombinatorial possibilities accordingly.

Experiments in Musical Intelligence also analyzes database music for signatures, earmarks, unifications, SPEAC, structure, and so on as described in previous chapters. Each of these analyses is stored in a separate lexicon for use at the appropriate time during composition. The order of using these lexicons should become clear during the following step-by-step description of the creation of a new piano sonata movement in the style of Mozart.

9 Themes and Variations

Assuming that the data of the previously discussed five Mozart sonata movements have been clarified and translated into events allows us to step through the processes described in chapters 4 through 6 and observe the creation of a new movement, arguably in the style of Mozart.

The Role of Pattern-Matching

For Experiments in Musical Intelligence to create a theme, or for that matter any stylistically credible music, first requires pattern-matching, as described in chapter 5. Figure 9.1 shows five examples of a Viennese signature used by Mozart in the second movement of his Piano Sonata, K. 284, and discovered by pattern-matching the five movements in the database. This signature can be described as a premature tonic bass note (A in A major) under a dominant chord (E–G-sharp–B in A major) or a late-sounding dominant over a tonic pedal point. This signature also appears in various guises in the second movements of K. 310 (mm. 32 and 54), K. 333 (mm. 75 and 82), and K. 545 (mm. 16, 24, 40, and 48).

Each iteration of the signature shown in figure 9.1 appears at the end of a two-phrase group whose first phrase does not cadence with the signature. Note how the spacing and number of dissonant notes provide differing tensions in the signatures, with the final signature providing the most prominent weight of the five shown. The tensions and locations help delineate the rondo form in this movement with tonic-functioned signatures (ending with A in the bass) more dissonant than dominant-functioned signatures (ending with E in the bass). Note that the first and last iterations of this signature also have very similar initial beats which help to give the movement a sense of closure. Hence, signatures may not only be location-dependent at the local phrase level but also structurally dependent according to section endings. Experienced listeners can hear these subtleties and know when composers—or machine-composing programs—misplace or leave out such important indicators of given styles.

The signature shown in figure 9.1 was used as a template by the Experiments in Musical Intelligence program in its creation of a new piano sonata slow movement in the style of Mozart. The various versions of this signature were fixed in place to form a structural framework to which the program then added requisite amounts of new music using recombinant techniques.

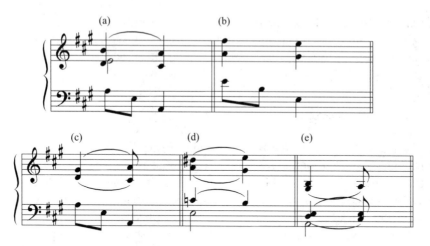

Figure 9.1
Versions of a signature found in Mozart's Piano Sonata, K. 284 (1775), mvt. 2: (a) m. 16; (b) m. 30;
(c) m. 46; (d) m. 69; (e) m. 92.

Object Orientation

After discovering and setting the signatures in place, Experiments in Musical Intelligence analyzed and stored the clarified events of the five chosen Mozart movements.
First, the program grouped the music appropriately, in this case using primarily
measure-sized groupings. Second, the program analyzed each resulting grouping
according to destination notes and defined its character. Finally, the program stored
these groupings in appropriate lexicons—repositories of like-analyzed music.

Understanding grouping, storage, and lexicons requires some knowledge of object
oriented programming, better known as OOP (see Keene 1989). Simply stated, OOP
allows data storage in objects with names, various attributes, and so on. Objects can
also contain, among others things, other objects. A lexicon is just such an object-
storing object.

As an example, the events of the first measure of Mozart's K. 330, second movement, could be stored in an object called Mozart-330-2-1, where the name represents
ever-narrowing pointers to the information the object holds. In this case the object
Mozart-330-2-1 stores the music of K. 330, movement 2, measure 1. This object also
contains the events for this measure as described in chapter 7, as well as important
information such as destination notes, accompaniment character of the destination
measure, and so on.

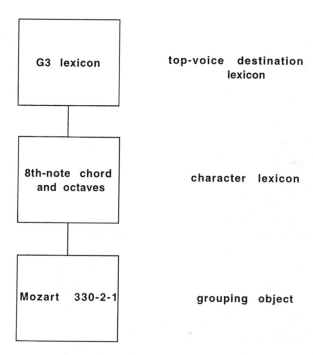

Figure 9.2
Graphic depicting lexicons in Experiments in Musical Intelligence.

Because the program eventually needs to select from a group of like measures, Mozart-330-2-1 is stored in a lexicon of measures which have one or more elements in common. For example, the version of Experiments in Musical Intelligence used for creating the music for this book uses the analysis of common onbeat notes as a lexicon type. This enables the program to consult this lexicon when making a next measure choice. To choose only those measures which have the same character as well as destination requires that the lexicon itself belong to specialized lexicons, as shown in figure 9.2.

To draw attention to the fact that the music in the database originally appears in different keys than the newly composed work, I have left the works in appendix A in the keys in which Mozart composed them. Readers should note, however, as expressed in chapter 7, that these database works were transposed to a single key (in this case F major) before the program composed the work discussed here.

Figure 9.3
A first-measure choice, m. 9 from K. 330, both transposed and transformed.

A First Theme

To begin a non-chorale composition, the Experiments in Musical Intelligence program selects a first measure. This measure may be chosen from an incipient lexicon in the case of music with predominant pickup notes or it may be chosen from appropriate first measure types. These measure types exclude cadences and signatures that have separate lexicons. This initial measure must also establish the key (in this case F major) which limits choices somewhat further.

Figure 9.3 shows Experiments in Musical Intelligence's first choice: measure 9 from K. 330. Note that comparing this measure with the actual measure of music in appendix A shows that the first note in the right hand and the entirety of the left hand appear transposed down a perfect fifth in the newer version. This revision results from the program's attempt to establish the key with more important key-establishing notes (the Fs in the program's revision clearly denote the key of F major). Such revisions, called transformations and discussed in chapter 4 (see figure 4.16 and related text), are rather routine at this stage and result from the program's attempt to model its new work after the music in the database. If the program were limited to choosing only first measures of actual database music, then the new work would immediately be recognizable and thus defeat the program's attempt at originality.

Experiments in Musical Intelligence begins its actual composing process by recognizing the destination pitch (G) and the accompaniment character from the measure object it has chosen and looks in the appropriate lexicon for a logical second measure. The program avoids accepting the actual measure which originally followed the one chosen unless no other possibility exists. In this case, apparently, the options included a transformed version of itself: measure 9 from K. 330 with the left hand intact but the right hand initially transposed down a fourth for the first note and then down a diatonic second for the remainder of the measure, as shown in figure 9.4. This process provides a good example of the program's use of unifications— developing motivic unity in the first two measures of music of a new work and

Figure 9.4
A second measure as a transformed version of m. 1.

Figure 9.5
A transposed version of m. 7 of K. 284 as m. 3 of the new movement.

SPEAC, as discussed in chapter 6. Note that these machinations, while seemingly complex, are routine in Experiments in Musical Intelligence. Simple transpositions to create new destinations to satisfy the program's search for the appropriate character of ensuing measures occur often in tonal composition and thus it seems natural to include them as routine processes in a computer-replicating program.

The destination note of the new measure 2 (F) and its associated character produce the music shown in figure 9.5, the first three measures of a new sonata movement. This new measure, measure 7 of K. 284, occurs intact but completely transposed so that the destination note continues the line of the previous measure and occurs in the key of the new music.

Having apparently exhausted all possibilities for a fourth measure, the program chose to continue with a similar transposition of measure 8 of K. 284, as shown in figure 9.6. This choice exemplifies the opposite process of that occurring in measures 1 and 2 of this new movement. Where these initial measures produce novel results, this new choice creates redundancy with the database. However, such repetitions seem more palatable when nestled in interior music compared to their exposure in opening measures.

The required destination note for measure 5 (F) occurs as the downbeat note of measure 71 of K. 284—transposed down a major third to the new key of F major—

Figure 9.6
A transposed version of m. 8 of K. 284 as m. 4 of the new movement.

Figure 9.7
A transposed version of m. 71 of K. 284 as m. 5 of the new movement.

as shown in figure 9.7. This new version has all but the first note of the upper line further transposed up an octave, a technique the program can impose whenever it encounters what appears as a range conflict. Here, the upper line in its original configuration apparently visits the bass register too often to suit the program; hence the transposition.

The choice for measure 6 of the new movement shown in figure 9.8 results not from recombination but rather from the program's hierarchical need for sequence which can be found in many of the analyzed movements in the database. In K. 284, for example, sequence occurs between measures 5 and 6 and between measures 71 and 73. However, the complexity of the various responsible code makes the absolute identification of the program's rationale here nearly impossible.

The new destination note (C, derived from mm. 73–4 of K. 284) now remains true for the selection of measure 7, a transposition of measure 59 of K. 284. This is

Figure 9.8
Use of sequence to create m. 6 of the new movement.

followed then by a transposed version of measure 60 of K. 284 for the same reasons that measures 3 and 4 remained intact. Figure 9.9, then, shows the entirety of the first phrase of the newly composed sonata movement. The phrase now consists of eight measures of music—the length of first phrases which all but K. 310 and K. 333 follow.

I have not carefully considered the program's possibilities for choosing measures in light of the impending cadence in measure 8. This omission is not due to oversight, but rather results from the near impossibility of following this particular process during machine composing. As important as cadential considerations are for the selection of measures and even their resulting transpositions, the complex interactions between the various rules governing these choices make such decisions impossible to reverse-engineer. However, my occasional indecision as to why certain transpositions occur or certain measures are chosen can probably be traced to one or more of the program's need for such hierarchical logic during the composing process.

Measures 9 through 14 of the newly composed movement are an exact repeat of measures 1 through 6 (see figure 9.10). The second movement of K. 545 seems to be the model for this choice, though Mozart includes significant variation in his repeat. Measure 15 duplicates measure 20 of K. 330. Measure 16, of course, is a transposed version of the signature from measure 16 of K. 284 derived by pattern-matching the movements in the database. The completed first sixteen measures of the new machine composition appear in figure 9.10.

Figure 9.9
The entirety of the first phrase of the newly composed sonata movement (transposed versions of mm. 59–60 of K. 284 completing the phrase).

A Second Theme

The Experiments in Musical Intelligence composition's second theme begins with a transposed—up a major second—version of measure 8 of K. 333, as shown in figure 9.11. This measure was chosen in a manner similar to the initial measure of the new work since it represents the beginning of a new section of the piece. The principal constraint governing such choices is contrast. Comparing measure 17 to measure 1 of the new work demonstrates their differences.

The second measure of the newly created second theme, a transposed version of measure 18 of K. 284, as shown in figure 9.12, begins with an F as prescribed by the original first measure's destination note, though down an octave. This new measure appears without its ornaments (see the original published version) as a result of clarification.

Figure 9.10
The completed first sixteen measures of the new sonata movement.

Figure 9.11
The second theme begins with a transposed version of m. 8 of K. 333.

Figure 9.12
A transposed version of m. 18 of K. 284 as the second measure of the new second theme.

Inexplicably, measure 3 of the new second theme (m. 19 of the new movement, derived from a transposed version of m. 21 of K. 333) does not adhere to the destination note prescribed by the previous measure, as shown in figure 9.13. The first note here should repeat the music's last note. Whenever such discrepancies occur, pattern-matching usually provides an answer. A careful review of the sonata movements in the database (see appendix A) shows that the melody here (top line only) occurs frequently, too frequently to be a signature, and when taken as a whole (all voices) occurs only once again (m. 71 of the same sonata movement, K. 333). Hence, this is most likely an earmark, denoting an important structural moment in the life of the first complete section of the movement, the exposition of the first two themes.

Measure 20 of the new computer-composed movement (m. 4 of the new theme) follows measure 19 with the proper destination note (G), also shown in figure 9.13. This measure derives from measure 20 of K. 284 with the right hand transposed up a sixth to create the proper destination note (G) and the left hand transposed down a third to keep it in proper register. The ensuing two measures of the second theme, measures 21 and 22 of the new movement, shown in figure 9.14, demonstrate how the program, apparently with no alternatives left, repeats the original—measures 21 and 22 of K. 284—in transposition.

The destination note of the last measure of figure 9.14 (G), measure 22 of the newly composed music, occurs as the first melodic note of the new selection for measure

Figure 9.13
A transposed version of m. 21 of K. 333 and m. 20 of K. 284 (the right hand transposed up a sixth and the left hand transposed down a third) as the third and fourth measures of the new second theme.

Figure 9.14
Transposed versions of mm. 21–2 of K. 284 as continuation of the second theme.

Figure 9.15
Transposed versions of mm. 14–5 of K. 333 as mm. 23–4 of the new movement.

23: a transposed version of measure 14 of K. 333. This in turn is followed by a transposed version of measure 15 of the same sonata movement—again necessitated by an apparent lack of alternatives. These measures appear in figure 9.15. The chromaticism here, suggesting a modulation to the key of C major—a fifth from the original, results from the program's large-scale form analysis. One finds such modulatory cadences in both K. 284 and K. 545.

Measure 25 of the newly composed music is a literal restatement of measure 50 of K. 330, a free choice since cadences disregard their destination notes. The connection of this measure to measure 26 of the new composition, presents a more elaborate transformation, as shown in figure 9.16. The first notes in the right hand of measure 26 represent both the first note of the newly chosen measure (a transposition of m. 52 of K. 284) and the proper destination note of measure 50 of K. 330 welded together. A small Experiments in Musical Intelligence subprogram which attempts to mold consistent textures probably created this transformation in the output.

Figure 9.16
A literal restatement of m. 50 of K. 330 and a transposition of m. 52 of K. 284 added to the music of figure 9.15.

Measure 27 of the newly composed music results from a transposition of measure 34 of K. 284 with the first note in the upper line transposed down an octave as well. This new measure, shown added to the second thematic area in figure 9.17, has the proper destination note, though interestingly its character seems far removed from the original destination measure. This character difference could result from a number of relevant factors which override destination character consistency. For example, the music at this point could follow contrasting character in the model being used or be constrained by structural limitations. More likely, the choice was formed by a lack of alternatives: rather than once again selecting the actual following measure, the program opted for what it perceived as the lesser of two evils.

The above-mentioned problem occurs once again in relating measure 27 to measure 28 of the newly composed music (shown grafted in place in figure 9.18). However, in this case the resolution is more clear: the program uses a transformed version of the second measure of the current phrase (m. 26) to fulfill a structural need. One finds similar transformations in Mozart, as in measures 26 and 28 of K. 545 and measures 14 and 16 of K. 333. Note that measure 28 of the new movement has also been transposed up one octave.

The ensuing measure 29 (a transposed version of m. 29 of K. 284) suffers the same problems for the same reason: the forcing of measure 28 into place to fulfill structural needs causes both its inception and its destination to lack proper connectivity, as shown in figure 9.19.

Almost counter to these successions of difficult transitions between measures, measure 30 is a transposition of measure 30 of K. 284, the measure which followed it in Mozart's original. This appears added to the second thematic region in figure 9.20. Measure 30 also presents a cadence of sorts which after only six measures creates a very short phrase (the previous cadence occurs in m. 24). Interestingly, however, Mozart often composed phrases of more or less than eight measures, though he is usually stereotyped as following a strict eight-bar phrase structure. For example, the opening phrase of K. 333 has seven measures (or 4+3) and the phrase in measures 8–13 of K. 333 has six measures.

The destination notes again match with the succession of measures 30 and 31 in the new music (shown in figure 9.21) with the latter being measure 43 of K. 284 transposed down a third. The same correspondence is true of measures 31 and 32 (a transposed version of m. 8 of K. 545) and measure 33 (m. 44 of K. 284 transposed down a third), as shown in figure 9.22. The relationship of the next two measures (mm. 33 and 34) involves a destination-note inversion since the new measure (m. 3 of K. 330) provides the right note but transposed an octave down. These relationships also appear in the music in figure 9.22.

Figure 9.17
A transposed version of m. 34 of K. 284 added to the second theme.

Figure 9.18
A transformed version of m. 26 as continuance of figure 9.17.

Figure 9.19
The addition of a transposed version of m. 29 of K. 284 as m. 29 of the new movement.

Figure 9.20
The new phrase and its cadence (a transposition of m. 30 of K. 284).

Variations

The music between measures 35 and 45 follows the same basic principles as thus far described with no significant compositional developments. Measure 35 is measure 4 of K. 330. Measure 36 is measure 50 of K. 330. Measures 37–9 repeat measures 26–8 of the computer composition as a structural reinforcement. Measure 40 represents a transposed version of measure 9 of K. 284 with the upper line transposed up one octave. Measure 41 is a transposed version of measure 40 of K. 284 with the first note of the upper line also transposed up one octave. Measure 42 is a transposed version of measure 11 of K. 284. Measure 43 is a transposed version of measure 42 of K. 284 with the first note of the upper line further transposed to the proper destination note. Measure 44 is a transposed version of measure 45 of K. 284. Measure 45 is a signa-

Figure 9.21
Measure 43 of K. 284 transposed down a third as the beginning of a new phrase (m. 31).

Figure 9.22
Measures 32–4 (a transposed version of m. 8 of K. 545; a transposed version of m. 44 of K. 284; and m. 3 of K. 330) added to the new phrase.

Figure 9.23
Beat-by-beat recombinance from K. 545 in mm. 46–50 of the new movement. Measure 46 consists of transpositions of m. 4, b. 2; m. 4, b. 1; m. 4, b. 2, with the right hand up one octave. The beats of m. 47 result from a recombination of transpositions of m. 26, b. 2; m. 25, b. 2; and m. 28, b. 1 from K. 545. Measure 48 consists of transpositions of m. 4, b. 2 (r.h. up an octave); m. 26, b. 1; and m. 26, b. 2 from K. 545. The beats of m. 49 result from a recombination of transpositions of m. 29, b. 1; m. 5, b. 2; and m. 5, b. 3 from K. 545. Measure 50 returns to measure-by-measure recombinance with a transposition of m. 28 from K. 545.

ture marking the midpoint of the movement. This signature also represents the introduction of a less developed third theme similar to the one found in the original model on which this new music is based (mm. 47–52 of K. 284). This point in the new movement also marks a significant departure from the measure-to-measure compositional approach taken thus far.

Measure 46 results from a beat-by-beat recombinance of measure parts from K. 545. The successive beats of measure 46 appear in the caption to figure 9.23 which also shows measures 47–50 of the new composition. Beat-by-beat recombinance usually requires strict adherence to character matching or else the music shifts from one accompaniment figure to another with such rapidity as to sound completely out of style. Ultimately, a carefully structured process produces a distinctly different third theme for the newly machine-composed slow movement.

Many Experiments in Musical Intelligence compositions result from processes such as the ones shown here making reverse engineering to discover the sources of their music virtually impossible. This new Mozart-like sonata movement has fewer such measures than most, making it more easily describable in terms of origins.

Measures 51–8 of the Experiments in Musical Intelligence Mozart-style new slow movement repeat measures 17–24 but transposed up a perfect fourth. This transpo-

Figure 9.24
Measures 64 and 65 of the new movement from mm. 66–7 of K. 284 transposed up a third.

sition resembles that of Mozart's own in K. 284 (see mm. 17–25 and mm. 53–61) and similar transposition-repeats in other of the sonata slow movements in the database. These nine measures of the new movement represent the first actual recapitulation and the first real indication of the unfolding form. These measures appear in the full score in appendix B.

Measure 59 of the new movement derives from measure 69 of K. 310 transposed up one octave. Measure 60 then continues with measure 70 of K. 310 up one octave with its third beat borrowed from measure 17 of K. 310 transposed up a perfect fourth. Measures 61–2 then repeat these two measures for unclear structural reasons. Measure 63 derives from measure 29 of the new movement transposed up a perfect fourth (again, for apparent structural reasons). Measures 64 and 65 of the new composition conclude this repeating music with, interestingly, measures 66 and 67 of Mozart's K. 284 transposed up a third. These measures appear in figure 9.24.

The next two measures of the new movement (mm. 66–7) represent some of the program's more novel and creative composition thus far observed. These two measures extend the previous measure by varying and transposing it by the intervals of a seventh (m. 66) and a fifth (m. 67) downward, respectively. All four of these measures appear in figure 9.25. In all probability, measures 66–7 represent individual transpositions of one or the other of the preceding two measures transposed by structural necessity in order to cadence on the fifth degree of F major. These seemingly haphazard arrangements of destination notes are made possible by the third-beat rests in each measure which relax the destination constraints. Measure 68 of the Experiments in Musical Intelligence Mozart is a transposed signature from K. 284 (m. 69) as noted previously.

The music beginning in measure 69 initiates what I think represents the most convincing transformational composition of the program's entire new movement. The upper voice of the first three measures here (mm. 69–71) repeat exactly the first three measures of the movement. The left-hand music, however, has been replaced by

Figure 9.25
Transposed extensions of m. 65 as mm. 66 and 67.

material from K. 545: measure 69 in the left hand is a transposed version of K. 545 measure 26, and measure 70 of the left hand derives from measure 29 of K. 545. These measures appear in figure 9.26. Intriguingly, Mozart achieves much the same effect in his K. 284 where measures 70 onward repeat the main theme (in Mozart's case with rather extraordinary variation) with a new left-hand figuration—the same kind of Alberti bass which Experiments in Musical Intelligence uses in its version. Measure 71 of the machine composition continues with a transposition of measure 30 of K. 545 as an accompanying figure. The music which follows this, measure 72, is more pedestrian—an exact repeat of measure 4 of the new work—as shown in figure 9.26.

Given the complicated right-hand–left-hand recombinations of the previous measures, the program opts for a simple transposition of measures 61–4 of K. 284 for its next musical choice. The program then repeats these eight measures (mm. 69–76) which can be seen in the full movement appearing in appendix B as measures 77–84.

Measures 85–7 represent a transposition of measures 71–3 of K. 545, as shown in figure 9.27. These measures in the new movement then move to the two-measure repeat of the final signature derived by pattern-matching and shown in figure 9.28. The approach to the final signature does not follow that shown in the original in K. 284. However, such dislocation often occurs when signatures have been set in place prior to normal recombinative composition. The program attempts to make its destinations follow the original, but failing that, makes the closest approach possible—here but the interval of a second removed.

Figure 9.26
The right hand repeats exactly the first three measures of the movement, while the left hand has been
replaced by material from K. 545.

Figure 9.27
Transpositions of mm. 71–3 of K. 545 as mm. 85–7 of the new movement.

Figure 9.28
Final signature derived from K. 284 and its approach.

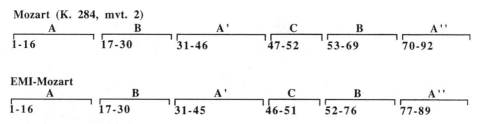

Figure 9.29
How the Mozart and Experiments in Musical Intelligence movements align in terms of material and key choice.

All five of the Mozart databases were accessed during the creation of this new Experiments in Musical Intelligence movement. Mozart's K. 284, the original source for the signatures used in this new movement, provided the most material, while K. 310 provided the least. Mozart's K. 330 and K. 545 were drawn upon almost equally, whereas K. 333, like K. 310, had almost no references. While imbalanced, this distribution of derivations across the entirety of a database generally produces the most unrecognizable and, usually, the most interesting, creative, and musical results.

Choice of key in Experiments in Musical Intelligence's output music results from the application of several criteria. First, key choice should not move notes beyond the range of the instrument(s) for which the music is intended. Having to transpose even a single note up or down an octave to enable a work's performance by a certain instrument can jeopardize stylistic continuity just as a single mistake in the database can. Second, given that all notes fall in range, keys are chosen which produce the most idiomatic performance possible. Keys of output music, however, can otherwise be changed arbitrarily with no real damage done to the music itself or to the integrity of the process which created that music.

The form of the new Experiments in Musical Intelligence slow movement (shown in its entirety in appendix B) parallels that of K. 284 rather closely. Figure 9.29 shows how the two movements align in terms of material and key choice with the letters indicating material repetition and variations (shown with additional single quotes). The actual Mozart movement from K. 284 has more subtle musical variations in its repeating sections. The original Mozart also has a well-placed fermata in its eighty-ninth measure as a preparation for the final cadence—a preparation missing from the replication. The first variation of the Experiments in Musical Intelligence's Mozart movement is tenuous at best and I mark it thusly here, since this clearly was the intent, however unsuccessful it may be. On balance, Mozart's style and this movement from K. 284 seem modestly well served by the program's output.

10 Interface

In order to give readers an opportunity to develop a feel of using the Experiments in Musical Intelligence program, I include here several screen images of the program in action. Currently the program requires a PowerPC computer with at least 64 megabytes of RAM and a hard disk drive with at least 8 megabytes of free space. A 1-megahertz MIDI interface is also required for performance. This interface should connect to a sampler with a generous selection of traditional musical instrument samples since timbral quality contributes to the overall aesthetic response to the output of the software.

Users of the program must have an acquaintance with Macintosh pull-down menus, windows, and how to connect MIDI devices. More advanced musical skills are highly recommended but not required. Users need not have any knowledge of programming. Most of the operation of Experiments in Musical Intelligence can be accomplished using point-and-click operations.

The Menu

The menubar of Experiments in Musical Intelligence appears in figure 10.1. The File menu contains most of the basic file accessing functions of the standard Macintosh interface, including open, close, save, and so on. The Edit menu contains most of the basic cut-and-paste functions, including cut, copy, and paste, among others. This menu item also contains the Abort command which interrupts most of the program's processes with no ill effect.

The Input menu allows individual music files and folders to be loaded as either Lisp or MIDI files. Lisp files are compiled files which include an analysis of the file's music placed there during the Save process. This storage and retrieval of analysis while saving and loading avoids having to analyze music during composition. The keyboard window shown in figure 10.2 provides another method of loading music into the program. Here users simply click notes on the screen keyboard while holding down designated keys on their external ASCII keyboard to determine duration. On-times accrue consecutively with rests added using the Rest button instead of the piano keyboard (necessary for input timing calculation and not for creating rest events). Many other input options exist as well, including a simple graphic music notation program and direct MIDI input from an external piano-style keyboard. Users can also create their own MIDI files using a separate sequencer program and then upload those files to the program. The input menu also determines (through a separate window not shown) which loaded database(s) will be used in composition.

The Patterns window provides user control of the selection of works for pattern-matching. This window and a modified form of the controller's window appear in

File   Edit   Input   Match   Compose   Output   Windows

Figure 10.1
The Experiments in Musical Intelligence menubar.

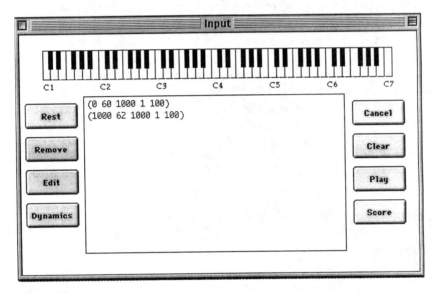

Figure 10.2
The Experiments in Musical Intelligence keyboard window.

figure 10.3a and b. Most of the meanings of the terms used here should be self-evident. High and low limits refer to the upper and lower extremes of numbers of matches for a pattern to qualify as a signature. Threshold indicates the maximum number of signatures allowable during a matching session. Many other types of controllers exist (see Cope 1996). I have limited the number here for the sake of clarity. Users can also relinquish controller settings to the program should they wish to avoid this part of the process. The Signatures window, shown in figure 10.3c, provides access to signatures for viewing (in traditional musical notation), playing, saving, and loading.

The Compose window (shown in figure 10.4a) allows users to initiate the composition process and to play the results. The Play variables window (shown in figure 10.4b) includes scrolling sliders for controlling the overall loudness, tempo, and key of performed databases and works. This window also allows determination of the region of music desired for performance. Changes in this window affect the current perfor-

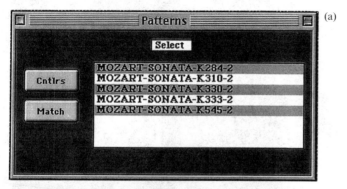

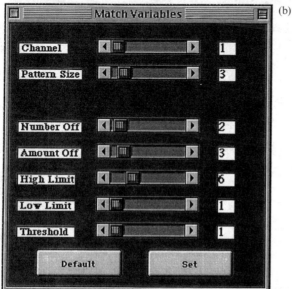

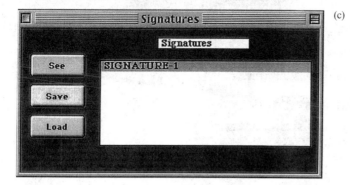

Figure 10.3
(a) The Experiments in Musical Intelligence Patterns window; (b) the Match Variables (controllers) window; (c) the Signatures window.

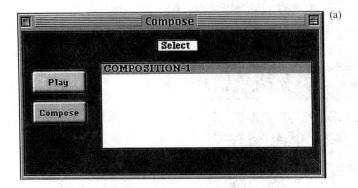

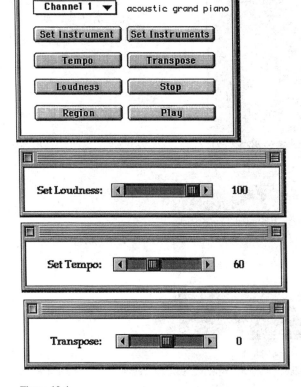

Figure 10.4
(a) The Experiments in Musical Intelligence Compose window; (b) the Play variables window with scrolling sliders for controlling the overall loudness, tempo, and transposition of performed databases and works.

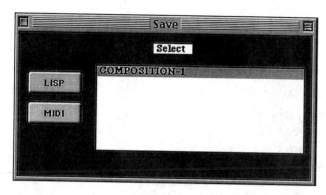

Figure 10.5
The Experiments in Musical Intelligence Save window.

mance only and do not appear in saved files. Note that while many of these settings are initially inherited from the music itself, they may be overridden manually here.

The Save window (shown in figure 10.5) allows works to be saved in two formats: as Experiments in Musical Intelligence databases for use in further composition or as standard MIDI files for performance with any sequencing software. The last menu item, Windows, shown in figure 10.1, presents a list of all open windows on the screen from which users can select one for activation. This menu item can be very helpful when the screen becomes cluttered with many open windows hidden from view.

Saving Experiments in Musical Intelligence works as MIDI files affords users the opportunity to view these works in many formats, including standard music notation. Generating scores from MIDI files, however, also presents a number of nontrivial problems. These problems include appropriately combining channels to two staves as in piano music, deriving a consistent and logical spelling of accidentals (even the best computer notation programs have trouble with this process), and the accurate representation of rhythm—triplets and other small-value notes can often become confused in translation to notation, especially when the tempo of the original is not aligned with the default tempo of the notation program. Aside from these fundamental problems, effective notation also relies on page layout, including note spacing, proper clef choices, metrically logical beaming, and appropriate page turns. While many of the Experiments in Musical Intelligence program's scores, such as those in appendix D, may be performed from such rectified notation, many works, especially orchestral music, also require crucial performance markings such as articulations, bowing, phrasing, and assorted other additions relating to the rendering of the final score and parts for rehearsals. These additions should follow the performance practice of the period or composer of the replicated work, which further requires research and comparison with original scores to achieve accuracy.

Performance

MIDI performances can create false illusions as to how works will actually sound when performed live. I have often been tempted to discard music based on hearing a MIDI performance, music which has ultimately proved to be highly successful. In order to verify the accuracy of my initial judgments, I often perform output myself at the piano, regardless of the type and size of ensemble originally intended. These human performances provide me with a better sense of the worth of the music.

The output shown in *Virtual Music* indicates what the Experiments in Musical Intelligence program *actually* composed. Some critics argue (see Cope 1996, chapter 7) that performance quality has contributed to the program's success in style emulation. Since this argument has some merit, I have since incorporated more and more performance elements into the compositional process. Currently the program composes using timbre and dynamics as well as pitch and duration. Future implementations will use a version of the currently nascent performance subprogram which attempts to humanize otherwise mechanical performances.

A Reject

I have included a computer-composed reject in appendix C to give readers an idea of a typical failed output from the Experiments in Musical Intelligence program. This reject was one of four I discarded in favor of the work presented in appendix B. This ratio compares favorably with the ratio of accepted to unaccepted of from 1:4 to 1:10. My reasons for considering the music in appendix C of less quality than that of the music in appendix B include its duplications of continuous measures of Mozart's originals (e.g., see mm. 47–56 borrowed from Mozart's K. 310 mm. 44–53), the fact that much of the work tends to develop scales and other less interesting material (e.g., see mm. 25–8 and 65–9), and this music sounding less stylistically and musically convincing to me than the acceptable movement found in appendix B. Obviously this latter distinction represents personal opinion rather than empirical judgment, though to some degree so do all the other judgments here. However, such intuitive responses have been important for me in deciding which of the program's works I release and which I do not.

I often save rejects, particularly since MIDI files require so little storage space. Revisiting such works helps me to understand more thoroughly why some works succeed, and provides a source of documentation otherwise lacking from the composing process. Failures also often prove more instructive for improving the program than do successes.

The completed compositions of Experiments in Musical Intelligence represented in appendix D are quite simple but occasionally startlingly effective. Even though a great deal of recombination and transformation has taken place, the program has based its output so effectively on the compositions it attempts to emulate at times that some (including myself) contend that part of the original message seems to be captured in the newly composed music. The program's Rachmaninoff Suite for Two Pianos (see appendix D), for example, is so convincing, for me at least, that I mistook its first performance for one of the actual Rachmaninoff works in the program's database.

A much-simplified version of Experiments in Musical Intelligence called SARA (Simple Analytic Recombinant Algorithm) is available in source code on the CD-ROM accompanying my book *Experiments in Musical Intelligence* (Cope 1996). Readers can experiment with SARA to get a feel for composing virtual music.

III COMMENTARY

Aside from Douglas Hofstadter, the colloquium on computers and creativity referenced in the Preface also included Steve Larson (who teaches music theory at the University of Oregon and who has published dozens of articles on music cognition and jazz, including a recently released compact disk with jazz flutist Cynthia Folio entitled Portfolio*); Daniel Dennett (director of the Center for Cognitive Studies at Tufts University, author of* Consciousness Explained; Darwin's Dangerous Idea; Kinds of Minds; *and co-editor, with Douglas Hofstadter, of* The Mind's I*); Eleanor Selfridge-Field (historical musicologist at Stanford University, a founding member of the Center for Computer Assisted Research in the Humanities, editor of* Beyond MIDI: The Handbook of Musical Codes *and co-editor of* Computing in Musicology*); Jonathan Berger (associate professor of music at Stanford University, composer, and music theorist whose research includes studies in music cognition, recognition, and transformation of musical patterns); and Bernard Greenberg (software engineer specializing in operating systems and LISP, a major contributor to the Multics and Symbolics Genera operating systems, organist, harpsichordist, composer, a lifelong student of the music of J. S. Bach, and currently technical director at Basis Technology in Cambridge, MA).*

The colloquium, which included papers by each of the above individuals, produced full-house audiences and created a stir in both local and national media. After the last panel concluded, the participants agreed that the two days of events deserved publication so that others besides those in attendance could better understand the project and hear the various views expressed. Part III of Virtual Music *represents just such a publication and I am delighted to help disseminate these diverse views with which I both agree and disagree, comments which praise and criticize, and ideas which explore the role of computers in music and creativity. Chapters 11 through 16 range from careful analyses and comparisons of Bach and machine-composed Bach inventions to the philosophical implications of computer creativity in the arts.*

Eleanor Selfridge-Field in chapter 11 presents an important historical perspective which frames the presentations to follow. Her views of the forerunners of virtual music extend and deepen the diversity of my own presentation in previous chapters.

Bernie Greenberg specializes in the music of Bach and in chapter 12 presents a passionate reflection on counterpoint, dissonance, and context in the Baroque master's music. Bernie describes what he feels is the intricate and deep religious backdrop of Bach's work.

In chapter 13 Steve Larson narrows the comparison of machine- vs. Bach-composed music to inventions, providing a theorist's view of the Experiments in Musical Intelligence program's output in the form of two letters to the program as if it were a living and ardent student of Bach's counterpoint. Note that the problems that Steve correctly identifies in the program's inventions partially result from its state as of 1987. Most if not all of the generating algorithms have improved significantly since the inventions which appear in appendix D were created.

Jonathan Berger in chapter 14 invites readers to consider the listener's role in the creative process. He presents a virtual listener *as a foil to Experiments in Musical Intelligence.*

Dan Dennett's overview of computer creation in chapter 15 describes how we might regard such creation in the mosaic of history and the future. Dan compares Experiments in Musical Intelligence output with musalot, *a variation of* gramelot, *where gibberish sounds as good as great ideas to the uninitiated.*

11 Composition, Combinatorics, and Simulation: A Historical and Philosophical Enquiry

Eleanor Selfridge-Field

What is Experiments in Musical Intelligence, this strange amalgam created from a long chain of human-and-machine cause-and-effect activities? How can it be understood in relation to entirely human procedures for creating musical works? How can it be understood in relation to traditional definitions of and procedures for composition? How can it be understood in relation to intuitive ideas of the hallowed "compositional process?" Or in relation to logical rationales of the piecing together of tones into works? Finally, how do the arguments about all of the above change depending on whether we speak of music read from notation, music heard, or music in which we ourselves perform (becoming thus reader, listener, and interpreter in one stroke)?

To explore these questions in an orderly way, we examine several historical models of both (1) musical composition and (2) combinatorics, a critical component of the program's procedural identity. Then we examine (3) an ahistorical model of compositional practice which is combinatoric: the biological paradigm. We also consider (4) selected uses of combinatorics in Experiments in Musical Intelligence's simulations and the epistemological questions they raise. By way of a tentative conclusion, (5) we look at the program's ontological status in relation to Peter Kivy's cognitive idealization of "music alone."

Composition: Some Historical Models

To consider some of the most important overall ideas of musical composition from the past two millennia (with an admitted skew toward our own time), at least five rubrics arguably have some relevance to Experiments in Musical Intelligence. These rubrics are (1) the celestial model, (2) the empirical model, (3) the dialectical model, (4) the Gestalt model, and (5) the cognitive model. Each contributes some essential points to a generalized idea of musical composition that may be usefully considered in relation to Experiments in Musical Intelligence.

The Celestial Model

From antiquity through the seventeenth century, one particular thought dominated much philosophical discussion of music: that music consisted of a set of relationships between moving tones. Among the seven liberal arts (grammar, rhetoric, logic, arithmetic, geometry, astronomy, and music) there was a close analogy between the science of moving objects (astronomy) and the science of moving tones (music). In common with many other civilizations of antiquity, Greek thinkers were fascinated by the rotation of heavenly bodies. That these bodies were considered to be revolving around Earth and, in some quarters, to influence the course of earthly activities, gave these bodies a stature which may be difficult to appreciate in our post-Copernican, post-Edisonian age. The dark, mysterious heavens provided a backdrop of dramatic awe to those who sought to understand their secrets.

The movement of tones within this manifold was a mysterious process into which the conscientious observer might gain occasional insight. Those who sought to compose tones (or, under ideal circumstances, to make them compose themselves) would be rendering a representation of their preordained movements that would be harmonious with the laws of celestial nature. Thus the composer's duty was to cultivate the ability to tune in to these natural phenomena.

Writings on music theory, from Boethius in the sixth century through the time of Zarlino in the sixteenth century, attest to this unwavering absorption in the primacy of planetary motion and the doctrine of physical correspondences to understand the inner workings of music. Scale degrees were frequently understood to exist in sets of the same extent as planets. In figure 11.1, from book I of Boethius's treatise *De institutione musica* (early sixth century; first published 1491–9), Earth (TERRA) is shown as the core of the universe. In the seven rings, moving from the center outward, we find (1) the moon, (2) Mercury, (3) Venus, (4) the Sun, (5) Mars, (6) Jupiter, and (7) Saturn. In the descending conjunct Ionian mode of ancient Greece these rings would have ruled the strings (1) D, or the *nete* (the lowest string of the lyre as the instrument was held produces the highest pitch), (2) C, the *paranete*, (3) Bb, the *trite*, (4) A, the *mese*, (5) G the *lic[h]anos*, (6) F, the *parhypate*, and (7) E, the *hypate*. The scale was called conjunct because two tetrachords, or four-note modules, overlapped.

In part 2 of Zarlino's *Le istitutioni harmoniche* (1558), one diagram shows the correspondences between three series of objects—the planets, shown by signs of the Zodiac; the muses, indicated by their names, Calliope, Thalia, Euterpe, Erato, Melpomene, Clio, Terpsichore, Polimnia, and Urania; and certain modes, as shown in figure 11.2. The bilateral arrangement shows how two modes were ruled by the same planets. Zarlino's diagram is designed to show the complexities of combining tetrachords (series of four notes) to form modes. In the *meson* system on the left, the designations correspond to the descending tones G, F, and E from the middle or *meson* tetrachord; D, C, and B from the highest or *hypaton* tetrachord, and A, known as the *proslambanomenos*, because it exceeded the limit of the preceding tetrachord and had to be added to complete the mode. The *synemmenon* system on the right coupled what was known as the conjunct tetrachord (here contributing D, C, Bb, A) with the middle tetrachord ([A,] G, F, E) and the first note of the highest tetrachord (D).

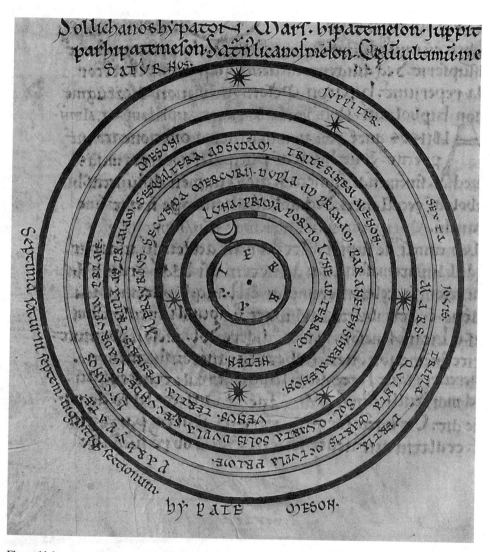

Figure 11.1
Boethius: explanation of scales and intervals by analogy with the planets (from the library of Trinity College, Cambridge University, MS R. 15.22 [944], f. 24v). Boethius's text was here indebted to the Arithmetic of Nicomachus and the Harmonics of Ptolemy. Used by permission of the Master and Fellows, Trinity College Cambridge.

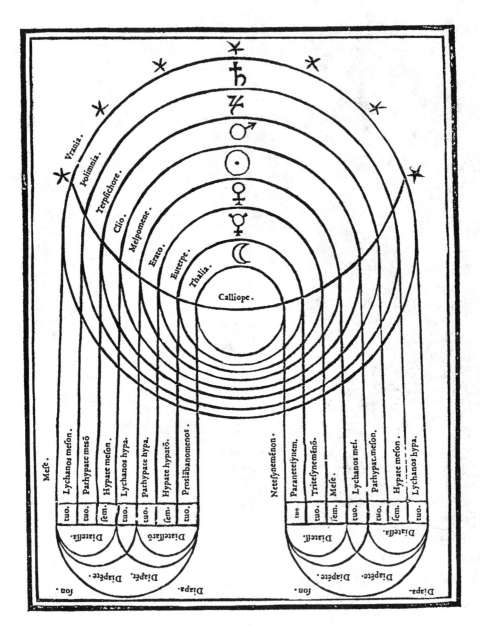

Figure 11.2
Zarlino: *Le istitutioni harmoniche* (Venice, 1558), pt. 2, chap. 29, p. 102.

In viewing both of the illustrations (figures 11.1 and 11.2), remember that these apparent descriptions of planetary motion and influence were writings not about astronomy or astrology but about music. These ideas continued into the seventeenth and eighteenth century, particularly in the works of theorists and mathematicians such as Johannes Kepler.

As the Renaissance dissolved in the Baroque era there was a new concern for performance and a new respect for sound. That is, real experience and practical advice gained ground over purely theoretical discussions of hypothetical compositions. Polemical arguments for and against music became more common. The concept of the harmony of the spheres acquired a new overlay of meaning. Composers of music for the church were encouraged to orient their listeners toward the spiritual, to wed the listener's attention to thoughts of celestial order and perfection. In other words, it was no longer simply a question of tuning in; it was now necessary to funnel listeners to the right channel.

In secular vocal music there was a similar orientation, but with a contrary aim: to enable listeners to become conscious of some Platonic states of the soul. Monteverdi's efforts in the seventeenth century to evoke the Platonic calm, warlike, and agitated states are well-known. To performers of the time, access to these states could be mediated by the use of corresponding musical affects—trills and other ornaments that simulated emotional response to the words associated with the musical score. Thus, to the concept of the harmony of the spheres there now adhered new associations of musical detail, of human gesture, of human perception, and of human emotion. Meaning was no longer confined to a distant heaven. The composer's task was to stir the emotions of the listener. These states were considered purgative, and early opera was a proving ground for their use.

The Empirical Model

By the early eighteenth century the roster of known affects was expanded. Almost coincidentally with the establishment of tonal harmony and equal temperament, theorists began to talk about rhetorical correspondences with particular keys. They suggested appropriate keys to express the happy, the sad, the noble, and so on. The rise of empiricism in the eighteenth century, with its quest for the tangible and the verifiable, directed their attention toward earth. The universe contained a host of observable forms which they could experience through verifiable sensations. Tonal relationships mirrored this universe and were governed by rules of content, procedure, and form.

Concurrent with the rise of empiricism in the philosophical sphere was the growing importance accorded to individual beings. Music theorists still believed that their rules described universal truths, which they were privileged to perceive or deduce. Beauty, form, and order were still in the "great chain of being" that constituted the natural world. Yet, while beauty was considered to be universally perceptible, they increasingly recognized that each individual might interpret it differently. For musical composition this meant on the one hand constructing concrete examples of universal beauty. On the other hand, however, it meant engaging individual talent to concoct the most illustrious examples of this universal beauty. The eighteenth-century German theorist Heinrich Christoph Koch (1983), in offering a series of mechanical rules for the creation of melodies, remarked that he considered "only genius to be capable of endowing a melody with beauty and only taste to be capable of perceiving this beauty."

Thus the development of empirical thought brought new importance to the role of the perceiver. In contrast to the Baroque ideal, according to which the listener was passively and unprotestingly steered toward a correct perception of universal truth, the listener now was socially and philosophically molded prior to involvement with a musical work. Through such cultivation of powers of discernment listeners might bring to the perception of musical works a sense of discrimination that would discard the overly ornate or self-important. Taste in the eighteenth century had a socially correct connotation that allied its acquisition and proper use with those of high birth and extensive learning. It favored simplicity, but simplicity of a particular kind modeled on classical examples.

The Dialectical Model

The notion that all art is expressive and that the expression of beauty is the highest goal of art is one largely grounded in the nineteenth century. In sculpture (the preeminent repository of the ideal model of "noble simplicity and serene greatness") this beauty resides in those isolated moments of flowing narrative which were frozen into concrete form, and thus preserved in time. Nineteenth-century aestheticians scanned the material world for such frozen moments, leaving aside the residuum of the narratives themselves. The meaningful and the beautiful were divorced from the continuum of living experience.

The straight line of narrative succumbed to the dialectical process of interchange and eventual synthesis in the thought of the philosopher Georg Wilhelm Friedrich Hegel. For Hegel, form and content were the aesthetically valid components of all works of art, and what validated them was the interaction between components. Hegel attempted to accommodate empirical ideas in his notion of aesthetics as a "science of beauty," although when he spoke of it instead as a "science of sensation or feelings," he was acknowledging the creator as a perceiver. The modern semiotic notion of a dialectic between the "plane of representation" and the "plane of meaning" is not entirely free of Hegelian leanings, and his ideas remained potent throughout the twentieth century.

In his writings on aesthetics, developed between 1818 and 1833, Hegel (1970) held that

The objection that works of art elude the treatment of scientific thought because they originate out of *unregulated fancy* and *out of feelings* ... and therefore take effect only on feelings and imagination ... raises a problem ... for the beauty of art ... appears in a form which is contrasted with abstract thought, and which the latter is forced to destroy in exerting the activity which is its nature. (p. 35)

Hegel credited Plato with the view (1970, p. 46) that "objects should be apprehended not in their particularity but in their universality." Generalizability was an essential component of the absolute that Hegel strove to describe. For Hegel the notion of beauty might be an abstract concept, but our encounters with it would require a material world to serve as a kind of vessel in which to contain the abstract. Hegel attempted to fend off the criticism that works of art originate in formless feelings, to which there is no empirical access. The greater problem was that they take effect only on feelings, that is, that they pass from one nonempirical universe to another.

With regard to tonal relationships in music, it was Hegel's view that a dialectical process wove together the abstraction of form with the concretization of content. A concrete universal was entirely possible in music. The composer's role was to shape this dialectic. The dialectic could best be achieved in instrumental music, which, to Hegel's mind, was a purer form of expression than the texted works of earlier centuries. The text was an impediment to abstraction; it distracted the listener from perceiving the universal ideal of form. Hegel's message pervaded Germanic culture and all the arts of its time. It was particularly influential on German music theory in the nineteenth century. Form became a fixture in the teaching of musical composition in conservatories. Instrumental music earned increasingly greater respect, as it was considered to express form more clearly, and to lie closer to the realm of abstraction.

The Gestalt Model

The emphasis of Gestalt psychology in the twentieth century focused on the perception of patterns. Many of these patterns are perceived incompletely by the observer and thus, in their most literal representations, they may seem ambiguous. The creation, perception, and interpretation of ambiguity has become an area of considerable fascination in the arts generally. Like form, patterns thus play an essential role in the arts.

In the thinking of Leonard Meyer, who leans toward the Gestalt model, tonal relationships are regulated by musical patterns. Two important aspects of musical patterns are that listeners identify them through extensive repetition and these patterns lack any external means of reference. Thus, musical patterns exist for their own sake. They occupy a sort of logical or mathematical space and are divorced from the invisible forces so dominant in the minds of Hegel's critics. Meyer (1956) writes,

Music ... employs no signs or symbols referring to the non-musical world of objects, concepts, and human desires. Thus the meanings which it imparts differ in important ways from those conveyed by literature, painting, biology, or physics. (p. 7)

Meyer attempts to avoid an atomistic view of music that considers each element of a work a static entity, because his emphasis is on process and its byproducts. Even when he writes of patterns he does not so much mean static patterns as the processes by which patterns evolve. It is precisely here that the notion of expectation becomes central, and the notion of human expectation is central to the link Meyer finds between meaning and emotion in music.

Meyer maintains (1956, p. 7) that music can convey "emotional and aesthetic meanings as well as purely intellectual ones" and that this differentiates it entirely from a "closed, non-referential mathematical system." He argues that musical expression consists of deviations from patterns (i.e., of the frustration of expectation), and certainly much of the growing literature in the field of music perception bears him out. A good way to attract a listener's attention is by changing the tempo, the meter, the key, the texture, the instrumentation, or the dynamic level. Although Meyer says much about performance, and although he gives some consideration to non-Western and non-notated repertories, the core of his theory necessarily addresses music that is, after its initial evolution, preserved in a fixed form. Thus those elements of deviation that lie principally within the control of the performer (dynamics, tempo, vibrato, and so forth), although acknowledged, cannot enjoy the same status as those that lie under the control of the composer (key, meter, and, of course, the pitches and durations of the notes that patterns contain). Thus, Meyer's essay is primarily concerned with composition and its artifacts, even though it springs from a psychological premise. This creates an interesting parallelism with Hegel, who also emphasizes process but whose influence seems to have fallen much more squarely on theories of form and structure.

The Cognitive Model

The rise of cognitive studies over the past two decades has fostered the development of a view that the universe is a pool of perceiving, conscious beings. Whatever the beauties of the natural world, whatever the elegance of mathematical models or of relationships between them, the recesses of the human mind form a dominant focus of study and an ultimate rubric of investigation for theories that range from the psychological (form and expression) to the philosophical (meaning). The objective world of antiquity and the Middle Ages has been entirely supplanted by an endlessly varied subjective domain operating in present time.

For cognitive psychologists, tonal relationships exist (or not) in the mind of the subject. That is, they exist only to the extent that they are perceived. Rapid evolution of thinking in the field permits few concrete overviews, but a range of questions currently under study exhibits the breadth and fecundity of its possibilities. Experimental research provides some fascinating insights into the inner workings of such human phenomena as musical memory, recognition, and attention. Cognitive linguists debate the proximity of musical language to grammars of speech. Cognitive philosophers grapple with fundamental questions associated with such things as artificial composition. For example, the philosophical underpinnings of theories of consciousness are a favorite subject of Daniel Dennett (see chapter 15).

In the symposium in which this chapter was first presented, the ultimate focus was on the Experiments in Musical Intelligence program's merits as a challenge to the notion of the superiority of human creativity. Creativity lies both within and without the domain of cognitive studies; my own observations on this subject will be left aside for a later airing. This exclusion occurs because so much of the discussion of creativity in the context of the live event was interleaved with discussions of emotion, which involves yet another set of values, basic definitions, and perceived truths. Yet some discussion of Experiments in Musical Intelligence in relation to certain aspects of the thought of Peter Kivy will be retained on account of its valuable clarification of one point.

In his book *Music Alone*, Kivy divides those who think about music in relation to emotion into two camps—the cognitivists and the emotivists. *Cognitivists*, according to Kivy (1990, p. 146), believe that the expression of particular emotions inheres in the music, while *emotivists* concentrate on emotions aroused in the listener by the music. Kivy sides largely with the cognitivists but attempts to deal with the questions of expressiveness, emotion, and meaning in relation to the music itself (hence his title). He excludes all theories requiring some external point of reference. He equates "expression" with the "heard properties of music" (p. 172); he does not equate expression with emotion. He does hold that "cognitivism is the correct analysis of musical expressiveness." The possible relevance of Kivy's thinking to the music produced by Experiments in Musical Intelligence is that ostensibly what the program produces is more fully isolated from all the points of reference which he rejects than humanly composed music would be. This point is taken up later.

Combinatorics: Some Historical Models

In discussions of Experiments in Musical Intelligence, the role of combinatoric principles is broadly acknowledged, but it may be helpful to acknowledge also that combinatorics has played a role in theorizing about a broad range of creative endeavors in fields other than music. Here I will briefly acknowledge its hypothetical involvement in mathematical, linguistic, and other musical activities.

Mathematical and Linguistic Combinatorial Prototypes

The earliest formal articulation of a theory of combinatorics seems to have come, appropriately enough, from the father of binary logic, the German philosopher and mathematician Gottfried Wilhelm Leibnitz. In his first published work, *Dissertatio de arte combinatoria* (1666), Leibnitz constructed an elaborate theory of the place of opposites in a general scheme of the elements constituting the universe. Heat and cold, moisture and dryness, fire and water, earth and air were combinable—or not—depending on a host of options, as shown in figure 11.3. All of Leibnitz's thought seems to have been dominated by the idea of binary oppositions, starting with the opposition of God (represented by the number 1) to nothingness (represented by the number 0). His emphasis was on the fundamentals of opposition rather than on the potential results of combination.

With the popularization of Leibnitz's thought, which made its impact after his death (1716), the *ars combinatoria* took on a life of its own. Something akin to it is evident in the satirist Jonathan Swift's elaboration (1726) of the mythical Laputan system for (re)creating all works of "philosophy, poetry, politicks, law, mathematics, and theology." These works were to be created from elements of language (pre-classified by their parts of speech [particles, nouns, ... verbs], moods, and tenses) pasted onto cubes arranged in a two-dimensional grid and equipped with handles for rotation. The Learned Academy of Laputa, we are told, employed forty boys to turn the handles and thus to explore all possible combinations of characters from several ancient and Oriental languages. Rotations would continue until meaningful combinations of characters produced works and phrases which conformed to the designated grammar. New works could be created "without the least assistance of genius or study." An illustration of the grid as shown in the first edition of *Gulliver's Travels* is given in figure 11.4.

Figure 11.3
Leibnitz: diagram showing the relationship of opposites in the *ars combinatoria*, from his "dissertation" on the same subject (before 1716).

The Prehistory of Musical Combinatorics

Designs for musical dice games probably had a different cultural point of departure, one that was inherently more numerically oriented than Swift's linguistic model. They could be understood as an appendix to the eighteenth-century's fascination with gambling, to resulting efforts to make moral distinctions between games of skill and games of chance, and to the unintended consequence of stimulating the development of theories of probability (to aid those who persisted in playing games of chance against the advice of the church). An enormous amount of paraphernalia was created for pseudogambling (i.e., activities dependent on the same logic as gambling but without wagering), and musical dice were simply one manifestation of this rage.

Leonard Ratner (1970) has traced the development of musical dice games based on the *ars combinatoria* as a device for musical composition. Kirnberger's model for generating six-bar melodies for polonnaises and minuets as shown in figure 11.5 is but one example (see Kirnberger 1757).

However, this fairly elaborate model is unlikely to produce identical results within a finite range of performances, so it is really quite highly evolved in comparison to

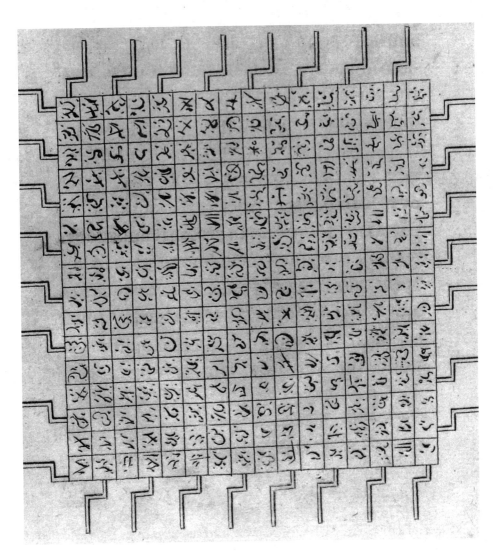

Figure 11.4
Jonathan Swift, *Gulliver's Travels* (London, 1726), vol. II, pt. iii, plate facing p. 74. Used by permission of the Librarian and Trustees of Stanford University.

Dice Roll	Measure					
	1	2	3	4	5	6
2	70	34	68	18	32	58
3	10	24	50	46	14	26
4	42	6	60	2	52	66
5	62	8	36	12	16	38
6	44	56	40	79	48	54
7	72	30	4	28	22	64
8	114	112	126	87	89	88
9	123	116	137	110	91	98
10	131	147	143	113	101	115
11	138	151	118	124	141	127
12	144	153	146	128	150	154

Figure 11.5
Kirnberger (1757): random-number table for the generation of six-measure melodies in the style of a polonaise or minuet.

Leibnitz's (1666) binary model of opposites, which can be related in more finite combinations much as many kinds of key relationships can be related by different geometrical shapes formed within the circle of fifths. Kirnberger's system generates one note at a time in one part at a time, so it is an atomic system of composition with no governing sense of overall order. It is thus incapable of paralleling the Experiments in Musical Intelligence program's grammatical sense of architecture because all of its elements are made available in a functionally equivalent way. It is apparent that had the grammatical sense of Swift's linguistic model and the logical choices offered by Kirnberger's game been used in combination with precomposed fragments of melody, the amalgam could have produced monophonic compositions that might have prefigured those of Experiments in Musical Intelligence.

In fact, a very brief summary of Experiments in Musical Intelligence's principal features comes down almost exactly to such a combination of models. The recombination of functional elements of language, reminiscent of the elements of Koch's theory of melody, govern the program's *sui generis* grammar, while the random selection of short passages supplies the content that enables this grammar to be self-realizing and thus to produce a structure of some specifically musical kind.

The Biological Model of Simulation

Genetics offers one paradigm that has no previous history of association with musical composition but is obviously applicable to the Experiments in Musical Intelligence's basic constituent parts and method of operation. Heinrich Schenker in the second chapter of his treatise on harmony described "The Biologic Foundation of the Process of Combination" (1954, p. 84) but not in ways that bear any relationship to the present considerations. His view was tied to various anthropomorphisms, so that when he spoke of "the truly biologic characteristics displayed by tones," he wished to call attention to the "procreative urge of the tones." In his search for means promoting "intense self-expression," Schenker identified the "egotism" of one tone in relation to another. This biological model relates to the simulation of musical styles, rather than to the natural composition of music.

Biological Combinatorics in Relation to Experiments in Musical Intelligence

The Experiments in Musical Intelligence program creates works according to an algorithmic system used in combination with the selection of specific traits for individual works from a large pool of signatures garnered from the works of past composers. Separate data pools are maintained for individual composers and specific genres. Generally, each data pool is kept pure by composer and genre: new Bach inventions are created from pools of signatures derived from two or more authentic inventions. Similarly, new works in the style of Mozart come only from Mozart and only from the genre desired (e.g., a sonata-allegro movement). New works can be crossbred, with a bias either toward horizontal morphing from one gene pool to another, as in the concert piece *Mozart in Bali*, or toward simultaneous recombination, for example, of left-hand and right-hand signatures from different sources. The former procedure is more congenial to the program's usual way of working, since signatures are usually stored as vertical time slices of sound-based information.

To what might be called the Experiments in Musical Intelligence paradox, elements of style are *particular* to genre as well as composer, but procedure, at the most abstract level of grammar, is *general* to all composers and even to repertories based on oral transmission. As in the model of procreation in the natural world, an element of randomness inheres in the program's governing grammar of possible procedures for the realization of a new piece. The external casing of the work, such as key and meter, and more subtle variables, such as a range of lengths for the signatures to be used, can be selected by the user before the constructive phase is initiated. Thus some constraints exist at the outset, but this is also true in natural reproduction: two brown-eyed parents are unlikely to produce a blue-eyed child.

In addition to signature selection, the program controls the realization of the grammar of the genre selected. How many antecedents will there be? Will they stand in some rational relationship to the number of statements? Because the signatures used by Experiments in Musical Intelligence are small relative to the size of a phrase in most repertories, small differences in the number or order of elements accrue to make substantial differences in the overall accumulation, such that two different realizations of a work based on the same signature pools can be quite different in length and form, as shown in figures 11.6a and b. One might consider them fraternal twins, but fraternal triplets, quadruplets, and so on are also conceivable.

The overarching relevance of the biological paradigm to explanations of what Experiments in Musical Intelligence is and how it works inheres in an implicit debate about artificial creation in general. Lying just beneath the surface of the facile analogies that can be drawn between the program's procedures and the procreative ones of the natural world are the ethical questions that are asked with increasing frequency in genetic research. For those to whom the cloning of sheep, the hybridization of vegetables, and in vitro fertilization raise moral questions, it is a short step to resisting the advent of mutant Bach inventions, hybridized musical styles, and labs full of musical signatures awaiting recombination in the virtual test tube of computer processing. Experiments in Musical Intelligence mimics the creation of new life without any of the transcendental authority to which such power of procreation has historically been attributed. Experiments in Musical Intelligence and all other programs that generate simulations can potentially be perceived as transgressors of sacrosanct territory. Musicians will realize that music itself is incapable of creating new life, but all experiments in the simulation of processes previously associated exclusively with the human race are vulnerable to being found guilty by association.

The Biological Model in Relation to Historical Models of Composition

In relation to the historical models of musical composition previously examined, Experiments in Musical Intelligence appears to be a void. The program certainly has no sense of the astronomy of the universe, no genius, no taste, no understanding of the dialectic of form and content, no notion of what makes a pattern a pattern, no access to a cognitive construction of its own realization, and no capacity for emotional expression. At least this much pertains to the computer that runs Experiments in Musical Intelligence. When it comes to delineating the role of the composer, the extensive analogies that can be drawn between the program and the biological paradigm do not necessarily exclude parallel readings of historical models. In fact, in some ways the biological paradigm enhances them.

Figure 11.6
Bach/Experiments in Musical Intelligence (c. 1988): Invention in Bb Major, versions a and b.

Figure 11.6 (continued)

Figure 11.6 (continued)

For example, in relation to accessing the music of the spheres, the envelope of virtual attributes acquired from user input into which each new work is poured segregates the material of which the work is composed from the process of its composition, removing it from association with the specifics which provide content and enable performance. It is these user-supplied external features by which we are accustomed to identifying musical works (e.g., sonata in D major, symphony in C minor, etc.). This terminology fails in the context of the Experiments in Musical Intelligence program's repertories, both because there may be multiple examples under a single rubric and because works are not wedded to their keys in the same way as natural works are. For works in tonal harmony, any of twelve keys may be chosen.

This variability of key choice introduces a set of potential problems for performers. Human composers instinctively avoid certain sequences of notes that are uncomfortable or impossible to perform on the specific instrument and in the specific key of the work that they have chosen. There is little codification of gestural rules (e.g., for fingering) because they are innate, thus inherently human. Among those designing computer studies, Morehen (1993–4) probed the area by storing fingering rules for Elizabethan keyboard works to facilitate the automatic editing (for performance) of such works. In both versions of the Experiments in Musical Intelligence program's Bach *Invention in B♭ Major* there is one problematical passage for those pianists taught the proscription never to use a thumb on a black key. It is difficult to avoid violating this rule for the circled notes in figures 11.6a, measure 9, and 11.6b, measure 11, although none of the alternative fingerings are gesturally idiomatic.

When I discussed these reservations with the program's creator, he responded that these works are not in B♭. It is only these specific realizations which are in this key. The user could have specified C or any other major key. Unlike compositions of the tonal period, which are so often wedded to a particular key, the program's works are merely generically tonal. The Experiments in Musical Intelligence program's role is to produce a set of relationships which are more or less manageable in virtual tonality. Any work produced by the program is therefore much less specific in its descriptive identity than the parent works on which it is based. It could not appropriately be described as the "Great G Minor Symphony," for example. It is really a metawork which requires a user's choices to bring it to life.

In relation to the *ars combinatoria*, the role of which is so central to the Experiments in Musical Intelligence program's processing, we need only consider that the number of paths that the program might pursue is potentially much greater than the models of the eighteenth century. In musical dice games, length and form were heavily constrained. Experiments in Musical Intelligence is not so constrained, but user constraint is feasible. The program could be promiscuous in a way that nature does not permit: it could regularly combine signatures from numerous signature pools. In most examples, however, the signatures of two works only have been used. It could be indifferent to questions of breeding, by dipping into the signatures of multiple genres or multiple composers, or both at the same time. Again, current activities do not subscribe to such practices.

In the relationship between the Experiments in Musical Intelligence program's signatures and the controlling grammar of their conjugation, we arguably meet a latter-day manifestation of Hegel's dialectic. From a practical viewpoint, the static notion of form is gone but the dynamic one of process is the essential framework in which the genes produce their material effects. The concepts that facilitate this dialectic have a genius of their own. Hegel's concepts, tied as they are to a world of fixed objects and finished products, do not stretch far enough to pertain to the program's conjugations, but a post-Hegelian theory in which elastic procedure was substituted for fixed form would express the overall relationship to content quite appropriately.

That the reciprocity between process and successive signatures works as well as it does suggests that the relationship between them has been very carefully worked out. There could be many more, or somewhat fewer, elements of the grammar than Experiments in Musical Intelligence employs. The gene pool could be much larger or somewhat smaller. The signatures could be defined in a host of other ways. They could be more or less composite; the signatures could be generally larger or smaller than they are. Traits of any degree of prevalence could be accepted. Users could have greater or lesser latitude in selecting specific features of as yet unborn works.

Combinatorics and Simulation

Combinatoric procedures seem to be well suited to musical simulation, but they are foreign to documented human methods of composition. That is, existing explanations of the compositional process tend to be both prescriptive and proscriptive ("Do this … don't do that"). The freedoms that are left to the composer are not usually represented as possible couplings of traits. In some cases they are seen to be amorphous selections from the black box of imagination. In other cases, they may arise from the prescriptive process itself (e.g., through the formation of an initial tone-row or set, or, in electronic composition, through the choice of a self-realizing random process or virtual instrument).

Combinatorics in Relation to Artificial Composition

Some systems of algorithmic simulation of known repertories or styles, especially those based entirely on sound materials such as MIDI files, are much cruder examples of the recombination of existing works to form new ones. Systems based on procedural principles and internal data representations, in contrast, have been largely focused on implementing the rule systems described in music theory treatises. Among the latter, one of the most thoughtful and most fully described systems for the simulation of historical repertories is that of Ulf Berggren (1995), a Swedish researcher. Considering that a short summary of his work might read very much like a short summary of Experiments in Musical Intelligence, the results are significantly different (and the pieces many fewer in number). The beginning of one of his system's approximations to the sonata-allegro movement of a Mozart piano sonata is shown in figure 11.7.

Despite being based on a rigorous procedural apparatus, the music shown in figure 11.7 seems somewhat episodic in its construction. It may suffer from being too faithful to the finite details of its models, too absorbed in obeying the rules. Berggren's system has too little sense of form to mimic complete movements convincingly. Herein lies a paradox: careful procedural definition does not seem to guarantee an integrated sense of structure.

What is most conspicuous in the comparison of Experiments in Musical Intelligence to most other systems is that Experiments in Musical Intelligence opts for more data and fewer rules. In a sense it invests almost all of its capacity for specificity in

Figure 11.7
Ulf Berggren (1995): simulation of a first movement of a Mozart piano sonata (bars 1–20). Used by permission. Work on this project continues. For current information please send e-mail to ulf.berggren @musik.uu.se.

patterns and very little in procedure. Contrary to expectation, this approach usually produces a recognizable semblance of the intended movement types. This imbalance may be a great strength in that it fosters a limitless sense of new combinations of patterns without a mesmerizing repetitiveness of form. The Experiments in Musical Intelligence program's freedom from procedural constraint makes it more nearly self-perpetuating than self-limiting. The fulcrum of the program's balance between data sets and their procedural (re)combination creates a very lopsided inclination favoring control of content and freedom of process. Because, however, these two components of the system must ultimately find their limits in each other, Experiments in Musical Intelligence satisfies many conditions of the Hegelian dialectic.

By being able to compare simulations of the same repertory made by different systems, we gain the ability to better understand these intricate balances. It is possible that the apparent simplicity of Mozart's music, and thus its assumed utility for experiments in simulation, is deceptive. The Experiments in Musical Intelligence program's imitations of Mozart's sonata-allegro movements are less convincing than its simulations of many other repertories. Mozart's style feeds our cognitive faculties very graciously with passages that are easily remembered for their salient points, but if only these residues are imitated, the result will be a poor approximation to the model.

Combinatorics in Relation to the Simulation of Diverse Styles

While the synthesis of particularity and universality used by Experiments in Musical Intelligence may not be uniformly congenial to all repertories, it is amazingly adaptable to musical genres that are stylistically diverse—Bach inventions and Joplin rags, Palestrina masses and Prokofiev piano sonatas, Mozart quartets and Rachmaninoff suites. This might be perceived not only from the bulk of music contained in this publication but also from a quick perusal of some highly divergent examples. Consider, for example, the Mozartean recitative in figure 11.8, which comes from the Experiments in Musical Intelligence opera called *Mozart* (1992).

The Experiments in Musical Intelligence program's simulation of recitative is in some ways more interesting than its simulation of aria, because there are no grand schemes in composition manuals for the construction of recitative. Recitative normally follows the text, paraphrasing the contours and accents of speech. The program's recent simulations of Broadway show tunes is an even better test of this ability with respect to an indirect response to textual contours, since in this case Experiments in Musical Intelligence simulates the text as well as the music. (The text of the opera *Mozart* is scripted from the composer's letters.)

Figure 11.8
Mozart/Experiments in Musical Intelligence: Recitative "I Could Hardly Have Supposed It" from the opera *Mozart* (1992). A cadence to D major occurs in the following measure.

Figure 11.9
Joplin/Experiments in Musical Intelligence (c. 1990): rag.

The harmony in measure 11 of the Experiments in Musical Intelligence simulation of a Joplin rag shown in figure 11.9 seemed odd on first hearing. This led to the examination of other works by Joplin where it can be seen that tertiary dominants—the dominant of the secondary dominant—could occur. Descriptions are not easily found in harmony textbooks, though, because Joplin does not belong to any recognized canon of distinguished harmonizers. Thus, fidelity to actual repertories can expand our working store of theoretical knowledge, where formal music theory has failed to do so.

How exactly does Experiments in Musical Intelligence manage to mimic uncodified practices? The program's multifaceted approach cannot be reduced to a single formula such as bottom-up or top-down, for its development has absorbed many accretions from diverse analytical approaches. Its methods of pattern identification bypass entirely the most heavily frequented path to style simulation: implementation of rule systems laid down by music theorists. If manuals on composition and music theory told us more than a small percentage of all we need to know to mimic music of the past, then programs for automatic composition based on codified rule systems would have been more successful than they have been. What Experiments in Musical Intelligence does store with its signatures, however, is contextual information that allows it to find more or less appropriate fits as it passes from one signature to another in the assembly of a new work.

Cognitive Issues Related to Simulation

Cognitive perspectives not only play a role in dealing with some aspects of musical understanding and performance, they also entice us to distinguish between composition and the simulation of composition. In the case of Experiments in Musical Intelligence, we encounter fascinating but unexplored questions at both the theoretical and practical levels. Beginning with the first, we might ask, Do the Experiments in Musical Intelligence program's procedures, as distinct from its results, in any way simulate the subconscious choices made by human composers in the process of composing? Is there any chance that combinatorics of the kind used by the program simulate real processes in the human brain? There is no way currently to prove or disprove these ideas, for there is no way to test them. In scientific terms, we cannot judge the degree to which the program does or does not approximate human conceptualization and processing, because we do not know enough about the human side of the equation. Thus we cannot determine which, if any, are the uniquely and necessarily human aspects of musical composition.

Simulation of composition introduces its own complexities. Much writing about music focuses on *divergence* from a common point of departure—the evolution of musical styles, the creation of new genres, or the existence of variant versions of works. The focus of style-simulation studies, such as the signature-identification algorithms of Experiments in Musical Intelligence, employs a reverse logic: the goal is to mimic a predefined style and genre as closely as possible. A set of parallel procedures that become *convergent* is essential. While human composers tend to diverge among themselves in their relation to a common point of departure, Experiments in Musical Intelligence marshals many points of departure together to converge on its compositional object. This is a model which can best be described by its individual parts and the recipe by which they are combined.

At the practical level, nothing so confuses the issue of the Experiments in Musical Intelligence program's merits as our customary failure to distinguish between traits of performance and traits of composition. This hypothesis has been tested informally in the context of another set of simulated works—the chorale harmonizations of Kemal Ebcioğlu's program called CHORAL. When a chorale harmonized by CHORAL (Ebcioğlu 1993) is played with mean-tone temperament by a human organist for a live audience, it is much more likely to be judged true Bach than when the same chorale is played by the same organist with equal temperament. Audiences seem to be responding to an "out-of-tune Baroque sound" rather than to textural and procedural details of the score being performed, for these require a more highly evolved critical faculty. The judgment of differences of timbre is, after all, a single one, whereas the comparison of chordal progressions requires that many judgments be made in rapid succession.

A similar effect can be noted with any natural repertory that is reproduced mechanically. The important point here is that the converse also appears to be true: when an artificially created piece is performed naturally, it is much less likely to be judged artificially composed than if it is reproduced automatically (see Cope 1994 and 1997b to hear this difference). When the B♭ major invention (see figure 11.6, either version) is played by a human performer with improvised ornaments, it is not so likely to be found to be false Bach as if it is pumped out of a synthesizer with no rhythmic variety and (in version b) a mechanically executed trill at the final cadence. Here the reaction against mechanization is precipitated by the lack of rhythmic variety of an absolutely metronomic performance. Recent research confirms that even when human subjects are asked to perform metronomically, a slight variance from the established tempo is normative (Repp 1996). Not surprisingly, numerous algorithms to humanize automatic performance are currently under development.

Questions arising from the performance of simulated works are compounded when the model repertory is one that is not closely scripted. Jazz and blues provide useful examples. In the case of such repertories, we might say that what Experiments in Musical Intelligence produces is a metascore: it is the skeleton for a work that may be more fully realized in natural performance. Once the program's music is left to the discretion of the performer, it is even more difficult to discriminate between simulations and the models on which they are based. This is true primarily because we are not accustomed to hearing the models performed exactly according to the score. In fact, we are not accustomed to hearing them performed exactly the same way twice. We expect only to notice those salient features which give a set of endless variants the sense of a common overall identity. Our ears are tuned to certain styles of perfor-

(a)

Figure 11.10
Broadway/Experiments in Musical Intelligence: "You Can't Blame Me," versions a (computer) and b (ES-F arrangement).

(b)

Figure 11.10 (continued)

mance that seem to fit the piece in question. By way of an example, the Experiments in Musical Intelligence program's output and my own preliminary arrangement of a pseudoblues tune called "You Can't Blame Me" are shown in figure 11.10.

Although considerable liberties have been taken with texture and rhythm and one of the program's harmonies has been changed (at m. 3), the same liberties might properly be taken with the repertory on which this work was modeled. Yet it is quite clear that if Experiments in Musical Intelligence were to mix signatures derived from both versions, the result would be quite uneven. Music of this kind produced by a style-simulation engine such as Experiments in Musical Intelligence is, by the time it is performed, the result of a multipass compositional system which includes not only the original compositions on which the simulation is based but also the simulation and the performer's arrangement. It is worth noting, however, that the model repertory is, at the time of performance, the result of the first and third of these passes.

Conclusions

Regarding the debate over whether the computer simulation of specific musical styles is a machine activity or a human activity, over time Experiments in Musical Intelligence has become increasingly automatic, so it has become progressively more allied with machine activity. However, a great deal of human activity and human judgment underlie its achievements and continue to accrue. The program could not have invented itself. It is entirely dependent on human existence for its own existence. To consider that what Experiments in Musical Intelligence does is an entirely automatic process is to miss the fact of this dependency. The program's functional context remains bounded by human values.

I noted earlier that a computer running Experiments in Musical Intelligence would be devoid of thought and self-reference, as well as feeling and expression. It is less clear that the same can be said of software, because a great deal of human thought and, in many cases, ingenuity is woven into the fabric of software. The same pertains to the human user in an interactive relationship with the software. Users may select keys, meters, or other constraints according to some long-honed set of personal tastes and preferences. The amalgam of human observation and ingenuity that encapsulates the machine's monotonous vocabulary of iteration and selection has all of the human characteristics that surfaced in our historical review of compositional values. Even the facile biological analog as a method of explaining Experiments in Musical Intelligence is constrained by the same long tradition as any music created today by human composers. It could be argued that Experiments in Musical Intelligence simulations are far more consciously constrained, because they attempt to simulate some very highly evolved repertories that require enormous study merely to recognize or describe, much less to attempt to replicate. Meanwhile they accrue more and more layers of human material.

The question of whether the computer simulation of musical styles is epistemologically the same as composition is less well explored. From a philosophical perspective, simulation is not the same as the activity being simulated. It is not the thing itself. It is an approximation, a representation, an abstraction. No one would argue that a photograph of the Mona Lisa is the same as the painting, or that the figure in the painting is the same as the woman who was once its model. Because the works of Experiments in Musical Intelligence are not intended to be exact replicas of precise preexisting works, they confuse this issue. They are suggestive of truly new objects. Yet both their newness and their objectiveness can be challenged. Ultimately, Experiments in Musical Intelligence is a reprocessing engine. It is generative without being directly creative. Another paradox of the program is that what it produces incorporates large elements of what might be called indirectly new materials.

The Experiments in Musical Intelligence program's simulations can apparently be situated within the context of Kivy's view that music is about specific musical procedures. If music is expressive at all, he maintains, then a chromatic fugue, for example, is expressive of chromaticism (and arguably of "fugalism"). Within the framework of Kivy's argument (1990, p. 195), that "the expressive properties of music alone are purely musical properties," it is apparent that the fundamentally "expressive properties" of these particular computer simulations are their being about musical composition in the round. What Experiments in Musical Intelligence produces is metacompositions—works that weave new threads of thought about compositional procedures together with strands recycled from the fabric of actual preexistent works. Is it then the case that the Experiments in Musical Intelligence program's methods, while resonating with some long and varied intellectual traditions, cannot constitute a true plane of composition? Are they simply mimetic imitations of such a plane? Such an ontological status would not prevent them from bringing pleasure to listeners and performers in their surface role as musical compositions.

The matter is too contorted to produce a simple answer. "Genius" in music created by Experiments in Musical Intelligence is a hybrid synthesized from multiple passes of human intelligence managed by machine. The genius of content remains entirely acquired from human sources. The genius of processing is implemented by machine but designed by human agents. The dialectic of form and process, so comparatively simple in Hegel's time, is now considerably more complex.

By way of summary, let us consider this complexity in relation to conventional ideas of the (human) compositional process. Figure 11.11 shows various modules of compositional activity that have been mentioned above. Previously acquired types of knowledge are itemized by number on the horizontal axis at the top. Steps in the procedure itself are itemized by letter on the vertical axis.

Cherished nineteenth-century notions of composition privilege A and C, the magical acquisition of ideas and their realization in new works. Both processes are vaguely defined. Our increasing awareness of the intellectual qualities of music and the cognitive faculties of composers suggest that mere ideas will not lead from A to C

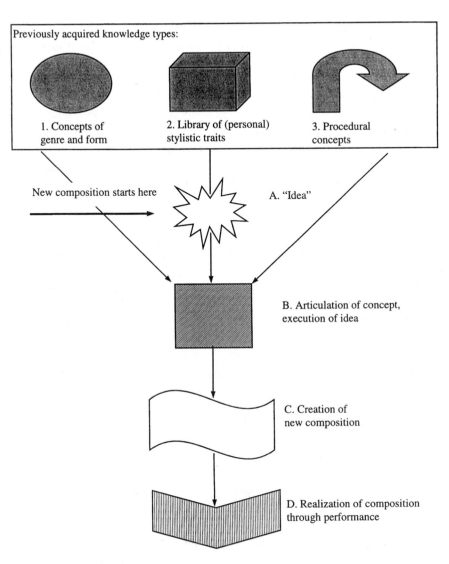

Figure 11.11
Various modules of compositional activity described in the text. Previously acquired types of knowledge are itemized by number (1, 2, 3) on the horizontal axis at the top. Steps in the procedure itself are itemized by letter (A, B, C) on the vertical axis.

without previously acquired knowledge of several kinds, including 1, 2, and 3. Any student of composition also appreciates that the path from A to C leads inevitably through B and that the composer may not have an entirely formed judgment of C without passing through D at least once.

In the kind of combinatorial composition facilitated by Experiments in Musical Intelligence, the crucial factor may be reprioritization of 1, 2, and 3. In the pedagogy of the eighteenth and nineteenth centuries, students were well prepared in 3 (e.g., via the study of harmony and counterpoint) and increasingly, from the nineteenth century on, in 1, while 2 was (and often still is) left to inspiration and other mystical processes. Experiments in Musical Intelligence, instead, privileges 2, because combinatorial procedures necessarily require a wealth of component parts on which to operate.

We do not know whether highly inventive human composers store a large 2 vocabulary, and there is no obvious way of exploring the question. We might suppose that they do not consciously entertain the possibility of exploring every conceivable combination of nodes, but rather rely, like Pavlovian rats, on following familiar pathways through what might otherwise seem an overwhelming array of choices. The downfall of aspiring composers, in fact, may sometimes be the lack of a big enough store of the idiomatic contents on which 3 and 1 depend for their success.

Experiments in Musical Intelligence also subverts the relation between 1 and 3. For many of the composers whose music is simulated by these procedures, musicians living today will readily perceive the form, because they have been well schooled to do this. Composers of the past may have been more conscious of procedural issues. Experiments in Musical Intelligence absorbs much of 1 into 3 by dealing with form at the level of evolving grammatical construction. Procedural selection is also combinatorial, but it moves on a much slower cog than feature selection.

Vis-à-vis other kinds of algorithmic composition by machine, Experiments in Musical Intelligence is conservative by comparison with those procedures in which 3 is the sole purpose of the exercise. Substance may vary from one composer to another but style is unlikely to vary from moment to moment within one work.

Partly because of the reprioritization of preexistent knowledge types, Experiments in Musical Intelligence could be said to be a system devoted to "composing about composition." But since knowledge types lie outside the work itself, Kivy's view is ultimately rendered moot—not only for repertories simulated by Experiments in Musical Intelligence but also for the "natural" examples he discusses. (For a chromatic fugue to be "about chromaticism," for example, some notion of "chromaticism" must reside in the mind of the composer, and, if the work is intended to communicate, it must reside in the mind of the listener also.) Even this kind of "expression" requires the involvement of something that lies outside the work and indeed outside the realm of music. However, while historical and philosophical perspectives shed light on so many details of its (their) operation, Experiments in Musical Intelligence collectively represents an activity of its own kind, not one which can be directly related to familiar categories, even those of recent vintage.

Final conclusions about Experiments in Musical Intelligence seem unwarranted at this time, particularly since the program is still evolving. Happily, the materials found herein can greatly enrich discussion of the issues—ontological, epistemological, and practical—raised in this and other contributions.

12 Experiments in Musical Intelligence and Bach

Bernard Greenberg

Artistic beauty is in the eye, ear, and mind of the beholder, not necessarily the artist, let alone the art. The electric fractal Buddhas of the Mandelbrot set, all the more striking in Peitgen's realizations,[1] offer us more enlightenment about the many complex planes of Beauty-Dharma than about the landscape of their native Himalaya of Number, mirroring to us the greater mystery of what it is we find interesting, evocative, and beautiful. As such still-unfathomed mystical beauty already wells up from the cold heart of the computer, in this case with minimal programming effort, one might take a cue from George Gamow[2] and quip that all we lack is criteria and tools for evaluating it. David Cope's stunning program, Experiments in Musical Intelligence (Cope 1991a), is the best attempt at credible automatic art I have yet seen, and confirms my faith that beautiful, arbitrarily interesting, emotionally challenging music can be created programmatically.

In spite of the uniquely convincing, interesting, and well-wrought compositions of David Cope's program, however, no music lover will deny that even this program is not now a likely candidate for a position with a major arts organization, parish, or university. I am convinced that this gap between the program and the great art of the past and present is a reflection of the fact that, to paraphrase a malapropism of a renowned DJ of the vinyl era, we have hardly scratched the surface of this new domain. I will examine here the nature of that gap. As a self-styled organist, improviser, and composer who has concentrated lifelong on the work of Johann Sebastian Bach, I will limit myself to a critique of David Cope's Experiments in Musical Intelligence program's putative Bach-like productions, which also seem at this time to be its calling card. Neither bemoaning nor begloating the purported differences, I will strive to characterize and analyze some of them, toward not only a better composition program but a better understanding of Bach, and a better understanding of the compositional process, three intimately conjoined domains. Having so limited myself, let my deep admiration for the Experiments in Musical Intelligence program's non-Bach creations not pass unstated. As a programmer, I will speculate about what Cope or others might do differently.

I will examine in detail a small sample of what I consider quintessentially Bachian counterpoint, and identify the concrete techniques wherein I find its greatness, ubiquitous in Bach but wholly lacking in the Bach-like output created by Cope's program to date. While none of these techniques are ineffable, much progress in cognitive science must precede their programmatic realization.

David Cope's Program: Experiments in Musical Intelligence

I am deeply impressed with the Experiments in Musical Intelligence program's oeuvre, representing doubtless the best attempt at automatic music known to me. Had I heard it in a situation where my concentration was elsewhere, I might well be "fooled" (although the connotations of that term demean the process of artistic learning). Cope's strategies of copying, cataloging, and deploying signatures and textures are remarkably effective of serving precisely this end. Some of the program's output is, to my taste, simply beautiful. The program's melding of Bach and Beethoven in its resynthesis of the *Moonlight Sonata* needs no credentials beyond its own manifest beauty. When I heard it on National Public Radio some weeks before the symposium absent any revelation of its genesis, I was moved by it as pure music.

Should a composing program's goal be to "fool" listeners, or to churn out predictable quanta of beauty on each run? In fact, "fooling the audience" is merely a vernacular paraphrase of the Turing test, the classic admissions exam for all putative AI endeavors, so I have no qualms about describing the charter of Cope's program as such. While I, fancying myself a composer enamored of antique styles and not a model of composition, would resent such a description of my work, or that of any human contemporary, this characterization seems both apt and complimentary when applied to a program (still) free of ego. On the other hand, does not the amateur or aspiring artist achieve the rank of "real artist" at precisely the moment when he or she has "fooled others into believing he or she is a 'real artist?'"

Rather than indict Cope's automatic composer with a picayune litany of niggling gaffes and gotchas that seem foreign to Bach, feeling more can be learned elsewhere, I will identify some substantive skills that this program still needs prior to employment as *ein wahrer Bach* in my ducal chapel. These skills fall into two major areas: high-level emotional architecture and low-level contrapuntal technique.

Architecture

Cope addresses the general issue of form, related to, but not quite the same as what I would call architecture, that is, a work's or movement's emotional and dramatic structure. The ostensible form of Bach's C Minor *Passacaglia*, BWV 582.1, is an eight-measure theme with twenty-one variations with the ostinato stated or outlined in the bass or occasionally other voices. The dramatic architecture, on the other hand, is that of a huge, tragic lament of carefully terraced intensity, with several respites of texture and tension framing and highlighting the climactic buildup, a cos-

Figure 12.1
From Bach's *C Minor Passacaglia*, BWV 582.1.

mic outpouring of grief in as close to pure harmonic texture as Bach ever comes in
the last three variations (see figure 12.1). With harmony, counterpoint, and texture,
the *Passacaglia* tells a story, and although there is no text, it seems clear to me that
the fabric of that story is spun of the warp and weft of human experience: fear, anxiety, longing, hope, crisis, and catharsis. I still do not know what the story is, but
since the first time I as a child crossed paths with the *Passacaglia* I have been swept
away by the tragedy of its mysterious drama.

I am not proposing that there is a hidden dramatic text behind the *Passacaglia*
or any other nontexted work, but rather that the *Passacaglia* itself meets all the
requirements for being one—the architecture of this work is that of a tragic drama.
Even if such crass eisegesis of a narrative be off base, I hope it is not utterly mis-
guided, for the *Passacaglia*, unlike the Mandelbrot set, was composed by one pos-
sessed and driven by the same passions we all share. BWV 582's ancestors, by the
way, the deeply touching minor-key chaconnes of Pachelbel and Buxtehude, tell
clearly related tales in a similar voice, albeit at lower intensity.

While Cope makes significant headway on the modeling of formal architecture
(the program's Mozartean works, the operatic overture in particular, achieve quite
remarkable success in this regard), that notion remains tantalizingly distinct from
emotional architecture. And, returning to Bach, all of its putative *Bachmusik* lacks
the raw emotional punch which is one of the *Thomaskantor*'s surest earmarks. A
devout so-called hard-line AI believer, I consider a deterministic modeling of emotional architecture not only eminently tractable but already under way. The best-
known effort in this domain is probably the modeling of drama (stories) by Roger
Schank (1982, and Abelson 1977). In texted works, Bach and other composers have
the help of not only the poet but the framework of the underlying psychodynamics of
the structures which motivated the poet. I posit that the models of drama that daily

assault us all in our everyday lives no less inform the rhetoric of successful free works than texted ones.

In Bach's case, that drama is usually the Christian mythos, with all its thorny ambiguity, contradiction, and cognitive dissonance. While drama in music surely need not be Christian, the unique psychodynamics of the Jesus drama, particularly its characteristic notions of glorious, redemptive suffering and the man/god, have everything to do with the emotional rhetoric and concomitant effect of the flats and sharps and canons of Bach. In this excerpt from the *Matthäuspassion* aria "Ich will bei meinem Jesu wachen," for instance, the kernel of this key idea is made manifest:

Tenor:

Meinen Tod	*My death is atoned*
Büßet seine Seelennot	*By His Soul-need*
Sein Trauren machet mich voll Freuden.	*His Sorrowing fills me with joy.*

Choral refrain:

Drum muß uns sein verdienstlich Leiden	*Thusly must His estimable Suffering*
Recht bitter und doch süße sein.	*Be for us right bitter and yet sweet.*

In the traditional Christology of the Cross, the supreme tragedy of the Crucifixion is neither a terrible mistake nor a grotesque miscarriage of justice, but God *qua* Jesus' deliberate, precious redemptive gift to mankind. In the excerpt above, the poet (Henrici, aka Picander) states plainly that Jesus' torture death on the Cross "fills me with joy," and what is more, confesses personal guilt for the very need for this sacrifice. The fundamental moral ambivalence of the Cross, simultaneously "right bitter and yet sweet," is the heart of Bach's religious Weltanschauung, as attested by every surviving libretto and document, and, I believe, the heart of his musical art as well. Comprehension of Bach's emotional architecture necessitates an understanding of his emotional building materials, most of all this difficult gravamen of traditional Christian faith.

This uniquely Christian crossing of values, wherein Jesus's horrific Passion is revealed as salvific, effects a pervasive and radical influence on Bach's dramaturgy comparable to that of a crystal of iodine tossed into a glass of starch, or the square root of two into the field of rational numbers. Upon this union of personal guilt, profound gratitude, and joy, Bach erects an emotional framework as removed from everyday life and experience as it is hauntingly compelling. How remarkably appropriate to the most sublime utterances of the *Thomaskantor*, from the Passions to the preludes and fugues of *Das wohltemperierte Klavier* (e.g., B minor no. 24, book I, whose pain-wracked fugue Spitta [1899] calls "a crown of thorns"), seems "Recht bitter und doch süß!" (Incidentally, Bach sets this singularly complex union of pain

Figure 12.2
From Bach's *Matthäuspassion.*

and sweetness to a singularly complex passage combining pain and sweetness, in my opinion a half-dozen of the most beautiful measures in the choral repertoire; see figure 12.2.)

What in human experience corresponds to the grandeur, voice, depth, and breadth of the opening chorus of the *Matthäuspassion,* let alone what other work of art? What can possibly be so grand and nobly tragic, so lacerated with agonizing pain, but yet sweetly beautiful? This incomparably conceptually, texturally, and technically complex movement, as Schweitzer (1905, p. 211) observed, befits (even if Schweitzer, with some justification, concludes from the text "depicts") a tortured, humbled god, hounded by a swirling crowd, dragging a cross up a hill to his own crucifixion. Even if there be equally grand and tragic scenes in other mythic systems, such as the destruction of Valhalla (but even Wagner is no Bach), whether or not imbued with redemptive subtext, acquisition of Bach's artistic vocabulary in particular mandates thorough comprehension and appreciation of the traditional Christian one. To paraphrase an old bread advertisement, you don't have to be a believing, committed Christian to understand Bach, but (in the words of a newer one) you at least have to know how to play one on TV.

Refocusing on automatic composition, I think David Cope's style-based composing program would benefit from a state network, or similar model of dramatic rhetoric, by which to regulate and deploy various parameters, some known to it now and some not. As I will illustrate with some Bach examples, the degree of harmonic and contrapuntal liberty, even from one measure to the next of the same movement, are powerful controls of emotional impact; Cope's program's published Bachian examples show no evidence of variance of technical constraints within a piece, nor is such control described in his books.

Without some attempt at modeling the space of emotional dynamics, that is, drama, one cannot hope to create emotionally fulfilling art. While successful hu-

man composers do this instinctively, digital ones must still be taught. I think Cope's
SPEAC model is already a probe into this type of space, and speaks well to the
tractability of a theory of drama, gesture, and statement. We should turn to Aristotle,
Aeschylus, Shakespeare, the Bible, Stanislavsky, Strindberg, and so on, for the raw
data to continue. The extreme nontriviality of this problem surely underlies our
appraisal of a work of art as great, but for those of us in the computer arts, assault on
nontrivial problems is our daily bread.

Counterpoint

In short, the counterpoint evidenced in the output of Cope's composing program is
far too timid for Bach. Nevertheless, while falling short of its model in some ways,
this computer counterpoint is quite, perhaps even too, smooth. While Cope speaks of
the generation and integration of additional voices as standard rule-based composition, that is, little more than a library subroutine, the results impress my eye and ear.
The program's "Bach-like" C major fugue displays what I think is the best of it
(although also some of the program's most typical deficiencies, as I will discuss).
Perhaps I overlooked the counterpoint subroutine in my compiler-vendor's C++
run-time library, but by my account, the contrapuntal accomplishments of this subroutine, apparently not even considered interesting, merit some acclaim.

The discussion of specific examples might almost seem a wasteful avenue to pursue, for if the rules by which the program's counterpoint are generated occasionally
lack salt or overabound in pepper, any such perceived deficiency or its fix sheds little
light on the burning questions of computer creativity. On the other hand, "Model the
entire Pathos, Bathos, and Mt. Athos of Human Experience by a network of finite-
state machines" admits of no ready solution; while my speculations about approaches
to this key problem might make good copy, they are of scant help in formulating any
plans that one could put into action.

It distresses me that Cope's program's contrapuntal skill is begotten, not made. In
keeping with its own philosophy, it ought to have an aptitude for harmony and
counterpoint, and learn it by example, as did Bach himself. The program learns
Bachian melodies and patterns, yet relies on "Cliff Notes" for putatively Bachian
counterpoint, and the result seems not quite Bachian enough. An obvious extrapolation of Cope's work is to formulate spaces for describing contrapuntal technique:
what intervals can appear in what sorts of context and so on, in which an autodidact
program, like Bach, could accumulate, characterize, and refine observations toward a
contrapuntal technique.

Figure 12.3
The *Sinfonia* (three-part invention) in C, BWV 787.

Looking at the automatically composed "Bach-style" fugue found in Cope (1991a, p. 191), we observe a severely limited style of counterpoint, or more accurately, accompanimental active voices. Cope seems to have constrained the program to contrapuntal stasis on every eighth-note, where a full triad or seventh chord seems to be mandated. Classical suspensions, although used beautifully in the computer-created Inventions nos. 2 and 8 in appendix D, seem absent everywhere else in its output, including here. In short, virtually none of the sources of contrapuntal energy in Bach can be seen at work.

Consider by comparison the second half of measure 12 of BWV 787, the *Sinfonia* (three-part invention) in C (see figure 12.3), ostensibly a much simpler texture than the program's C major fugue described above (Cope 1991a, p. 191). In the second half of the measure there are three distinct harmonies operating simultaneously: A7, B diminished, and E diminished, producing the most violent discord imaginable (at *) when taken out of context. These extremely bold dissonances arise from three very independent voices responding contrapuntally to an unstated figured bass in half-notes, and their astonishing and wonder are key to the emotional impact of this measure, perhaps the darkest and most twisted alley of the generally sunny landscape of this *Sinfonia*.

There is a bit more contrapuntal freedom in the two-voiced inventions composed by the program, seen every now and then, such as in the accented passing tone in its Invention no. 12 (in appendix D), and its wordless C minor chorale (Cope 1991a, pp. 194–5) bespeaks a whole third paradigm, perhaps the closest to the reality it is trying to model (for reasons of space, I will not analyze or comment further on it here). In short, Bach's underlying model of what Fux (1725) calls the *contrapunctus floridus* is far from the program's model, which seems caught up in a rather anemic reading of the Viennese theorist.

I fully appreciate the difficulties of writing a program that attempts such work—I certainly have tried several times and failed to carry it through to anywhere near this degree of success, and stand in awe of this accomplishment. And I will preemptively acknowledge the inevitable disclaimer that the current versions of the program are mere prototypes from the viewpoint of what lies ahead. But if this example's raison d'être is that it arguably sounds like a Bach fugue, I feel justified in arguing to that point. If the *novum* here is supposed be that it sounds like Bach, it doesn't, at least not to this long-term student of that master's technique. And the ways in which it falls short are nontrivial—strategic deployment of this larger palette of contrapuntal gesture and freedom is no mere corollary to an enhanced rule set.

One of the greatest miracles of Bach is his ability to wield counterpoint as emotional bricks and mortar—to build love and fear, shepherds and devils, cathedrals, crosses, and kisses, out of raw counterpoint. If you want to traffic in the marketplace of putative Bachs, you will need not merely counterpoint far more vibrant than that utilized in the current version of this program but the knowledge of how to vary and wield it for dramatic effect. Not just the powdered wig is required, but what's under it, too.

In summary, although the program's métier is the modeling of all musics of all eras, modeling of the music of the contrapuntal eras without either a so-called learning strategy for counterpoint, a more sophisticated model of contrapuntal gesture, or both, misses what I consider the lifeblood of this music. Cope seems to acknowledge this in his justification of the use of ad hoc code to provide this facility where his pattern processing strategies fall short (Cope 1991), and I concur.

Some Bach Analyzed

Although not without their occasional charms and sweet surprises, I find Bach's two-part inventions, the basis and obvious comparand of the program's showpieces, among the weakest and most formulaic Bach I know. I never play them or listen to them, as they seem to offer little of what I value or admire about Bach. I think the "three-voice inventions" (*Sinfonie*), two-voiced movements of *Das wohltemperiertes Klavier*, and the *Klavierübung* duets qualify as red-blooded Bach. The alto aria, BWV 177.2, "Ich bitt' noch mehr, o Herre Gott," in particular, is a stunning example of a first-rate two-voice Bach movement. (In fairness to Bach, his inventions were explicitly conceived as didactic tools.)

Wishing to bring to the fore the most relevant examples possible, but not having space to even scratch any of the eight vinyl surfaces of the *Passion According to St.*

Matthew, I will focus on two short excerpts from a smaller but quite related master-piece, dubbed "this most celebrated of Organ Chorales" by Peter Williams (1980), the *Orgelbüchlein* setting of "O Mensch, bewein' dein' Sünde groß," BWV 622, as it demonstrates much of what I think is terrific about Bach—especially features missing from his two-part inventions, let alone the output of Cope's program.

The technical features which instantly proclaim this masterpiece as Bach's are not arcane canons or the like, but contrapuntal gestures arising from a sophisticated, hierarchical conceptualization of harmony and counterpoint, which, paradoxically, almost predictably generates surprise and freshness in a way Cope's program, or for that matter any currently known to me, does not.

The screenplay of this short work is the brief and dramatic earthly life of Christ, as related by Sebaldus Heyden's 1525 hymn exhorting the hearer to bewail his or her contribution to mankind's sins, for which Christ has come to earth and been cruci-fied. The rather lengthy stanza describes the career of Jesus from the Nativity, *usque ad mortem in cruce.* As Jesus nears his Cross, the texture grows in chromatic and contrapuntal daring, as the *Affekt* heightens its agony; that is, the contrapuntal and harmonic rule sets change from measure to measure.

The words of the chorale (not performed, but presumed to be known to knowl-edgeable listeners) in the above measures are "Den Toten er das Leben gab, und liegt dabei all' Krankheit ab"—(to the dead He gave life, and thereby cast away all sick-ness), forming the critical link between the narratives of the Incarnation and the Crucifixion in this panoramic miniature. In the last quarter of measure 14 and the first of measure 15 (see figure 12.4), almost every eighth-note is so colored by the disso-nant cluster C–D–E-flat as to remind one of Ligeti's *Lux Aeterna* and the music of Arvo Pärt. Such impressionistic coloration is uncommon for the Baroque, although it

Figure 12.4
From the *Orgelbüchlein* setting of "O Mensch, bewein' dein' Sünde groß," BWV 622.

does occur in the lute repertoire, as in Kapsberger, and its keyboard and violin imitations. One will not find it often, if at all, even in Buxtehude or Pachelbel chorale preludes, or in Handel, yet, it is utterly typical of Bach's contrapuntal workbench and the uniqueness of his sound. The French *organistes-clavecinistes* whom Bach loved and studied, De Grigny, Marchand, Louis Couperin, and so on, however, reveled in similar sounds.

Considering the alto alone over the bass, a seventh resolves "incorrectly" to a ninth on the last eighth-note of measure 14, and a fourth to a seventh on the second eighth-note of measure 15, as notes to which other notes are supposed to resolve routinely disappear before they get the chance. Looking at the soprano and the bass, an augmented fifth resolves to a minor seventh on the last eighth-note of measure 14, which never resolves in any sense that the contrapuntal model of Fux, or what I see in any of the putative *Bachmusik* of Cope's program, does. Just what kind of counterpoint is this?

Such counterpoint can all be accounted for by the proper model—it is not a mystery after 250 years. Play the chorale as a chorale, with the bass in quarter-notes, add the eighteenth-century chord symbols, that is, figured bass, and work it out as the traditional chorale it is—then loose four independent jazz musicians, contractually enjoined against parallel perfect consonance, to wail their four laments against the harmony and bass, with extra pay for more mutual dissonance, and this will be the result. The soprano and the alto, as a matter of fact, are playing chords in sixteenth-notes that successfully create an almost Ivesian polytonality on the second sixteenth of the last quarter of measure 14.

These remarkable chains of unresolved dissonances, protoimpressionistic colorings, and tonal ambiguity are the very soul of this style of counterpoint, and uniquely Bach's in his era. They arise from a hierarchical model born of the figured bass and close to the heart of jazz—better modeled by Schenker[3] than Fux. Their effective use relies on assignment of emotional color values to individual audacities, and on their controlled, metered deployment to expound the drama of the work. Contrapuntal technique here is not a constant rule set, but a dynamically parameterized one. The settings of the dials change from measure to measure. This is no mere dissonance, but imaginative, creative, dynamic dissonance. Appropriating Schickele's witticism, *Mirabilis facta est chutspa tua.*

Two lines ahead lie one of the—justly—most renowned passages in the organ literature, at the words "Daß er für uns geopfert würd" (that He might be sacrificed for us), the central *mysterium et sacramentum* of the Christian faith (see figure 12.5). This remarkable passage sustains continuous chromatic movement for the first time in the piece, a sequence of wholly unprepared sevenths treated as essential chords,

Figure 12.5
"Daß er für uns geopfert würd'" from BWV 622.

painted in inner voices based on the repeated motive of the unprepared en passant crunch of a second, treated very nonclassically: the upper voice goes up, instead of the lower down. The last element is the first over a bass which has freed itself from the harmony into nonharmonic passing tones, producing clashing simultaneous dissonance as seen in the previous example. This climactic dissonance is one of the most characteristically Bachian sounds. The harmonic spectrum in key space, the cycle of fifths, covered by this measure is broad—G minor and B-flat minor abut here, for an unusual, powerful, disorienting effect.

One of the most renowned appearances of this juxtaposition is in the lush, romantic, chromatic leitmotif of Amfortas' agony (also related, albeit murkily, to the Crucifixion) in Wagner's *Parsifal* (see figure 12.6), whose harmonic outline is prefigured here. And let us not leave the above Bach excerpt without noticing the so-called *Tristan* chords on the last sixteenths of the first quarter—the heavily emotionally loaded root-position half-diminished seventh (compare the most disorienting chord at "**" *in* "Recht bitter above). Let no one ever dismiss Bach as the icy antithesis of Romanticism. Deeply felt agony pours out of these measures like blood.

I have presented the above not only as examples of some of the features I expect when I hear a claim that some texture sounds like Bach counterpoint, let alone sounds like Bach per se, but to illustrate the control of harmonic and contrapuntal liberties, or style, as rhetorical parameters, dials that are to be skillfully twisted within a single movement, or measure, for that matter, to narrate a drama. The problem of adding appropriate rules to the rule-based composer seems less interesting than that of knowing when to engage them.

There are further areas that deserve exploration, such as Bach's remarkable post–major-minor approach to church-modal harmony, but space here is short.

Figure 12.6
Leitmotif of Amfortas' agony in Wagner's *Parsifal*.

Further Speculations and Musings

The style of David Cope's composing program resides as much in its rule sets as in its acquired signature patterns. Although this conjunction succeeds admirably at generating in-style music, its technology for the former is not within its domain of innovation. It is therefore hardly remarkable that the **compose-invention** function composes a two-voice invention—it can do little else. And one's awe at how well its two-voice inventions so resemble Bach's must be tempered, as it were, by the knowledge that Bach originated the form, rendering the qualifier "Bach's" before "two-part inventions as a model" largely redundant.

The "style of Bach," or Chopin, Mozart, or Hendrix, is not one, but many. Consider the *Orgelbüchlein*, as revealed by its title page, or the set of Chopin études, as illustrated in the sheer visual variety of Douglas Hofstadter's beautiful panorama (see figure 12.7). Where is the common Bach style between the tender *Matthäuspassion* soprano-and-flute aria "Aus Liebe will mein Heiland sterben" and the cathedral of *stile antico* chromatically fortified "quasimodal" counterpoint "Aus tiefer Not schrei' ich zu dir" (BWV 686)? Is there a hidden eigenfunction, or even a statistical average that can be distilled out of a composer's total oeuvre? Taking a cue from the calculus of variations of Bach's contemporary, Leonhard Euler, the variation between styles, within a collection, within a movement, within a measure, within a lifetime oeuvre, and how that variation is conscripted into the service of artistic effect, is a major part of what I consider style.

And the usual concept of a composer's style does not equal the greatness for which we admire him or her. The style of Bach is, for me, to mount excruciatingly difficult expository and technical challenges and meet them. For example, Bach succeeds in conveying the story of the bureaucratic lynching of a Roman-era Jewish hippie with

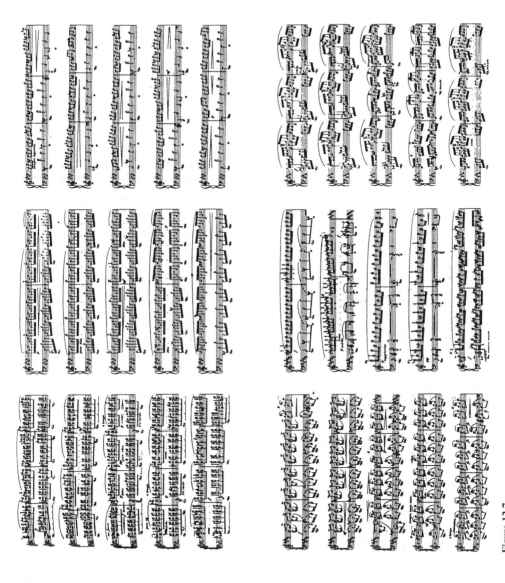

Figure 12.7
The Chopin études as illustrated in Douglas Hofstadter's panorama from *Metamagical Themas* (1985).

such majesty, glory, grace, and sheer panache that even lifelong atheists are repeatedly moved to tears by the counterrational fable of a God offering himself as a sacrifice for the sins of the world. And Bach pulls this off with a technical facility and intellectual depth not seen before or since in music, over and over again. Handel and Telemann were not able to do this, nor, for that matter, Matthew, Mark, Luke, John, nor Luther. The style of Bach is, *vor allem*, the routine application of titanic, incomparable, multilayered conceptual and intellectual depth to the problem of making music speak. J. S. Bach is one tough act for *any* computer program to follow.

Nonetheless, few successful acts start out with top billing. Let us remember that we are come to celebrate the wondrous birth of credible automatic music, not its long-foretold triumph. Having grown up in front of a vacuum-tube TV as my father told of iceboxes and horse carts on New York's Lower East Side, I am daily in awe of my privilege to be present at the dawn of the Era of Information, surely the most profound technological and social change in centuries. I must therefore dismiss with laughter any attempt to extrapolate the maturity of this wholly novel titan who has just crawled out of its egg. As I wrote this *stretto* hurtling 35,000 feet above the Midwest in an aluminum cigar tube powered by burning dead dinosaurs, the patent folly of attempting to circumscribe a priori the recursive progeny of human ingenuity seemed particularly keen and poignant. With the quest for understanding having just begun, I wonder not whether the computer can create great and beautiful art but only how great and how beautiful and how soon and, of course, how, if we do not destroy the planet first.

And as for Herr Bach, late of the *Thomaskirche Lipsiæ*, and his music, we have yet to be able to explain to one another how to write music that so at once awes, exalts, bedazzles, and refreshes the human spirit, which is surely prerequisite to explaining it in Lisp code. We have yet much to learn from Sebastian Bach of Leipzig, not merely of counterpoint, the implementation language of his choice, but of his use of it as a tool to craft miracles of insight into the depths of the human mind and heart.

Acknowledgments

I offer my heartfelt thanks to David Cope and James R. Davis for their critiques and other help with the distillation of this chapter out of my 1997 Stanford presentation whence it arose, to Daniel Dennett and Walter Hewlett for their enthusiasm for my ideas and work, and to Douglas Hofstader for this opportunity and his support over many years.

Notes

1. See Heinz-Otto Peitgen and Peter H. Richter's *The Beauty of Fractals—Images of Complex Systems* (Berlin: Springer Verlag, 1986) for one. Peitgen's evocative images have seeped into the popular media since the mid-1980s.

2. In his classic *One Two Three ... Infinity* (1961), Gamow posits an automatic printing press producing all strings the length of its platen, starting with *aaaaaaaaaaaaaaaaa ... aaa* and including (memorably) *A horse has six legs*, and *I like apples cooked in turpentine*, and the like amid the signal insights of Shakespeare and previously unknown cures for dread diseases, noting that only the lack of appropriate editing criteria and resources withholds its bounty from us.

3. The best and most readily available presentation of the ideas of theorist Heinrich Schenker (1868–1935) is the venerable conservatory workhorse, Felix Salzer and Carl Schachter's, *Counterpoint in Composition*. New York: McGraw-Hill, 1969 (and later revisions).

13 Dear Emmy: A Counterpoint Teacher's Thoughts on the Experiments in Musical Intelligence Program's Two-Part Inventions

Steve Larson

Dear Emmy,

Professor Cope dropped off a set of pieces that you wrote—fifteen two-part inventions in the style of Bach. He said my comments on these pieces would be of interest, so I have jotted down some of my thoughts for both of you. I assume that you are a student at our university. Please forgive me if I am mistaken, but I don't recall having met you. In any case, I hope that you enjoy reading my remarks as much as I enjoyed playing through, and thinking about, your compositions.

First, let me say that I am impressed. Fifteen inventions represents a great deal of work. How did you do this? I ask because the students in my ten-week course devote a considerable amount of time to studying Bach's inventions and to composing some of their own. After ten weeks, most have written only one or two. Yet, you've written fifteen! I've enclosed a course outline so you can see some of the things we do (see figure 13.1).

There are things about your inventions that I like very much. For example, I think that your Invention no. 5 begins very nicely (see figure 13.2). The subject is a simple but attractive one. The opposition of the athletic ascending eighth-note leaps balanced by descending sixteenth-note steps (which opposition is, of course, typical in Bach's inventions) generates a compelling momentum and makes a nice dance or dialogue between the hands. And the sequence that begins in measure 3, with embellished parallel tenths, is elegant and engaging.

It really seems as though you share the desire that my students and I develop in studying Bach's inventions—the desire to write music that sounds like Bach! In fact, you went so far as to imitate the overall scheme of Bach's inventions: fifteen two-part pieces, each in a different major or minor key, using the more common keys only, and ordered so that their keynotes form an ascending scale. This leads to my next question: the order of keys and meters you use differs only very slightly from Bach's (see figure 13.3)—why didn't you follow his scheme more exactly?

However, in some places, what you wrote reminds me not just of Bach's music in general but of a single specific Bach piece; in some places, you quote big chunks of motivically distinctive material. For example, your Invention no. 8 (figure 13.4b) begins very much like Bach's Invention no. 9 (figure 13.4a). And measures 25–6 of Bach's Invention no. 9 (figure 13.5a) appear verbatim (with only a change of octave) as measures 4–5 of your Invention no. 8 (figure 13.5b) despite the fact that the material quoted clearly implies the 3/4 meter in which Bach's invention is written, but does not agree with the 4/4 meter in which your invention is written.

WEEK	TOPICS	ASSIGNMENTS
1	Bach's style Rhythmic momentum	Improvise rhythms Compose 7 inv-motive rhythms
2	Musical forces Melody as embellished pattern	Improvise on given melodic patterns Compose 7 invention motives in major
3	Minor mode	Improvise on given minor patterns Compose 7 invention motives in minor
4	Chromaticism in the Baroque	Choose 10 best motives (5 major, 5 minor)
5	Invention expositions	Compose 3 major-key expositions Compose 3 minor-key expositions
6	Cadences Harmonic progression "map"	Write 2 endings (1 major, 1 minor) Transpose model harm progressions
7	Sequences	Transpose given linear intervallic patterns Improvise sequences on given patterns
8	Episodes	Write 4-6 sequences derived from motives
9	Form	Analyze form of 2 Bach inventions Write 2 draft inventions (1 major, 1 minor)
10	Revising drafts	
Final		Performance of one final invention

Figure 13.1
Course outline, Writing Inventions in the Style of Bach.

In other cases, you seem to have *recycled* some of Bach's ideas with only minimal alterations. For example, your Invention no. 13 (figure 13.6b) alters the notation, but does little to change the sound of, Bach's Invention no. 14 (figure 13.6a).

In a couple of cases, the alteration consists of shifting something from major to minor (see figures 13.7 and 13.8). Perhaps you know that Bach used these same techniques of "recycling." For example, several of the fugues from the *Well-Tempered Clavier* are based on subjects that appeared in an earlier composer's collection of fugues (see figure 13.9).

And Bach recycled his own material, too. The subject of Bach's Invention no. 15 strongly resembles the subject of his C minor fugue from the *Well-Tempered Clavier* (see figure 13.10). One could say that the only difference between the motives of Bach's Invention no. 7 and his Invention no. 9 is that the rhythm has been changed (see figure 13.11).

Of course, I'm not saying that I think Bach consciously (or even unconsciously) transformed one of these motives to get the other. But it is interesting to think about them as if he had. For example, take the beginning of Bach's Invention no. 8 (figure 13.12a). Remove the embellishing sixteenth-notes in the second measure (creating figure 13.12b). Now make all the notes the same length (the 4/4 sixteenth-notes in c).

Figure 13.2
Emmy's Invention no. 5, measures 1–13.

#	Bach's keys	Bach's meters	your keys	your meters
1	C major	C	C major	C
2	C minor	C	C minor	C
3	D major	3/8	D major	3/8
4	D minor	3/8	D minor	3/4
5	Eb major	C	Eb major	3/4
6	E major	3/8	E major	C
7	E minor	C	E minor	12/8
8	F major	3/4	F minor	4/4
9	F minor	3/4	G minor	C
10	G major	9/8	A major	C
11	G minor	C	A minor	2/4
12	A major	12/8	Bb major	3/4
13	A minor	C	Bb major	C
14	Bb major	C	B major	C
15	B minor	C	B minor	C

Figure 13.3
Table of keys and meters in Bach's and Emmy's inventions.

Figure 13.4
The beginning of Bach's Invention no. 9 (a) and Emmy's Invention no. 8 (b) are similar.

Figure 13.5
A passage from (a) Bach's Invention no. 9 appears verbatim in (b) Emmy's Invention no. 8.

Figure 13.6
The beginnings of (a) Bach's Invention no. 14 and (b) Emmy's Invention no. 13.

Figure 13.7
The beginnings of (a) Bach's Invention 13 and (b) Emmy's Invention no. 6.

Figure 13.8
The beginnings of (a) Bach's Invention no. 6 and (b) Emmy's Invention no. 2.

Figure 13.9
The beginnings of (a) J. K. F. Fischer's Fugue in E Major (from Ariadne Musica) and (b) Bach's Fugue in E major (from book 2 of the *Well-Tempered Clavier*).

Figure 13.10
The beginnings of (a) Bach's Fugue in C Major (from book 1 of the *Well-Tempered Clavier*) and (b) Bach's Invention in B Minor.

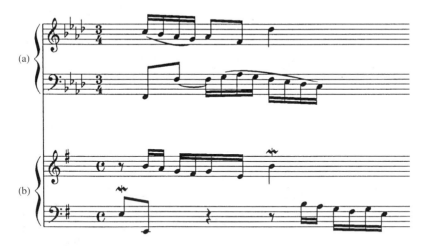

Figure 13.11
The beginnings of (a) Bach's Invention no. 7 and (b) Bach's Invention no. 9.

Figure 13.12
Transforming (a) Bach's Invention no. 8 into (f) Bach's Invention no. 14.

Now change the fifth note so that the melody follows a slightly different rule: before, every other note was a leap down to the tonic; now, it is a leap down to the next lower chord tone (d). Now add a couple of passing tones (the Gs in e) and transpose to Bb major (f) and we have Bach's Invention no. 14. Or remove the third note from figure 13.12d, transpose the last note up an octave, and write the whole thing in eighth-notes instead of sixteenths, and we have your Invention no. 5 (figure 13.2, above)!

The transformations are simple ones:

· take out embellishing tones
· add embellishing tones
· change triple to duple
· change duple to triple
· renotate sixteenths as eighths
· renotate eighths as sixteenths

- make all the note-values equal
- make some downbeats longer
- in a series of notes generated by a simple rule, make a slight change to the rule

Once such a similarity is pointed out, it is easy enough to hear. But that doesn't mean that Bach purposely created his Invention no. 14 subject by making these alterations to his Invention no. 8 subject. Nor does it mean that he created no. 8 out of no. 14—the procedures are essentially reversible (that's why I listed them in pairs above). But it does suggest that it's okay if we find such a relation between something you wrote and something Bach wrote.

However, we do know from one of Bach's manuscripts that he (or someone else who had access to that manuscript) transformed his Invention no. 1 in one or two of these ways. Figure 13.13 demonstrates what I am thinking of. Note how the motive of his Invention no. 1 is rhythmically transformed by the insertion of passing tones.

What happens if we apply the same transformations to the beginning of Bach's Invention no. 1 that turned his Invention no. 8 subject into his Invention no. 14 subject? If we take the beginning of Bach's Invention no. 1 (figure 13.14a) and change it from duple meter to triple meter, we get figure 13.14b. But we've lost the characteristic opposition of sixteenths against eighth-notes. So let's create eighth-notes in the countersubject (mm. 3–4) by adding passing tones. The result in measure 3 has the same eighth-eighth-quarter rhythm that we had in measure 2. Doing something analogous in measure 4 gives us figure 13.14c.

Now, to create sixteenth-notes in the subject against these countersubject eighth-notes (and to disguise the eighth-eighth-quarter rhythm still left in m. 2), we can start by adding the embellishing notes shown in measure 2 of figure 13.14d. But, as you can see and hear from the parallel fifths in the third measure of d, we need to make a more substantial change to the first measure of the subject. Our task is to find a string of sixteenth-notes that spans this same C–E third, but does not create the effect of parallel fifths. Fortunately, the very sixteenth-notes that we began with (the sixteenth-notes from a are reproduced in e) fit this description. If we reverse the D–F third and fill in the E–C third just as Bach did (in figure 13.13), we solve the parallel-fifths problem and create a motivic shape in which measure 1 nicely mirrors measure 2 (f). Transpose the result up to D major and we have Bach's Invention no. 3!

When I think of such transformations, it reminds me of cooking. One can create new dishes out of old recipes if one understands how the recipes work. A recipe can be thought of as a list of ingredients and a list of instructions. If your recipe is for making chocolate-chip cookies, then its list of ingredients may include things like sugar, butter, flour, salt, chocolate chips, and so on; and its list of instructions may

Inventio 1

Figure 13.13
Bach's autograph of his Invention no. 1 shows inserted passing tones.

Figure 13.14
Transforming (a) Bach's Invention no. 1 into (g) Bach's Invention no. 3.

include things like preheating the oven, beating the eggs, chopping the nuts, stirring the batter, and so on. To get a new dish out of an old recipe, you could change the ingredients or the instructions or both. You might change the ingredients by substituting raisins for chocolate chips, to create raisin cookies. You might try changing the cooking time and cooking temperature, to create a softer cookie.

But if your recipe is for making an invention, it is a little less clear which are the ingredients and which are the instructions. Notes might seem like ingredients, but I don't think composers really work with anything as microscopic as notes. Perhaps the ingredients include motives or, even better, the pitch and rhythm patterns that make up motives or that combine them in various ways.

Of course, recipes are hierarchical in the same way that music is. For example, a recipe for soup might be constructed so that one of its ingredients is a special broth, which has its own recipe, one ingredient of which might be particular kind of stock, which has its own recipe, one ingredient of which might be a *bouquet garni*, which has its own recipe, and so on.

But let's assume that Bach's recipes do include motives as ingredients. What, then, are the instructions? Let's consider Bach's inventions nos. 1 and 7. We could consider them as having similar ingredients in one sense: we might think of the subject of his Invention no. 1 as having been inverted to create the subject of Invention no. 7. Figure 13.15a shows the subject of Bach's Invention no. 1. Figure 13.15b shows what happens when we start on the C but go in the opposite direction the same number of half-steps. The result suggests F minor, and strongly resembles the subject of Bach's Invention no. 9 (see c, which adjusts the rhythm by taking out some embellishing leaps, starting on the downbeat, and evening out the rhythm). As I pointed out above (figure 13.11), the subjects of Bach's inventions nos. 7 and 9 are also similar.

But the similarities between Bach's Invention no. 1 and Invention no. 7 run deeper (see figure 13.16). Instead of paying attention to the ingredients, let's consider the instructions. Here's a list of instructions for a recipe that creates the opening of Bach's Invention no. 1:

1. In the first half of measure 1, state the sixteenth-note subject in the right hand.

2. In the second half of measure 1, state the eighth-note countersubject in the right hand (with a trill on the leading tone), against the subject, now an octave lower, in the left hand.

3. In the first half of measure 2, state the sixteenth-note subject, now on the dominant, in the right hand, against a descending octave leap on the dominant, in eighth-notes, in the left hand.

Figure 13.15
The subject of Bach's Invention no. 1 (a) transformed into the subjects of his Inventions nos. 7 (c) and 8 (d).

4. In the second half of measure 2, state the eighth-note countersubject, now on the dominant, in the right hand, against the subject in the left hand.

5. Resolve that dominant so that it leads to the third degree on the downbeat of the third measure and initiates a sequence there.

Figure 13.16 lines up these instructions with these two Bach inventions. In this figure, in order to make the point clearer, I have lined up Bach's Invention no. 1 (figure 13.16a) with a transposition (from E minor to C minor) of Bach's Invention no. 7 (b). Beneath these, I have placed a Schenkerian analysis (c and d), which shows the basic "skeleton" embellished by both of these melodies. The fact that both melodies have the same skeleton describes a similarity between them (the difficulty of saying whether this is a similarity of ingredients or of instructions is part of what I was thinking of above when I wrote about patterns that underlie and connect subjects). Have you studied Schenkerian analysis? Even if you are not consciously aware of Schenker's theories, aspects of your pieces suggest to me that some of the structures he described play an important role, at least at the intuitive level, in your compositional process, too.

I always feel more creative (or at least that my "theft" is less recognizable as such) when I steal Bach's "instructions" (altering the "ingredients") rather than when I steal

RH: subject   countersubj   subj on V   countersubj   3
LH: (rests)   subject   desc 8va   subj on V   I

Figure 13.16
Bach's Invention no. 1 (a) and his Invention no. 7 (b) share the same structure (c–d).

Figure 13.17
A common sequence in Bach's Invention no. 15, mm. 8–10.

his "ingredients" (especially if we equate ingredients with specific melodic material instead of underlying patterns of rhythm or pitch). For example, one instruction I like might be stated as follows: write two voices so that one moves by step in eighth-notes while the other moves in sixteenth-notes, every other sixteenth-note making a tenth with the other voice and the remaining sixteenths repeating a single pitch or clearly embellishing the line in parallel tenths. Bach uses this recipe in his Invention no. 15 (see figure 13.17).

You use the same sequence in several of your inventions. For example, this same sequence appears in your Invention no. 1, measures 22–3; Invention no. 3, measures 4, 7–10, 12–5, 38–40, 45, 6, 48–59 (also in sixths in measures 22, 3, 25–32, 34, 5, 41, 2); Invention no. 5, measures 4–6, 10–2, 18–20; and Invention no. 11, measure 2 (see appendix D). This is a sequence that bears repetition; you can use it in a lot of different situations without people getting tired of it and without them thinking that you "stole" it from somewhere.

On the other hand, there is a sequence in Bach's Invention no. 13, which I am also quite fond of (see figure 13.18), that seems so distinctive that I cannot hear it without thinking of that particular invention. This sequence is actually two sequences combined. The second begins in measure 5 and may be thought of as compressing the first, accelerating the sequence, and propelling it elegantly to its goal, the cadence in measure 6.

It appears that you also like this passage. The same sequence appears in your Invention no. 6, measures 3–6, measures 10–3 (note acceleration 13–), and measures 27–9; Invention no. 11 measures 17–21 (note acceleration 21–) and measures 35–9 (note acceleration 39–); and Invention no. 14, measures 3–15 (note acceleration 15–) and measures 24–8 (note acceleration 28–) (see appendix D). In fact, in your Invention no. 14 there are more measures that include this sequence than there are measures without it!

Figure 13.20
Bach's Invention no. 10 is based on a framework of parallel tenths.

Figure 13.23
Revising Emmy's Invention no. 3, mm. 4–8.

lished where "home" is, we will now begin our journey. But in measure 6, we're right back where we started, with the subject in the tonic. Furthermore, that subject begins on a downbeat octave. The tonal stability of a downbeat octave suggests a point of arrival. For this reason, Bach usually avoids downbeat octaves in the middle of a phrase, and he usually reserves downbeat octaves on the tonic for the final cadence of an invention. Yet, just two measures after setting out on our journey, we've cadenced back home in the tonic.

And the measure that leads to that cadence stumbles a bit. If you look at each eighth-note in your measure 3 as an independent chord, then there is nothing wrong here. But if you listen to the harmonic rhythm, you will hear that what you've written implies one chord per measure. Measure 4 is tonic and measure 5 is dominant. That means that the D on the second beat of measure 5 really needs to resolve to C♯, but it leaps down to A. In a context where the harmony is so simple and the other dissonances resolve, this unresolved D creates an awkward effect. One immediate solution not only resolves the D to C♯ but also changes the repeating offbeat sixteenths from D to A (figure 13.23b). When you use this repeated-note embellishment of parallel tenths, you often have a choice between repeating a root or a fifth, but if you consider pairs of chords joined by this pattern, you will often want to choose a repeated note common to both chords (that's why the last right-hand note in measure 8 sounds bad—not so much because it is a minor ninth, but because the repeated note in that bar should be A instead of D). And here, in order to get away from the tonic, it might be better to prefer a repeated note that will lead us to the dominant. Another possibility would be to allow the pattern to retain the repeated D and take measure 5 a third higher (c), which naturally reverses the right and left hand for measure 6. Note that the result is that the subject now appears in rhythmic augmentation in the left hand in measures 4–5. And, once again, note that this is exactly what you've written in measures 22–3 and (in inversion) in measures 12–3 (though, by this time, we're in B minor). But this solution, even with changing the octave of the repeated notes in measures 7–8 as you have done, seems too repetitive. You might wish to experiment with alternative episodes based on the repeated A, or based on a sequence in which the repeated note changes. Going first to the dominant would be a good idea (just save the material you've written in the relative minor for later). Nevertheless, B minor is a natural place to go, so if (or when) you go there, I recommend that you avoid the G–A♯ melodic augmented second (which you now have in mm. 14 and 15), which doesn't fit the character of this piece.

In measures 17–22 you have written a sequence (figure 13.24a). Sequences impart momentum to the music, and a sequence is just what is called for here. However, this particular sequence could be improved: the right and left hands disagree, downbeat octaves weaken the texture, the sequence fails to reach its goal, and the relation of the sequence to the subject is not clear.

The right hand in measure 17 implies the chord A7. But the left hand in the same measure implies a G major chord. The sequence (a circle of fifths) seems to call for A7, so the left hand could state the first half of the subject ABC♯ (see figure 13.24b). This also leads quite naturally to D on the downbeat of measure 18, avoiding the downbeat octave there that weakens your version of this sequence. If the same portion of the subject is quoted in measure 18, the sequence has a good sense of direction to it (c). Note that this also reverses the hands for measure 22. The underlying

Figure 13.24
Revising Emmy's Invention no. 3, mm. 17–22.

structure of these measures (d) implies continuation to D in the right hand of measure 22. The sequence now leads all the way to its goal.

But in Bach's inventions, one can usually *hear* a clear relationship between the melodic material of such a sequence and the invention's subject or countersubject. In your sequence, I can *reason* out such relationships, but those relationships are hard to *hear*. Like the subject, measure 17 gives us four notes in one direction and then reverses direction; but we're two steps removed: both the directions (down-then-up instead of up-then-down) and the interval size (leaps instead of steps) are different.

Like the countersubject, measure 17 begins with a descending chord arpeggiation; but, again, we're two steps removed: both the chord (dominant seventh from its seventh instead of tonic triad from its third) and the speed (sixteenths instead of eighth-notes) are different. We could alter the second measure of the sequence (mm. 18, 20, and 22) so that it is an inversion of the subject (figure 13.24e), but the result lacks the rhythmic interest (with its implied two against three) of your sequence. I leave it up to you to come up with other possibilities.

Steve

surprise realization occurs either when the realization fails to match the expectation or fails to occur when expected.

In the example from Haydn's String Quartet, op. 33 no. 3, shown in figure 14.2, the strong and specific expectation for a tonic resolution following a cadential leading tone is subverted, leading to a surprise. The first violin's F-sharp in beat 3 of measure 7 strongly points toward a resolution to G. Instead, Haydn takes advantage of the reversed-accented dominant-unaccented tonic relationship, placing the root in the viola and creating a sequence that transforms the expected eight-measure half-period to a self-contained ten-measure period.

A surprise is patent if the expected event is replaced by an anomaly. Anomalies can be either rare events that are syntactically foreign, or contextual surprises in which a grammatical or contextual misplacement of a syntactically known event occurs. A rarity does not diminish the "validity" of the expectation. That is, although there may be no correspondence between the expectation and the realization, the fact that the event is anomalous strengthens rather than subverts the sense of expectation. Rarities are often used for local dramatic or humorous effect. They sometimes carry extramusical connotations.

Expectational targets that correspond with the expectation but whose occurrence is temporally offset either by occurring earlier than anticipated or by being delayed are called *latent* surprises and are defined as an event that is sequentially correct but temporally misplaced. A latent *ambiguity* is a series of events in which a normative event within a normative sequence occurs in an unexpected temporal position. A common example of a latent ambiguity is a hemiola, in which melodic or harmonic patterns conflict with periodic metric schematic inference.

A specific type of surprise results in a forced reinterpretation of the initial expectation. Although retrospective ambiguities share a term with expectational ambiguities, the cognitive effect is entirely different. Multiply projective and nonprojective expectations cause a certain anxiety about the future. Retrospective ambiguities are disruptive to the temporal flow of music in that they demand a reevaluation of a past event. Ambiguities fail to create or continue schematic expectations. Surprises fail to meet schematic expectations.

As expectations are described in physical strength, surprises are often described in terms of energetic strength—they are "shocking" or come "like a thunderclap," they can be "electrifying" or "jolting." The energy felt, perhaps as a result of a demand for increased attentiveness or reevaluation of the past, can be measured in terms of the disparity between expectation and realization. This measure of correspondence is termed the *degree of realized expectation* (DRE). The graphic symbols shown in figure 14.3 represent various expectation and realization states.

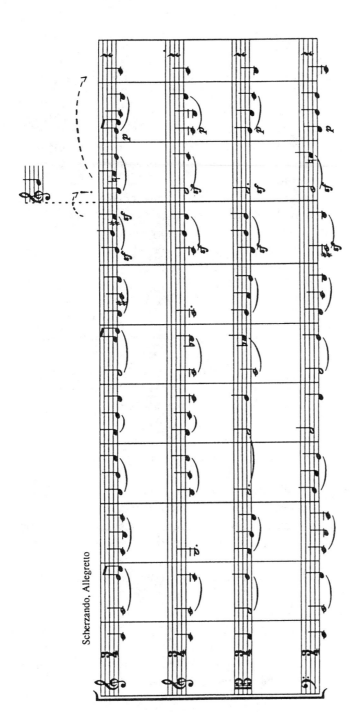

Figure 14.2
Singularly projective expectation and resulting patent surprise in Haydn's String Quartet, op. 33, no. 3.

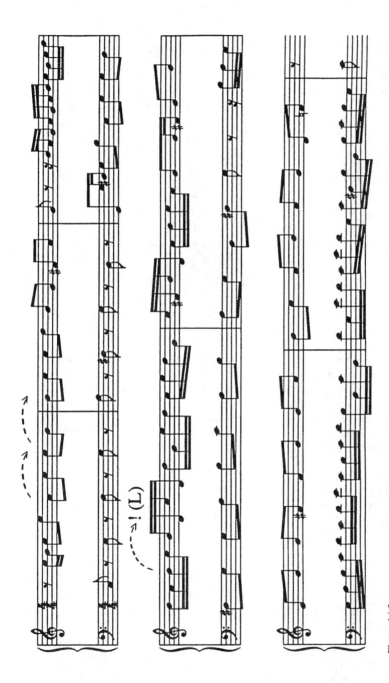

Figure 14.3
The graphic symbols representing various expectation and realization states of the *degree of realized expectation* (DRE).

Building expectations involves recognizing and adapting patterns. The ability to deduce and abstract structures and patterns is fundamental to all cognition. When involved with everyday interaction in our environment, this ability is one part of a web of activities that constitute cognition. When applied to a generally orderly and structured data set such as a piece of music, this ability becomes tantamount to experience. By extracting and adapting patterns we can keep a constantly updated schema against which we perform best-fit comparisons. This allows us to create categories of patterns, which, in turn, assists us in reducing the amount and frequency of incoming stimuli to a manageable flow. "Categorization," writes Reybrouck, "is not a passive registration of ready made stimuli, but a constructive process that integrates sensation, perception, and cognition" (Reybrouck 1995). Thus, as Hucbald infers, the *continuous* flow of sound becomes perceived as *discrete* patterns that are organized categorically. In an effort to simplify sensory input we are forced to integrate information in order to formulate one percept from much information. Failing to do so, we attempt to sort and segregate the input into the minimal number of items or streams that we can.

The implications of this discrete-continuous dichotomy in cognition is suggested in Arnold Schoenberg's definition of *motive* as

a unit which contains one or more features of interval and rhythm. Its presence is manifested in its constant use throughout a piece. Its usage consists of frequent repetitions, some of them unchanged, most of them varied. The variations of a motif produce motif-forms, which are the material for continuations, contrasts, new segments, new themes, even new sections within a piece. Not all the features are to be retained in a variation: but some, guaranteeing coherence, will always be present. Sometimes remotely related derivatives of a motif become independent and can then be employed like a motif.   (Schoenberg 1948, p. 221)

Schoenberg hints here at each link in the chain of cognitive tasks enumerated above: pattern detection, abstraction, classification, best-fit matching, and schema adoption.

Discretization of the temporal continuum is referred to as adaptive matching by Edelman. In his theory of neuronal group selection the process of categorization that drives adaptive matching facilitates recognition of familiarity even in previously unmet objects. The process is inherently evolutionary (Edelman [1987] calls this neural Darwinism), and promotes sensory data reduction by grouping and rating data according to a degree of fit and role in distinguishing the object with which the datum has been grouped. Rather than determining overly specific categories, these ratings serve as constraints.

These opposite abilities, to segregate and categorize under certain conditions, and to integrate and fuse under others, pose a peculiar contradiction. Creativity involves two opposing thought processes that interact simultaneously. Divergent think-

ing involves the generation of multiple, often loosely related thoughts. Covergent thought is the process of comparing and selecting the best idea produced by divergent thinking. Grouping principles describe how covergent thought is applied to interpret divergent thought generated by music.

In summary, we perceive categorically. We break down the continuity of a rainbow into bounded and distinct colors. A slow continuous frequency sweep is perceived as entering and leaving distinct pitch boundaries, and thus segregated into components. There exists, however, a threshold beyond which we fuse rather than categorize. A rapid frequency sweep (or one that is contextualized as in a musical glissando) is perceived as a single event.

Experiments in Musical Listening: Modeling Expectations and Realizations

Neural networks provide techniques for modeling experiential learning. Connectionist approaches have been used to model timbre classification, for cochlear modeling, for modeling pitch perception, and for modeling melodic tendency. They have also been used for generating compositions. Predictive models of music perception and cognition are proving to play a tremendously vital role in music theory. Models of pitch recognition and pitch acuity have given rise to new theories of perception that will influence many aspects of music theory. Models of performance timing and articulation (Repp 1989, Sundberg 1983) have raised issues of music performance in theories of phrasing, metric structures, and tonal analysis. Similar contributions have been made by models of melodic implications (Narmour 1992), timbral classification (Grey 1977, Keislar and Blum 1996), and others.

Catherine Stevens uses a simple recurrent network to predict subsequent events in a melody. The network consists of twenty-five input and output units, and twenty hidden and context units. As in the work described here, activations in the output layer map to input one step later, thus forming a prediction for what is to come next. In Stevens's study Johann Strauss' *Blue Danube* was input. Stevens traces the developmental performance of the network over more than 4000 passes. The aim in training the network was "to study the way in which effects of temporal transitions between events were incorporated into the representation constructed gradually by the network" (Stevens and Latimer 1992, 1993).

Experiments in Musical Listening is a neural network trained to reproduce common practice chord progressions and associated metric markers. The trained network represents a listener who has experientially acquired the listening skills needed to create a plausible expectation for each event in the music.

In the learning phase, errors in reproduction of an event are used to correctively manage the learning process. In the generalization phase, output errors are interpreted as the "listener's" predictions for the next event. These errors suggest a visualization of fluctuations in expectations during the course of listening to music. The relative strengths and distributions of the output vector indicate the strength and the specificity of a prediction. These two indicators represent the measurements of expectation described above. The disparity between the expectation and the realization results from specific realization states.

It is important to stress that in this model, expectations are not directly learned but rather are an emergent property of the process of learning harmonic progressions. A performance of a new and hitherto unheard progression is therefore sequentially fed to the state units of this model listener. Experiments in Musical Listening provides visualization of the expectation of the virtual listener as each event is sounded. In these sequences, patent or latent surprises are introduced to the listener.

The network considers each representation of a chord in a harmonic progression and predicts the next element of the sequence in the output. This prediction follows the current context which consists of the entire history of the sequence modified by a decay parameter. This decay parameter represents short-term memory. Each prediction is fed from the output back into the input layer. By combining the sequential element with the accumulation in the state units, conflicts between a listener's contextualized inferences and expectations modify the composer's actual continuation in such a way that the interplay of implication and realization or disappointment of these expectations is visualized. Thus the approach serves both as a method of visualizing the process of contextualization, and as a method of classifying and quantifying expectations. Introducing anomalous and ambiguous situations demonstrates that the system convincingly expresses these surprises and ambiguities. These cases of surprise and ambiguity are qualified in terms of the strength and specificity previously described. Ambiguities result from strong or weak and unspecific expectations, while surprise is qualified by strong and specific but incorrect predictions. Experiments in Musical Listening thus simulates a musical context that taps the listener's experience to influence predictions.

Jamshed Bharucha's work in neural net–based expectancy modeling in music relies on comparing the target and output. Bharucha writes, "Learning musical signals is a task for which error signals are both available and necessary. They are available because each event is the target to be compared with the expectation generated prior to that event. They are necessary because the error signal plays an important role in the aesthetic or emotional response to music. It is widely held that expectancy violation is an important aspect of the aesthetics of music" (Bharucha and Todd 1990,

p. 129). This insight was expanded by considering the difference between the target and the output (Bharucha's error signal) not just as the mathematical error that drives the learning process in the net but rather as embodying a special meaning representing a quantitative index of an emotional response to music. This model is (to borrow Bharucha's term) a human network which charts the dynamic changes of expectation of the listener. Furthermore, the model may account for how a listener corrects and recontextualizes expectations during the act of music audition.

Experiments in Musical Listening was developed in three distinct stages. The three stages allowed us to progressively create a virtual listener. The neural network simulates experiential acquisition of knowledge and the processing of new information in light of this experience. This visualization provides a means to hypothesize how context is created and adapted. It also suggests a modeling approach that represents different types and scopes of memory, captures the dynamic processes involved in memory and context, and visualizes how expectations are influenced by and affect context.

The first stage of Experiments in Musical Listening involved the visualization of cognition of a tonal sequence that is unambiguous both in its harmonic progression as well as in the metric placement of harmonic events; that is, both what occurs and where it occurs in time conforms to experientially derived expectations. The result was a visualization of strong and specific expectations with a high DRE due to consistently corespondent realizations. The results demonstrated an awareness of sequential expectations without, however, any sensitivity to temporal placement. Simply stated, without a sense of periodic metric organization, the system was making expectations without any plausible musical contexts to guide it.

In the following examples the simulated listener is trained with harmonic progressions found in J. S. Bach's two-part inventions. The network is then given harmonic reductions found in Experiments in Musical Intelligence's Bach Invention no. 3 (see figure 14.3).

Figure 14.4 shows an example of stage 1. This example visualizes the formulation of expectations as the first five beats of Experiments in Musical Intelligence's Bach Invention no. 3 are sequentially sounded. Above the music is the graphic representation of the network output. The squares represent activations of expected pitch classes (PCs), with relative strengths of expectation represented by the size of the square. The harmonic progression [I I IV V | vi ...] represents a normative progression that supports formulation of strong and specific expectations which are correspondingly realized with a high DRE.

Above the score in figure 14.4 is a harmonic reduction used as input to the net. Above the reduction is the network's output. The black squares represent activations

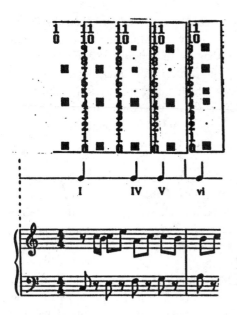

Figure 14.4
The simulated listener's surprise as it encounters the irregular harmonic rhythm corresponding to Experiments in Musical Intelligence's Bach Invention no. 3, measures 4–5.

of expected PCs. The larger the square, the stronger the expectation. Since the network is trained with sequences that begin with a tonic downbeat, the strong expectation for a tonic as the first harmonic event will always occur. The expectation for I to repeat in beat 2 is qualified only by a weak activation of PC 9 (suggesting a weaker expectation for a subdominant harmonization). The realization of I drives the network to strengthen its expectation for change to a subdominant in the next beat. Activations for PCs 7 and 9 are virtually equal, implying that the expectation for I or vi is equally felt. These activations suggest multiple projections for realization. This represents an ambiguity, albeit a very common and thus not strongly felt one. The division of specificity to include $[0, 4, 7]$ and $[0, 4, 9]$ visualizes the proximity of tonic and submediant and their interchangeability. It is in the fourth beat of the measure where we encounter our first surprise. The network, trained primarily with the expectation that a change to a subdominant will persist through the measure, presents strong and specific activations for a repeat of the submediant. The target chord is a dominant and the network reacts to this surprise in its expectation that the downbeat will either be a tonic or a submediant. Of interest here is that the expectation for harmonic change across the bar line is visualized as a reaction to the dominant at

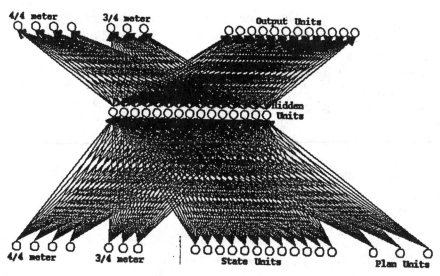

Figure 14.5
The ELI program's network architecture.

the upbeat position, while the awareness that the harmony previously expected may repeat is evident in the strong activations of $[0, 4, 9]$.

The visualization in figure 14.4 reflects how a high DRE is established by strong and specific expectations accompanied by correct corresponding realizations. The strength results from use of syntactically common events, and the specificity results primarily from grammatical placement in commonly occurring situations.

Figure 14.5 represents the simulated listener's surprise as it encounters the irregular harmonic rhythm corresponding to Experiments in Musical Intelligence's Bach Invention no. 3, measures 4–5. The addition of metric awareness to stage 2 makes the "listener" aware of this irregularity. Although the progression itself (regardless of metric placement) should show a high DRE, the rate of harmonic change itself creates a surprise. The role of the metric subnet is critical in the network's sensitivity to this irregularity.

The second stage of experimentation integrates a second subnet with that of the chord sequence learning mechanism. The added subnet provides a simple metrical organizer by supplying a constant periodic beat stream modulo the meter. The output layer of the meter subnet represents the index of the meter for one measure. The decomposition of the task and the existence of the subnet for meter enabled us to extend the functionality of this component and to learn changes in the meter. The two integrated subnets facilitated learning the sequence of chords, with consideration of the index of the meter that is propagated from the metrical subnet. The output layer of the subnet for meter is fully connected to a hidden-unit layer of the sequential net. All of the connections are learnable. The imposition of metric constraints on the hidden layer of the sequential net influences the prediction of the next chord. Each chord in the sequence is represented by twelve units for the PCs in the state and the output layers. The meter in the second stage was represented by four units, a unit for each beat in a measure in common meter.

The third stage involved revising the architecture to represent the inference of meter by the listener, schematic metric expectations, and the mutual influence of meter and harmonic expectations. In order to represent the interaction between a musical surface and meter, the two subnetworks were integrated. Together these networks represent distinct yet mutually influential and complexly intertwined entities, that of harmony and that of meter. These two schematic entities combine to formulate context. The first of these is a sequential harmonic tonal progression (which, serves as a reductive and simplified representation of a musical work) and the second serves as quadruple and triple metric pools (which, combined, represent the temporal organizing process inferred by the listener). It should be noted that harmony is based on the physical presence of musical sound while meter is an inferred psychological state. The mutual influence of these contextual entities are established and learned during the course of formulating corresponding harmonic and metric predictions. These predictions are output in three distinct vectors, one with twelve activations corresponding to each PC, and two for metric pulse units in vectors of three (representing triple meter) and four (representing quadruple meter) units. By dividing tasks into cooperating modules, complex cognitive tasks into schemata, like components were categorized.

The fluctuations of musical expectations that arise as a consequence of the dynamically changing musical context were also visualized. The learning phase again trained the network with harmonic progressions but this time with metric and beat position represented. All the examples are in major keys and in duple or triple meter. The modularity of integrated subnets not only allows for progressively adding complexities but also for modeling diverse theories of schema-based cognition, as well as modeling the intricate interactions of schemata. The two schematic entities, harmony and meter, combine to formulate context. Figure 14.5 shows the program's network architecture at stage 3.

Figure 14.6 visualizes the temporal offset of measure 4 of the Experiments in Musical Intelligence Bach Invention no. 3. This example visualizes the surprise resulting from a conflict between harmonic rhythm and the sense of meter established by the progression prior to this point. The distinct conflict between harmonic rhythm and

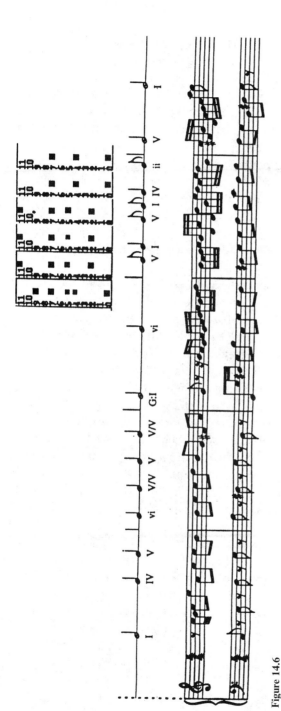

Figure 14.6
Shifting harmonic rhythm in the Experiments in Musical Intelligence Invention no. 3.

meter results in significant drops in DRE. The hastened harmonic rhythm (a chord already on the second beat, setting up a quarter-note harmonic rhythm) is resisted in the output's expectation for continued subdominant harmony in beat 3. The arrival of a tonic on beat 4 of measure 1 throws both the metric counter and the harmonic expectations into flux. The drop in DRE is particularly interesting in that the distribution of expectations is not random but rather reflective of an ambiguity, in which conflicting functional regions (tonic/dominant) are confused.

Experiments in Musical Listening produces graphic visualizations of dynamically changing musical contexts, and a means for qualifying and quantifying the fluctuations of expectations that result from and affect these changes. The representation allows us to visualize parallel interpretations of tonal expectation as well as multiple interpretations of metric organization. The hybrid approach to modeling music cognition addresses numerous issues in cognitive science, including theories of contextualization and memory.

The Experiments in Musical Listening schema-based model of metric cognition is inherently context-dependent. The cognition of meter is interpreted to be largely the result of prediction of consequential events based upon hierarchical relationships or sequential patterns, or both. Simultaneously, the effect of meter on activations of chord tone representations suggests that meter promotes the creation of contextual "windows of expectations." These windows facilitate the creation of schematic expectations that advance far beyond predictions of immediate consequence.

The primary mechanism for organizing the musical continuum into discrete units is the listener-invoked implication of a periodic cycle of time. Joel Lester states the issue simply. "We not only expect harmonies to resolve," he writes, "we expect them to resolve at specific points in time" (Lester 1986, p. 52). Meter cognition is deceptive in its seeming simplicity. The mechanism that causes listeners to tap their feet is elusive in that it is rarely a conscious activity. Experiments in Musical Listening provides a visualization for how metric expectations and contexts are established and how these expectations affect expectations for patterns in the music. Modeling premonitory bias of tonal and metric expectations introduces the concept of external schemas and long-term memory that affects the way we perceive and interpret music.

The hierarchical network architecture seems to be a very promising model of cognition of metered and rhythmicized functional tonal harmonic progressions. The metric index encoding differentiates between identical elements that are sounded in different metric positions. Thus, for example, a tonic triad that appears on a downbeat generates entirely different expectations from one that falls on an upbeat. Furthermore, the functional role of specific harmonies seems to be responded to in meaningful ways. This is most clearly evident in the results of submitting a deceptive cadence as target input to the architecture.

Since the network is now sensitive not only to what and how changes should occur but also to when they should occur, the architecture models how combinations of expectational strength and specificity combine to provide a measure with which to compare the realization of the prediction with the expectation itself.

Prominent among Experiments in Musical Listening's (numerous) limitations is the inability to visualize scope in meaningful ways. The decay character of memory is not context-dependent in the current model and suggests an important path for future research. Another direction for further research is the formulation of a method of quantification of expectations.

The Complement of Experiments in Musical Listening and Experiments in Musical Intelligence

Experiments in Musical Intelligence is a significant example of a symbolic approach to music analysis and stylistic replication. Experiments in Musical Intelligence involves stages of extracting, archiving, interpolating, and adapting musical patterns. The system generates compositions in specific genres or in crossbreeds of multiple genres. Cope finds a certain grounding in the cognitively based writings of Leonard Meyer. Cope's aim is not to model cognition but rather to produce convincing replications of style or original works created by consciously crossbreeding existing works. It can be argued that although it may not shed direct light upon the creative process, the program's ability to convincingly replicate style implies much about cognition.

Functional tonality, the lingua franca of Western music for over 200 years, has instigated a large corpus of theoretical descriptions. Some of these have a cognitive rationale rooted in the overtone series (Rameau 1985, Schenker 1926); others are rule-based abstractions that implicitly describe such cognitive attributes as tension and repose (Riemann 1911). Still others implicitly describe the cognitive aspect of tonality as a hierarchical system of relationships based upon the circle of fifths (Schoenberg 1948), or from a linguistic perspective. However, only recently have there been efforts to describe the grammatical and syntactic attributes of the tonal language from a purely cognitive perspective (Schmuckler 1989, Bharucha and Todd 1990). Experiments in Musical Listening rests upon the linguistic integrity of tonality from the perspective of a listener rather than from that of a composer.

Because computational models are limited first and foremost by issues of representation, a valid criticism of any model is the inability of any single model to reveal the rich multidimensionality of music. A listener's quest for organization does not stop at the musical surface of notes and rhythms but rather concurrently occurs at many levels of nested abstraction. Cope and I both depart from and confine ourselves to a note-level surface. For Cope the limitation is patterns of pitch and rhythm; in Experiments in Musical Listening, combinations of simultaneously sounding PCs in a beat-oriented temporal layout. Similar processes of reductive pattern recognition and categorization occur at the levels of pitch identification and timbral recognition.

Needless to say, harmonic progression and harmonic rhythm are but two aspects of music. Melodic, rhythmic, dynamic, phrase, and articulatory attributes also contribute to contexts. These other attributes can themselves carry their own sets of implications. They can also support or detract from implications suggested by harmonic progression or the harmonic rhythm. Furthermore, Experiments in Musical Listening resolves only at the beat level.

Conclusions

I have argued that the essence of creativity lies in the act of listening. Composition at its best provides a framework within which a listener's attention is drawn, sometimes by seduction, other times by force, but always by manipulation of expectations and realizations. Defining the processes involved in formulating expectations and evaluating realizations touches this essential core of creativity.

Expert and symbolic system approaches to model compositional practice succeed to varying degrees in replicating stylistic features of music. Introducing a theoretical framework and visualization tools to describe the creativity of listening enriches the ability to discuss creativity. Artificial neural networks provide a flexible environment within which the mechanics and implied associated cognitive processes involved in human prediction of time-ordered sequential elements can be simulated and visualized.

The interplay of expectation and realization demands creative mental processing. Any definition, characterization, or replication of style that fails to capture this interplay will fail to produce anything beyond a local musical surface with convincing stylistic identity.

The ongoing controversy surrounding the title of Milton Babbitt's 1964 article "Who Cares if You Listen?" (to which the title of this chapter alludes) suggests a superficial disdain for the notion of music written in a vacuum, in disregard for the audience. The communicative aspect of music is not simply an issue of accessibility but rather demands a broader definition of creativity. This deeper definition must include the intentional control of the degree of realized expectations. It reflects the profound difficulty of either Experiments in Musical Intelligence or Experiments in Musical Listening to arrive at a comprehensive model of creativity. The definition harkens back to the discrete-continuous paradox that differentiates the two models, and finds its roots in the dynamic nature of realized expectations described by Hucbald at the close of the first millennium.

Acknowledgments

The neural network experiments described in this paper were done in collaboration with Dan Gang, currently a Fulbright Postdoctoral Fellow at the Center for Computer Research in Music and Acoustics at Stanford University.

15 Collision Detection, Muselot, and Scribble: Some Reflections on Creativity

Daniel Dennett

In this chapter I want to stress the continuity between all sorts of creativity. Life on earth has been generated over billions of years in a single branching tree—the tree of life—by one algorithmic process or another. Figure 15.1 shows a recent picture of the tree of life (Morell 1997, p. 701). Note that a relatively recent branching on the eukaryotic limb, which bears all multicellular organisms, divides the plants from the animals. Among the plants are apple trees, which make apples, and among the animals are spiders, which make webs, and beavers, which make dams. Apple trees and apples, spiders and webs, beavers and dams—these are all fruits of the tree of life, directly or indirectly.

Also among the animals are three magnificent composition makers: J. S. Bach, David Cope, and Bernard Greenberg (who performed a number of his works patterned after Bach at the conference). They and their compositions are also among the fruits of the tree of life, and one of these composition makers, David Cope, has also created a composition maker, Experiments in Musical Intelligence. Its products are doubly indirect, being products of a product of a product of the tree of life, but, I want to argue, its means of production are simply special cases of the very same processes that created both the compositions by Bach and Greenberg, the apples and spider webs, and the organisms that made them.

According to the poet Paul Valéry,

It takes two to invent anything. The one makes up combinations; the other one chooses, recognizes what he wishes and what is important to him in the mass of the things which the former has imparted to him. What we call genius is much less the work of the first one than the readiness of the second one to grasp the value of what has been laid before him and to choose it. (quoted in Hadamard 1949, p. 30)

This making up of combinations is also known as generating diversity, and the choosing is also known, of course, as selection—as in natural selection. Valéry was right. All invention, all creation, proceeds by trial and error of one sort or another, and all such processes are what are known as generate-and-test algorithms (Dennett 1975). Since the processes are algorithmic, we ought to be able to take them apart and see how they work. How many layers of generate-and-test does it take to create an apple tree, or a Bach, or the *St. Matthew Passion*, or Experiments in Musical Intelligence, or one of that program's inventions?

Many find this vision of creativity deeply unsettling—some would add that it is not just unsettling, it is crass, shallow, philistine, despicable, or even obscene. I am always

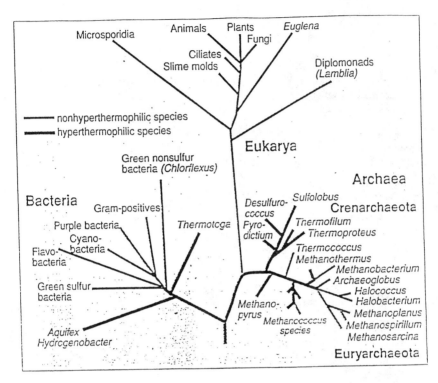

Figure 15.1
A recent picture of the Tree of Life (Morell 1997, p. 701).

more than a little quizzical about these emotional reactions, since they seem to me to betray a certain parochialism. It is apparently *not* crass, philistine, obscene ... to declare that all the first-order products of the tree of life—the birds and the bees and the spiders and the beavers—are designed and created by such algorithmic processes, but outrageous to consider the hypothesis that creations of human genius might themselves be products of such algorithmic processes. Is an ode to a nightingale really that much more marvelous than a nightingale itself? I would certainly be prouder of having created the latter! And of course no human being, no matter how great a genius, does all the creative work that goes into a work of art.

How long did it take Johann Sebastian Bach to create the *St. Matthew Passion*? An early version was performed in 1727 or 1729, but the version we listen to today dates from ten years later, and incorporates many revisions. How long did it take to create Johann Sebastian Bach? He had the benefit of forty-two years of living when the first version was heard, and more than half a century when the later version was completed. How long did it take to create the Christianity without which the *St. Matthew Passion* would have been literally inconceivable by Bach or anyone else? Roughly two millennia. How long did it take to create the social and cultural context in which Christianity could be born? Somewhere between a hundred millennia and three million years—depending on when we decide to date the birth of human culture. And how long did it take to create *Homo sapiens*? Between three and four billion years, roughly the same length of time it took to create daisies and snail darters, blue whales and spotted owls. Billions of years of *irreplaceable* design work.   (Dennett 1995, p. 511)

The contribution of Christianity to Bach's work is, in one sense obvious, but it is made particularly vivid by Bernard Greenberg (see chapter 12), who has analyzed his own reliance on the memes of Christianity to enrich his own Bach-inspired compositions. For those interested in theories of cultural evolution, Greenberg provides a particularly clear-cut example of a type of cultural vector (and locus of combination) that has been overlooked by many theorists: he is a meme vector, and meme exploiter, without being a believer. He harbors an elaborate virtual machine, the well-designed, field-tested, debugged culture machine of Christianity, and he has gone to considerable lengths to acquire this machinery. It enables him to do things that he could not do if he hadn't incorporated that virtual machine into his architecture, but he does not believe its doctrines. You don't have to believe in a system of memes to transmit them, or to benefit from them. (This has been typically overlooked by Darwinian theorists of culture. For some details, see Dennett, forthcoming.) And one of the remarkable contributions of Greenberg's presentation to the conference is his willingness to let us go backstage and see how the process works—for him, and by extrapolation, for others. Unlike Greenberg, most artists conceal their creative processes from us as if they were magicians. Picasso famously said, "Je ne cherche pas. Je trouve," but if he was sincere (which I doubt), this only means that he had less access to, and less insight into, the search procedures (or generation procedures) that actually went into his own formidable artistic production.

Here is a recipe, then, for making the *St. Matthew Passion*. First, make a Bach, and educate it, installing all the best products of the contemporary culture. Then sit back. Pretty soon it will be punching out cantatas one a week, for years. From there it is a large but not miraculous step to a more ambitious work like the *St. Matthew Passion*. J. S. Bach was prolific, but not as prolific as the Experiments in Musical Intelligence program—but then Bach was running on a much slower architecture, using old-fashioned technology. What an algorithm can do in principle, and what it can do in jig time (or just in real time in real life) is entirely a matter of the architecture on which it is run. When Danny Hillis, the founder of Thinking Machines, Inc., wanted to show off the huge advance in computing power of his Connection

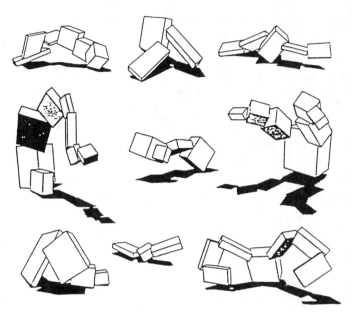

Figure 15.2
Evolved virtual creatures (Sims 1994a,b), an artificial evolution program that produced strikingly biological-like phenomena.

Machines, he commissioned Karl Sims to create some demos. One of the best was his Evolved Virtual Creatures (Sims 1994a,b), an artificial evolution program that produced strikingly biological-like phenomena in only a few hundred generations (see figure 15.2). Like Experiments in Musical Intelligence, this program is itself the work of a brilliant creator, but also like Experiments in Musical Intelligence, its creations include many features undreamt of—even antecedently unimaginable—by its creator. But for all its brilliance—and my admiration for Sims's work is unstinting—the program does have some striking limitations. By drawing attention to them, I want to suggest a ground for residual misgivings about Experiments in Musical Intelligence, which has—to date—the same limitations.

What's missing in Sims's world of evolving virtual creatures, is, in a word, *concreteness*. For instance, although the bodies of these virtual creatures are exposed to selective pressure in the virtual world they inhabit, their genomes are offstage, and hence not subject to any selective pressure. That means that their genomes could not grow longer or shorter under any realistic circumstances. While there are a Vast (Dennett 1995) number of possible virtual creatures in Sims's world, the search space is open-ended in a strictly limited number of dimensions. When Sims wanted to see if his creatures could evolve phototropism (heading for the light, the way moths close in on lamps and candle flames), he had to reach in, godlike, and add the genes for a photosensor element, increasing the dimensionality of his simulation. Another evolutionary simulation, John Holland's (1995) ECHO, does put the genome itself in the virtual world; organisms in ECHO have to acquire the necessary raw materials to make offspring, including the offspring's genome, before they can reproduce. This dramatically widens the scope of evolutionary possibilities, but still falls short of the open-endedness that only a fully concrete phenomenon can enjoy.

Consider the difference between virtual worlds and real worlds. If you want to make a real hotel, you will have to put a lot of time, energy, and materials into arranging matters so that the people in adjacent rooms can't overhear each other. When you go to make a virtual hotel, you get that insulation for free. In a virtual hotel, if you want the people in adjacent rooms to be able to overhear each other, you have to add that capacity. You have to add noninsulation. You also have to add shadows, aromas, vibration, dirt, footprints, and wear and tear. All these nonfunctional features come for free in the real, concrete world. The generic term for what must be added to virtual worlds to make them more realistic is *collision detection*. If you have ever played around with the task of making a computer video game, you soon realize that putting shapes in motion on the screen is not enough. Shapes will pass right through each other without any effect unless you build collision detection into the update loop.

In his book *Le Ton Beau de Marot*, Hofstadter (1997) draws attention to the role of what he calls *spontaneous intrusions* into a creative process. In the real world, almost everything that happens leaves a wake, makes shadows, has an aroma, makes noise, and this provides a bounty of opportunities for spontaneous intrusions. It is also precisely what is in short supply in a virtual world. Indeed, one of the chief beauties of virtual worlds from the point of view of computer modelers is that quietness: nothing happens except what you provide for, one way or another. This permits you to start with a clean slate and add features to your model one at a time, seeing what the minimal model is that will produce the sought-for effects.

Sims's Evolved Virtual Creatures is a spectacular example of getting a lot from a *relatively* simple model, but it also serves to show that when you're modeling creativity, there should be junk lying around that your creative processes can bump into, noises that your creative processes can't help overhearing. The spontaneous intrusion of that little noise from the next room may tweak what those processes are doing in a way that is serendipitous, or in a way that is destructive, but either way, this opens up new possibilities. The exploitation of accidents is the key to creativity, whether what is being made is a new genome, a new behavior, or a new melody.

Let me clarify what I'm *not* saying. The problem with Sims's evolved creatures is not that they are not made of carbon, or that they contain no protein or hemoglobin. The problem is that they are virtual. And by being virtual, they live in a world many orders of magnitude simpler than the world of biological evolution. I think exactly the same thing is true of Experiments in Musical Intelligence. Wonderful as it is, it is orders of magnitude simpler than the world of human musical composition. What is delightful about both cases is the discovery of just how much you can get from something so clean, so noise-free, so abstract.

We can imagine improving Experiments in Musical Intelligence, or Karl Sims's work, or any other such project in artificial life or artificial creativity, by adding more and more and more junk, more and more opportunities for collisions, into the world. But consider how counterintuitive such advice would appear:

No matter what you're modeling, make sure that every phenomenon, every subroutine, everything that happens in that world makes extraneous noises, leaves a wake, broadcasts a variety of nonfunctional effects through the world.

Why? What is all this noise for? It's not for anything; it's just there so that every other process has that noise as a potential source of signal, as an *objet trouvé* that it *might* turn, by the alchemy of the creative algorithm, into function, into art, into meaning. Every increment of design in the universe begins with a moment of serendipity, the undesigned intersection of two trajectories that yield something that turns out, retrospectively, to be more than a mere collision. But to the extent that computer modelers follow this advice, they squander the efficiency that makes computers such great tools. So there is a sort of homeostasis here. We can see that, not for any mysterious reason, computer modeling of creativity confronts diminishing returns. In order to get closer and closer to the creativity of a human composer, your model has to become ever more concrete; it has to model more and more of the incidental collisions that impinge on an embodied composer.

In other words, I want to follow Greenberg and Hofstadter in insisting that the shortcomings—such as they are—of Experiments in Musical Intelligence have nothing to do with carbon vs. silicon, biology vs. engineering, humanity vs. robotity. Concentrating on these familiar—indeed threadbare—candidates for crucial disqualifiers is succumbing to misdirection. What, though, about another all-too-familiar theme: what about consciousness? Experiments in Musical Intelligence is not conscious—at least not in any way that significantly models human consciousness. Isn't the consciousness of the human artist a crucial ingredient? One might think that there could not possibly be any *meaning* in the product of an unconscious process. Interestingly, some of the most creative human beings of all time have already thrown cold water on this hunch. (I have discussed these cases before, in Dennett 1975, from which the following paragraph—with minor revisions—is taken.)

> When the great 19th century mathematician, Henri Poincaré, reflected on this topic, he saw only two alternatives and they were both disheartening to him. The unconscious self that generates the candidates "is capable of discernment; it has tact, delicacy; it knows how to choose, to divine. What do I say? It knows better how to divine than the conscious self since it succeeds where that has failed. In a word, is not the subliminal self superior to the conscious self? I confess that, for my part, I should hate to accept this" (Koestler 1964, p. 164). The other extreme, of course, is that the generator is just an automaton, an ultimately absurd, blind trier of all possibilities. And that's no more of a homunculus with whom to identify oneself. So you don't want to be the generator. As Mozart is reputed to have said (in an oft-quoted but possibly spurious passage): "Whence and how do they come? I don't know and I have nothing to do with it."   (p. 86)

One of my favorite contemporary creators, the novelist and essayist Nicholson Baker (1996), has this to say on the way we go about changing our minds:

> Our opinions, gently nudged by circumstance, revise themselves under cover of inattention. We tell them, in a steady voice, No, I'm not interested in a change at present. But there is no stopping opinions. They don't care about whether we want to hold them or not, they do what they have to do.   (p. 4)

What these reflections have in common is a vision that many find deeply repugnant, even alarming: the self disappears, or at least shrinks, as Thomas Nagel once said, to a dimensionless point (Nagel 1979, p. 35). The active, responsible, farseeing, genuinely creative self is replaced by willful opinions or unconscious automatic selves that go right on generating and testing *without authorial supervision*. That the generation might be unconscious is recognized by Poincaré and Mozart; Baker adds that even the test is typically something that can happen outside of our control. Looked at from so close up, I seem to vanish. As Doug Hofstadter asks, in the last of his list of worries, "Am I not as deep as I thought I was?" But once asked, the question's answer is not far to seek. Indeed, another of my favorite novelists, Peter DeVries, has a character express just the right sentiment for this impasse: "Superficially he's deep, but deep down he's shallow."

Of course. How could it be otherwise? Hofstadter recognizes that although his self has many, many layers, it does not have an infinite number of layers, so when our analysis bottoms out, we find nothing but shallow, mechanical processes built on shallow, mechanical processes, built on shallow, mechanical processes. Completing the analysis, even in sketchy, speculative fashion, as we are doing here, should be an

occasion for joy, not despair. Is it not wonderful that a cascade of algorithmic processes should look really deep from a superficial point of view? What else could depth
be, in the end? Hofstadter understands this, of course. His disappointment is rather
the reaction of somebody who would have guessed that a musical mind had at least,
say, seventeen layers, instead of "just" thirteen.

Here, for once, I think I disagree somewhat with Hofstadter. It seems to me that he
is hoping to sustain a view of meaning *in music* that is one (or two or three) layers too
deep. We can frame the issue by comparing music to speech, and considering a fascinating variety of ersatz speech invented—or at least named—by Dario Fo, the
Italian poet, dramatist, and comedian (and 1997 Nobel laureate in literature).
Among his comedic tours de force are his exercises in what he calls *gramelot*. The art
of gramelot is the art of *seeming* to speak a foreign language that one is in fact not
speaking. In *Mistero Buffo*, his gramelot Elizabethan English judge sounds just like
genuine Shakespearean English to Fo's non-Anglophone Italian audiences—but
sounds marvelously strange and alien to us Anglophones. Gramelot has been invented
time and again by comedians. Danny Kaye and Mel Brooks have done hilarious
phony French and German, and then there is the Swedish chef on the Muppet Show,
and the exquisite mouthings of the proprietor of the Café Boeuf on Prairie Home
Companion.

What, then, is Hofstadter's worry? It is that Experiments in Musical Intelligence is
just producing musical gramelot, what we might call *muselot*—and that that is all
there is to music! Music just *sounds as if* it really means something! The reasoning
that leads Hofstadter to this quandary is quite straightforward.

Premise 1: Experiments in Musical Intelligence's music doesn't mean anything, however wonderful it is.
Premise 2: Either there is a *fundamental* difference between the Experiments in Musical Intelligence program's music and Bach's (and Schubert's, and Puccini's ...) music or there isn't.
Premise 3: There isn't.

(For Hofstadter, as for me, this premise follows from our conviction that strong AI is
possible in principle, however impossible it may turn out to be in grubby, economic
fact.)

Conclusion: Human music doesn't mean anything, however wonderful it is.

How could it possibly be that music means nothing, if untold generations of
musicians and composers have thought that it does have meaning? This rhetorical
question is easy to answer. Consider what linguists sometimes call *scribble*, the mixture of babbling and meaningful words that young children enthusiastically emit for
a brief period in their language acquisition process. As has often been pointed out,
there is no reason to suppose that these infants have any idea that their production is

falling short *in any way* from what they hear adults saying. After all, from their point of view, what adults are speaking is a lot of gibberish interspersed on occasion by a familiar, meaningful word. In the case of scribble, infants soon learn that even the gibberish part—the impressive gramelot—has meaning, but we can imagine (I think) a quite stable linguistic practice that never went beyond scribble. I harbor the suspicion that the fashionable works of recent French philosophy and literary studies are just such productions, and Hofstadter's examples of randomly generated Heidegger and Hegel indirectly support my dire conjecture.[1] But whether or not a *linguistic* institution of partial meanings embedded in delicious-sounding nonsense could survive, I see no reason why music could not consist of just such a matrix of occasionally (and obviously) meaningful elements set in structures that had no semantic interpretation at all.

The meaning that we know music can have is hardly negligible. Greenberg responds directly to Hofstadter in his discussion of Bach's use of counterpoint as a building system, a structure for incorporating meaning in music. But I think the elements of meaning that he shows to be incorporated in Bach's work still fall short of providing a standard of musical meaning that would permit us to draw a distinction between music and muselot, analogous to the difference between meaningful speech and gramelot. Even if we grant—what is surely true—that there is wide variation in the competence of human listeners to discriminate, abstract, and appreciate the music that they hear, this variation is not radical enough to parallel the imagined race of people who are speaking scribble and not realizing that other people are actually talking. The background fear that there might be a musically elite class that actually performed and appreciated music, while the rest of us were just content with muselot, is an empty fear. It couldn't be true. If it were true, there would be differences in the things some of us could do with music that would be as manifest to us as the differences between a good cookbook and a cookbook composed of randomized recipes. Music can "speak to us" but it can't give us directions, or explain phenomena, or codify laws, or tell stories (without the help of lots of verbal signposts, titles, and labels). Music is deep, music is wonderful, but not *that* wonderful.

Note

1. Doug Hofstadter coined the word "templagiarism" at the Stanford conference; it inspires me to attempt a coining of my own: *eumerdification*. John Searle once told me about a conversation he had with the late Michel Foucault: "Michel, you're so clear in conversation; why is your written work so obscure?" To which Foucault replied: "That's because, in order to be taken seriously by French philosophers, 25 percent of what you write has to be impenetrable nonsense." So, according to Searle, Foucault claimed that he deliberately added 25 percent *eumerdification*, so he would be taken seriously in France.

16 A Few Standard Questions and Answers

Douglas Hofstadter

Since this chapter is an attempt to convey the real-time flavor of my many Emmy lectures, I think it only appropriate to include a question-and-answer session with some of the most commonly raised points. Most of them are of the form, "Don't worry, Doug—your dire fears are totally unfounded. Emmy is great, and she's not in the slightest a threat to human dignity. Let me tell you why ..." So here we go.

Q: I'm a musician by training, and I remember how in undergraduate school my peers and I were required in various courses to copy many composers' styles. We all learned to do this without too much trouble, and some of the pieces we composed were pretty decent. It doesn't upset or worry me to think that stylistic imitation can result in pieces that are fairly effective, because I know that this can only occur *after* a composer has produced a body of material that establishes the style. The original, creative act must occur first. Indeed, I would propose that the most profound act of musical creation lies precisely in the invention of a novel and highly personal idiom or style. Thus I subscribe more or less to the Lew Rowell viewpoint—that the hard part, the only part requiring creative genius, is coming up with a new "grammar"; the easy part is then spinning off pieces that obey that grammar. Mastering musical mimicry may take a bit of talent, but it doesn't take creative genius.

A: First off, let me agree with you that coming up with a novel and highly personal idiom, as virtually all great composers have done, is definitely a greater achievement than writing one piece, or several pieces, even very high-quality pieces, that can pass for the composer's own but in fact are forgeries. Emmy apes previous styles, but she does not explore her very own stylistic worlds, nor was she ever intended to do so. In that sense, Emmy does not represent an assault on what I see as the very highest peak in the rugged mountain chain of musical achievement. So there is some agreement between our positions.

On the other hand, I would take issue with the imagery in your statement, which seems to suggest (although I doubt that you meant it this way) that a composer starts out spending a good deal of time devising a grammar, and then, that having been done, just turns into a drone who spins off piece after piece using the rules of the grammar. Well, the composers that I respect never did anything like create an explicit grammar. They just composed piece after piece, and as they composed, a set of statistical regularities emerged. Creating rules and then sticking to those rules was probably the furthest thing from their minds!

As a very minor composer, in fact, I might add a brief comment about my own feeling about remaining true to my own style, or staying within my own patterns. I almost always compose at the piano, and most of the time it is my fingers that guide me, in the sense that they are constantly trying out all sorts of small patterns on the keyboard, and after each such little unpremeditated motoric foray, I judge whether or not I like it, as well as whether or not it fits the piece's evolving and not-totally-stabilized mood. On the basis of such blurry considerations, I somehow decide whether or not to incorporate what my fingers just spontaneously came up with. What's interesting is that quite often my fingers will play a pattern that "I" would *never* have come up with, so to speak. Perhaps they stumble across a wrong note, or perhaps they just make a strange dissonance that I would never have thought of. At that point, my composer's mind enters the picture, and sometimes it says to me, "Hey, Doug—now *that* really was interesting, it was so unlike you, so why don't you incorporate it?" The logic of such a suggestion is that by using "un–Doug-like stuff" I sound more original than I really am, and I somehow break out of ruts. Perhaps over time I come to incorporate these un–Doug-like stylistic patterns and, somewhat ironically, they become Doug-like, at which point it is time for me to break out yet further. So much for a "Hofstadter grammar."

But I would like to answer this question in another way as well. Suppose that Lew Rowell really were able to distill a "Chopin grammar" from all of Chopin's oeuvre, and that he then sat down to write new pieces using this grammar—say, a fifth ballade, for example (Chopin's four extant ballades being generally regarded as among his most powerful expressive efforts ever). The key question, in my mind, is the degree to which this new Rowell–Chopin ballade will sound like an equal sibling to the other four—something worthy of the name "Chopin's fifth ballade." Will listeners be moved to tears by it? Will pianists flock to perform it? Will audiences clamor for more—for a whole set of new "Chopin ballades"? Will this music move people, in short, with all the power with which the first four Chopin ballades move people?

The reason I raise this scenario is that my impression has always been that for Chopin himself to come up with each of his four ballades was itself a mighty act of creativity, not anything even remotely like the spinning-off of a rule-bound piece from a fixed grammar. The four ballades are enormously different from each other, and not in any sense a bunch of pieces sharing an abstract skeletal structure.

If I might be excused for making the following rather presumptuous analogy, Chopin's four ballades are as different from each other as are, say, four of my most diverse articles, such as this one, or an article on the subliminal connotations of the word "you guys," or an article on a class of geometries related to projective geometry, or a humorous article gently mocking John Cage's Zen attitude toward music. Such a collection of articles certainly do not seem to have been cast from the same mold. Likewise, one would hope that anything meriting the name "Chopin's fifth ballade," whether concocted by Lew Rowell or by Emmy (or whoever or whatever), would be just as different from its four progenitors as they are different from one another, and that the sixth and seventh and eighth ballades likewise would all differ among themselves in just as significant a way. *If* Emmy–Chopin ballades did pass this test, and *if* audiences clamored for more and more of them, then I would feel I would have to despondently throw in the towel as a researcher who is seeking the mechanisms of creativity, for everything that I could ever have imagined seeking would already have been found, and the book on the human mind's mysteries would be closed.

For a sharply contrasting case, though, consider the so-called "prairie houses" designed by the famous American architect Frank Lloyd Wright. He designed many houses in this family, and they all share a certain fairly clear set of properties—so much so that some years ago, a group of professors of architecture at SUNY Buffalo distilled from them a "prairie-house grammar," which they conveyed to a computer, which then came up with dozens of new "Frank Lloyd Wright prairie houses." When I first saw this, I was quite astonished, but the more I thought about it, the more I realized that the original set of prairie houses itself was pretty formulaic, and therefore lent itself to "grammaticization." It would be entirely another matter, however, for a computer to come up with a Frank Lloyd Wright–style house that lay far outside the bounds of the prairie houses.

As this shows, even a great artistic mind can go into a temporary mode in which a certain fairly formulaic vein is explored for a while, and such explorations may lend themselves relatively easily to mechanical mimicking—but that is not the essence of being a great creator. For all I know—and though it pains me to say this—maybe some of Chopin's weaker mazurkas bear this kind of formulaic stamp. I certainly wouldn't hesitate for a moment to shout "Formulaic!" about many works of certain other hallowed names in music, such as Mozart and Beethoven, so why not Chopin as well? That might explain, at least in part, why an Emmy mazurka can sound better, in some ways, than a few Chopin mazurkas.

One last point about humans mimicking style and computers mimicking style. You say that you and your peers were pretty good at coming up with pieces in, say, "the Brahms style" or whatever. Well, part of what allowed you to do that is that *you all were human beings*, as Brahms himself was. Built into being human is the fact of living life and having all the sorts of experiences that—to my mind—underlie what musical expression is all about. And so, part of the power of *your* musical expressions came straight from your humanity. For an Emmy-type program to perform credibly at this type of task, however, is another matter entirely, because it does not have any human experience to draw on. So I don't buy into the viewpoint that says, "Stylistic imitation is a routine thing in music schools, ergo it's no big deal that we can get a computer program to do it, too." To the contrary, it is indeed a big deal, because a program like Emmy, although I facetiously call it "she," is not a person.

The question that Emmy ultimately raises is whether people who come out of music schools and who become famous composers are really just masters of a difficult *craft*, people who have absorbed all sorts of complex traditions and styles, and who now practice their craft exactly in the way that a carpenter makes fine tables and bookcases and so forth—*or*, contrariwise, whether composers are constantly, though surely unconsciously, plumbing the furthest depths of their psyches, discovering mysterious yearnings and sighs, and putting a voice to them. These two images are unbelievably different pictures of what music is all about, and I must say Emmy is forcing me personally to confront this question in a way that I never imagined I would have to—and making me squirm much more than I would like.

Q: Programs have been written that produce poetry based in rather simple ways on the poems of a human poet, and one can feel meaning in the output, but one realizes that such meaning is due to the input material. Thus if in a computer poem one finds the phrase "her haunting grace," it may be that this phrase was present as such in some poem, or if not, then its component words all were, and the machine stuck them together on the basis of some syntactic rules, maybe with a few rudimentary semantic guidelines as well. But a reader who feels depth in such phrases can also realize that it is basically *borrowed* depth, not *original* depth. It's just echoes and parrotings, not primordial screams from the depths of a feeling soul. Isn't that really what's going on in Emmy? If so, why worry?

A: If Emmy were just a plagiarizer or reshuffler at the level of simplisticness that you have suggested, then all over the place we would hear traces and echoes of the input pieces. And of course then we would chuckle at its obvious borrowings, and not be in the slightest impressed. What is impressive is that in many of her pieces, we *do not* hear where the elements are coming from. There is no wholesale borrowing of big phrases; rather, the elements of the composer's input have been chopped up into very fine-grained pieces, and those pieces have been reassembled in large structures in such a manner as to disguise their origins. And the reassembly process is faithful enough and subtle enough that at least some of the resulting compositions are good enough to fool excellent musicians—such as students and faculty at Eastman Rochester, for example. They cannot tell that the power has been borrowed.

Indeed, that's precisely the nub of the question: Is it fair to say that the power of a composer has been *borrowed* when Emmy dissects the input pieces into such tiny fragments that, effectively, the accusation of plagiarism is no longer viable, in that even a sophisticated listener cannot put their finger on where the phrases and gestures in an output piece have come from? If the reshuffling is so fine-grained as to make it virtually untraceable, then in what sense is *borrowing* taking place?

Emmy is not a coarse-grained plagiarizer. If you hear a Mozart-style Emmy piano concerto, it will *remind* you all over the place of Mozart concertos, but you won't, in general, be able to point to a particular phrase and say, for example, "Ah!—*that* was borrowed from the A Major Concerto, Köchel 488, second movement!" Admittedly, there are episodes in some of Emmy's two-part inventions that clearly come from specific Bach inventions, but that is probably because only a couple of inventions were being drawn on in those cases.

Analogously, I remember that when I first heard Mary Jane Cope perform "Nope" (Emmy's pseudo-Hofstadter piece) in front of me and the Santa Cruz audience, I had to try to suppress a smile at virtually every measure, because I could just hear its sources so easily. But the reason for that is very simple: it turns out that Dave was unable to use all twelve of the pieces I sent him as input to Emmy, but instead he selected just *two* of them, and it was on the basis of just those that Emmy composed "Nope." Well, obviously, if you have such a sparse database on which to draw, your output is going to reek of its sources in a conspicuous manner. If Dave had been able to use all twelve of the pieces I sent him (or better yet, all forty of the pieces I've composed), then of course the mixture would have been far, far subtler and the aroma surrounding any particular harmony or phrase would have been far more elusive.

I must add parenthetically that here we are forced to confront an amazing rigidity on Emmy's part, particularly when perceived in contrast to all her complexity and flexibility. Namely, Emmy cannot take a 3/4 piece and a 4/4 piece and use them both as inputs on which to base an output piece. All input pieces that are used together have to have the same time signature! Only if you convert your 3/4 piece into a 12/4 piece (putting four measures at a time into a "supermeasure") and also convert your 4/4 piece into a 12/4 piece (three measures making a supermeasure) will Emmy be able to deal with both of them at once. But you have to force-fit the pieces in this unnatural way for Emmy to be able to extract "style" from both at once.

It seems implausible in the extreme that a human musician would be stymied by the challenge of hearing stylistic similarities in a waltz and a 4/4 piece. But in any case it was this kind of rigidity that barred Dave from using all twelve pieces on my diskette as input to Emmy, and it was therefore clear as day to me, as composer, where each tiny part of "Nope" was coming from. But, to take a contrasting case, I know all the Chopin mazurkas well, and yet in many cases, I cannot pinpoint where the fragments of Emmy's mazurkas are coming from. It is too blurry, because the breakdown is too fine to allow easy traceability.

To recap, then, Emmy's power of course comes, in *some* sense, from borrowing, for by definition and by intention, that is all that Emmy is—a borrower. But the dissolving and recrystallization processes inside Emmy involve "musical molecules" at such a fine-grained level that how the emotions of the input pieces retain their power through it all is not in the slightest obvious. If you eat fish day after day, you do not thereby turn into a fish or come to resemble a fish in any way, because the fish cells are broken down far beyond the level of fishiness. Nonetheless, you do borrow from the power of fish life, because you don't break the biomolecules all the way down into pure chemical elements. Emmy likewise "digests" its input pieces using metabolic processes that chop its food apart at a fine level, but not so fine a level as to lose all coherence. It's an exquisite balancing act, that's for sure, and I would be the first to insist that Dave Cope deserves enormous credit for having stuck with it for so many years, and for having refined it with such loving care.

Q: Having just heard a human perform music by Emmy and by human composers, and having myself just taken a pseudo-Bach piece for genuine Bach (for which I am not ashamed or crestfallen because I do not pride myself on being a connoisseur of classical music), I am led to musing as to whether, rather than the composition itself, it is not its *performance* by a human with a heart and soul that gives meaning to the piece, whether that piece was composed by a person or by a machine. And thus the more sensitively a piece is performed, the greater will be its meaning, and conversely, the more mechanically performed, the less will be its meaning—no matter what its provenance might be.

A: To me, your suggestion seems analogous to claiming that unless a short story (say) is written out by hand by a human, what it says will be unable to convey any emotion. In other words, a story typeset by machine is empty, but the same story copied out by hand by someone will be rife with meaning. To me, that seems absurd. What contains the meaning is the set of *ideas* behind the notes or behind the words. How those notes or words are rendered is but a minor tweak in the story's effectiveness.

Let's shift back to music itself, rather than stories. I do not feel, as you seem to feel, that one needs a great performance of a piece in order to be able to hear its depths. Consider the first time I heard a mazurka by Emmy. Who was the performer? Myself—I was clumsily sight-reading it at my own piano, out of Cope's book. The notes were printed smaller than usual, which made it even more difficult to sight-read. Nonetheless, despite making mistakes left and right and playing it far too slowly and unevenly, I was able to discern a truly unexpected amount of "Chopinity" in that piece, and it was that experience—my own totally junky performance—that really made me feel something eerie was going on with this Emmy program. One might put it this way: since the performance was greatly lacking, whatever meaning I found in the piece could come from only one other source—the composer.

A few days later, I received in the mail from Dave a copy of *Bach by Design* (the first CD of Emmy's music), and on it there were very mechanical-sounding computer-produced performances of various Emmy pieces (including that same mazurka). I got a great deal out of hearing those pieces, despite the wooden quality of the playing. Such awkwardnesses are mildly annoying, to be sure, but it makes me think of reading a great poem typed on a typewriter rather than in a beautifully typeset edition, and perhaps with a few typos in it, to boot. What's the problem with that? It doesn't seem to me that beautiful typesetting makes the poem any better.

To me, adding the surface gloss of a virtuoso performer is not critical at all (in fact, confusing such glossiness with the depths conveyed by the notes alone is one big problem that plagues discussions of this sort). Where I would be troubled is if the piano on which I was sight-reading an Emmy (or human-written) piece were really out of tune, because then I couldn't really hear the resonances intended. But a decently played rendition on a decent piano will come through loud and clear, to me, in terms of the heart and soul behind the scenes (i.e., the heart and soul of the composer). The fewer the actual errors, of course, the better—but a great performance is not needed. Adequate is just fine.

Q: Why are you upset at the idea that Emmy can come up with great new pieces that sound as if they were by Chopin? There's no threat here to human dignity, for it was Chopin himself who created the database out of which these pieces are coming. The power and the genius reside, thus, entirely in the database, not in Emmy. Emmy can do no better than the data she is fed with. So you don't need to worry about threats to human dignity or human genius; after all, if wonderful new mazurkas emanate from Emmy, nearly all of the credit should go to Frédéric Chopin, and only a small portion of credit to Emmy—or perhaps to Dave Cope.

A: This amounts to saying "old genius in, new genius out," which I certainly do not subscribe to. Given a database that is filled with works produced by a genius, it would still take a fantastic program to come up with *new* works that exhibited flashes of that same genius. To make this more concrete, let's imagine that you were to input the famous *Nine Stories* by J. D. Salinger into a 9-gram text-imitation program (or whatever value of *n* you like). What kind of output would you get? A genius-level short story worthy of Salinger, as different from the *Nine* as each one of them is from the others? Of course not. It would be incoherent garbage, and even at its best, just a series of grammatical clauses that regurgitated bits and pieces from the previous stories—hardly a brand-new story filled with events involving new characters in new situations and new locations. Does genius input always give rise to genius output? Certainly not. To make "old genius in, new genius out" work, it would take a program whose depth is commensurate with (i.e., worthy of) the depth of its databases.

Consider literary translation, for example—something that I know quite a lot about, having just spent this past year quite obsessedly translating Alexander Pushkin's celebrated novel-in-verse *Eugene Onegin* from Russian sonnets into English sonnets. Without doubt the database I was working on—the Russian original—was a work of genius. But does that guarantee that my output will also be a work of genius? Obviously not in the slightest. In fact, if you want to see genius turned into utter garbage, try running a stanza or two of *Eugene Onegin* through one of today's highly touted machine-translation programs (an experiment I recently carried out with four state-of-the-art programs, by the way). The English that comes out is ludicrous and at times absolutely incomprehensible. It would be a mind-boggling achievement if a machine-translation program came up with so much as a *coherent* English-language rendition of *Eugene Onegin*, let alone a rhymed and metric version!

I might add that I devoted every ounce of my intellectual power for a full year to this translation effort, and I would say without hesitation that in so doing, I was constantly drawing on all of that which makes me human: my life experiences in the fullest—my struggles, my yearnings, my triumphs, my defeats, and so forth and so on. It took all of that to *understand* the Russian deeply enough that I could fully internalize the ideas, reflect on them, turn them around in my head, and then slowly reinstantiate them in a new and alien linguistic medium. If my translation has any merit, it is precisely because I put my whole self—mind, heart, and soul—into it.

And now consider the fact that translation is a darn sight easier than creation *ab ovo*. We are not talking about Doug Hofstadter writing a *new* Pushkin novel—just about reconstructing the poetry of the original in a new medium. How much more would it take for me to write a brand-new novel-in-verse "by Pushkin" (in the same sense that Emmy, given Prokofiev input, composed a brand-new piano sonata "by Prokofiev")? Quite frankly, I wouldn't have the foggiest idea how to write even the first sentence. The mere idea makes me laugh.

So what are we to conclude here? That although today's state-of-the-art machine-translation programs can't come anywhere close to giving us a decent or even comprehensible anglicization of a Pushkin novel, today's state-of-the-art pattern-recombination engines can quite handily produce for us any arbitrary number of new Prokofiev sonatas, Mozart concertos, Bach arias, Gershwin songs, and Chopin mazurkas? This would seem to suggest an astonishing and heretofore totally unsuspected discrepancy between the depths of the two different arts (music and literature). Does Pushkin's genius really tower above that of Chopin? Is music basically no more than suave pattern-play, whereas literature is something else altogether? I just can't buy into this view, for to me, throughout my entire life, music has always been just as deep as, indeed even deeper than, any kind of literature.

Q: As a composer, I find Cope's music-composition program quite interesting, but frankly, I think your worry over it is a tempest in a teapot. Decades ago, John Cage taught us that music happens in the brain of the hearer; all a composer can do is create a situation in which music will happen in some of the audience members' minds. I, by some fluke, have the ability to hear music in my head and I've trained myself to put it into a reproducible form (a score). But I have no control over whether it is heard as music! A babbling brook, ocean waves breaking on boulders, or an oriole singing at dusk can create the same experience for the right listener. So what if a machine's output pleases someone's mind through their auditory input channel? That's not the *machine's* doing! So don't worry—music is just as great as you've always thought—it's just that you've been looking to someone *else* (the composer) for the greatness, when in truth the wonder of it all happens in *you.*

A: Sorry, but I think this is a grotesque twist on the truth. I would agree that notes in the air can be thought of as vibrations drained of meaning, and the receiver's brain as adding the meaning back to them. But the phrases "drained of meaning" and "adding the meaning back" suggest that there once was meaning in the notes, and that it has been "sucked out" and requires the metaphorical "adding of water" to re-create it—namely, the processing by a listener's brain. And I will agree that as listeners, we find (or create) meaning in sequences of sounds in much the same way that, as readers, we find (or create) meaning in a bunch of black splotches on white paper when we read a novel. However, to claim that the active involvement of our recipient brains transfers all credit for greatness and depth from the creator to the recipient is nonsense. Such a viewpoint would imply that we can find greatness in anything at all, simply by using our receiving brains' power.

Want to savor a great novel? Then pick up a Jacqueline Susann paperback at the grocery store, sit down, and just turn your mind on *real hard*—greatness will come oozing right out of it. For that matter, take *anything at all* and read it, and in your hands it will turn into great literature—merely provided that you can find it in *yourself* to make it so. Who cares what thoughts and ideas went into its mere *making*? There's really no need for deep and powerful insight at the creation end of things.

Leo Tolstoy, you are fully dispensable, because *my brain* is what makes you powerful and deep. (It will also make Erich Segal's banal *Love Story* powerful and deep.)

Frédéric Chopin, you too are dispensable, because it is my great brain, yes, my *brain*, that gives your humble notes meaning. Moreover, my brain, in its infinite wisdom and power, will find (if I so choose) just as much meaning in Michael Jackson or Elvis Presley or Madonna—or for that matter, in random squawks.

Speaking of random squawks, I think it is sloppy thinking to equate babbling brooks and birds chirping at twilight with music (at least with traditional tonal music), which is produced deliberately by a human being in order to express or communicate something to other humans. Or is that not so? Does a composer have no intent to communicate, nothing to say? I think you will find the case is quite the contrary, if you read the biographies of any composers of note.

Given the absurdity of the notion that the creator/sender's role is irrelevant to the meaning produced in the receiver's brain, what is left but to shift the burden back to the creator/sender? *That* is where the power resides. To be sure, my listening brain— my "inner ear," so to speak—"adds water," but the level of quality of what results is not due to my *added water*; it is due to the *seeds*, or the recipe, or whatever it is that you are adding water to (our metaphor is a little blurry). After all, my water is the same, whether I add it to Chopin, to Elvis Presley, or to the sound of garbage cans being picked up in the early morning; what makes one recipe appealing and addictive and another recipe flat and boring to me is not the "water" used in preparing them— it is the difference between the two recipes!

No, the meaning of a piece of music (or literature) is not invented out of nothing by us receivers; it resides in the mysterious catalytic power of *the sequence of notes* that somehow that composer was able to find, and which other people had never stumbled across before. Yes, "catalytic"—yes, we *realize* the meaning (both in the sense of "come to understand" and in the sense of "manufacture") that lurks in the notes, but the true responsibility and credit redound to the *sender's* brain, not the *receiver's* brain. To rank listener above composer as the source of musical meaning is, I'm sorry to say, no more than extravagantly self-indulgent, egomaniacal, solipsistic silliness.

Q: Might it not be the case that *composing* music is easier than *appreciating* music? Maybe you should only start to feel threatened if Emmy (or some cousin program) can listen to pieces and decide which ones are good and which ones are weak. Perhaps Cope's achievement can even be taken as constituting a proof that *composition of music* is, in some sense, relatively simple, compared to *understanding* music.

A: Whew! That's a bizarre claim. I'd start out by saying, "Composing is not a free lunch courtesy of a big database or a predefined grammar." By this, I mean that composing involves genuine musical intelligence, and in fact musical intelligence of the highest degree of refinement and subtlety. How could a composer know that a piece was coming along well without being able to make positive or negative judgments? How could listening, understanding, and judging be bypassed? Well, of course, your retort may be: "Just as in Emmy, that's how."

And to this retort, I guess I would have to say, "Emmy's compositions are precisely as deep as her capacity to listen to and understand music." Which forces us to ask, "Does Emmy listen to music, or understand music, at all?" Well, of course Emmy doesn't *hear* music, in the sense of having eardrums that vibrate in response to complex waveforms—Emmy's way of perceiving music involves just the ability to deal with *numbers* that represent pitches and times and so forth. This may seem a funny sensory modality to us, but in a sense, it *is* an abstract kind of "listening." After all, our eardrums also produce a set of numbers that then affect the neurons in our auditory cortex. And remember that there are highly trained musicians who can merely *look* at a score and "hear" the music in their heads.

Hearing music really means accepting some representation of pitches and timings and so forth, and producing the proper end result in the brain (or in the computer analogue thereof). Exactly which kind of representation kicks off the process is not crucial. In some sense, Emmy ingests notes (even though they don't have the rich timbres that we hear), and she makes sense of those notes by chunking them into larger and larger structures, labeling such structures with SPEAC labels, discovering signatures, detecting motive templates, and so forth. That's how Emmy "listens" to her databases. What Emmy *doesn't* do, as we know, is to associate the structures she finds with emotional experiences drawn from life. But in any case, Emmy's compositional ability is proportional to her ability to understand or find order in what she "hears." You can only be a composer to the extent that you are a good listener.

Once again, going back to literature, can you really imagine a writer who could churn out superlative short stories by the dozens, and yet who was at the same time incapable of reading a single story with comprehension? Give me a break! Reading is to writing as walking is to running, and the same goes for listening and composing. Don't put the cart before the horse, please!

Q: How does musical *meaning* differ from musical *style*?

A: Your question points straight at the heart of the issue raised so marvelously clearly by Cope's work—namely, *Is there such a thing as musical meaning?* Or is music just a set of elaborate, ornate gestures that for some reason please us aesthetically but no more?

This reminds me of a wonderful but very rare book that I was lucky enough to get a copy of some years ago—the *Codex Seraphinianus* by Luigi Serafini (1981). This book poses as an encyclopedia, but of a totally fantastic world. Every two-page spread has one page that is filled with delightfully curly squiggles that seem to form words, sentences, paragraphs, and full articles on subjects of every sort imaginable. But given that you can't read the squiggles, how do you know what the subject under discussion is? Because the facing page is an elaborate picture of some aspect of this bizarre world—flora, fauna, engineering, culture, science, the arts, clothes, foods, and so forth and so on. The question one naturally asks oneself, on looking at this wondrously idiosyncratic book, is, Do the complex arrays of symbols actually *mean* anything, or are they just curly squiggles, end of story?

Although I've looked through the entire book many dozens of times, I have no knowledge of whether Serafini's "language" actually means anything. My guess would be that, although it is very carefully and self-consistently structured, it is nonetheless just empty scribbling. But it's the question, not its answer, that interests me here. What would make us feel that those arrays of squiggles were something *other* than just "empty scribbling"? What would make those squiggles "actually mean" something?

Presumably, we would have to figure out *how to decode them*. We would have to have some kind of objective way of finding meaning in them. If one notices a piece of paper in the gutter and picks the paper up and finds a series of roman letters on it that one cannot read, one can tackle the implicit challenge in various ways, such as asking people who know various foreign languages if they can read it, or attempting to decode it by trying out various substitution ciphers (letter-to-letter codes), and so forth. Eventually, one may find the key and a message emerges clearly and unambiguously. Then you feel you have found the meaning. But what if you do not succeed? Have you thereby shown there is no meaning there? Obviously not—you may just not yet have hit on the right decipherment scheme.

I personally think that I hear meaning all over the place in music, although it is very hard for me to explain this meaningfulness in words. That's what makes music so important in my life. Were it just formal gestures, I would tire of it very quickly. But I cannot explain what it is, exactly, that I hear in a given piece, no matter how much I love that piece. I believe, as much as I believe anything, that musical semantics exists, but I don't think it is much like linguistic semantics. I think that when we understand musical semantics—and Dave's many years of hard work and loving devotion to Emmy, especially his SPEAC notions, may be a significant step in that direction—we will know a great deal more about how human emotionality is constituted. But I think that will be a long time in the coming.

Q: Why aren't you ecstatic, instead of very depressed, at the prospect of soon being able to have an unlimited new supply of great Chopin, whom you admire unboundedly?

A: If I believed Emmy's Chopin simulation would soon be capable of producing a raft of Chopin-style pieces that would make chills run up and down my spine, I would have to revise my entire opinion of what music is about, and that would destroy something profound inside me.

Consider this analogy. Suppose that my beloved father, who died some years ago, were to walk into my study right now as I sit here typing. Would I not be overjoyed? Well, think of what that event would do to my belief system. Virtually everything that I have come to understand about the world would all go down the drain in one split second. Death would not exist. All the things I thought were true about biology would be instantly overturned. Pretty much all of science as I know it (and in fact as I learned it from my father) would be destroyed in a flash. Would I want to trade the joy of the return of my father for the destruction of my entire belief system?

There is, admittedly, one alternative reaction that I could have, were Emmy to spout forth new pieces that touched me to the core. Instead of revising my entire opinion of what music is about, I could conclude that I'm just a shallow listener—a sucker for lightweight aping—and drastically downgrade my opinion of my own personal depth as a perceiver of music, thus coming up with a very different kind of pessimism from the three listed above—namely, this one: "*I* am a lot shallower than I had ever thought." Maybe that's the ultimate explanation of my Emmy perplexity. If so, I'd just as soon not know it.

IV RESPONSE AND PERSPECTIVES

In these last chapters I discuss possible implications and ramifications of the Experiments in Musical Intelligence program. This is a difficult task to attempt without sounding arrogant. Therefore, I hope that you will forgive me by mentally inserting an "I think," or a variation of your preference, before each statement. By so doing you will save me having to repeat myself and, I hope, help me sound less presumptuous.

As I stated in the opening paragraph of this book, I feel that many of the principles incorporated into Experiments in Musical Intelligence imitate principles found in nature. One of the reasons I feel this way is that Experiments in Musical Intelligence actually works. My theories are not just abstract ideas; they have produced a body of results. I believe that we live in a recombinant universe and I continue to explore the wonder of what I believe are its myriad and compelling mysteries.

17 Response to Commentaries

In this chapter I respond to the various commentaries presented in chapters 11 through 16. I reference each commentary in chapter order followed by a few comparative analyses. I do not attempt to finalize matters with my responses, but rather express my opinion wherever it seems important to do so. I also do not pretend to be thorough, but rather deal with the issues which I feel require a response.

Eleanor Selfridge-Field

Eleanor Selfridge-Field makes a number of key points in her articulate philosophical contextualization of the Experiments in Musical Intelligence program. Like many others who have studied the program's output, she focuses on comparisons between its processes and those of human composers.

How can it [Experiments in Musical Intelligence] be understood in relation to entirely human procedures for creating musical works? How can it be understood in relation to traditional definitions of and procedures for composition? How can it be understood in relation to intuitive ideas of the hallowed "compositional process?" Or in relation to logical rationales of the piecing together of tones into works?

I believe that to some extent all composers use recombinancy as a compositional process (see Cope 1996, chapter 1). Certainly, at the simplest level, composers create by recombining notes and durations. Rudolph Réti (1962) and others have made similar cases for motivic recombination. I suggest that transformational recombinancy represents an important approach to composition, even composition involving highly formalistic models such as fugues or serialism. I discuss this further and in more depth under Music Composition and Theory in chapter 18.

Eleanor later rephrases her questions, adding a revealing word:

Do the Experiments in Musical Intelligence program's procedures, as distinct from its results, in any way *simulate* the subconscious choices made by human composers in the process of composing? Is there any chance that combinatorics of the kind used by the program *simulate* real processes in the human brain?   (Italics mine)

Note here Eleanor's use of the word "simulate." Near the end of her commentary she continues to ask:

The question of whether the computer simulation of musical styles is epistemologically the same as composition is less well explored. From a philosophical perspective, simulation is not the same as the activity being simulated. It is not the thing itself. It is an approximation, a representation, an abstraction.

Just because I use Experiments in Musical Intelligence to create new instances of music in various known styles, it does not follow for me that the program's processes are approximations, representations, or abstractions of individual works rather than musical styles. However, from this point on in her commentary, Eleanor refers to Experiments in Musical Intelligence's works as "simulations." She thus separates these works from what she apparently perceives as more *legitimate* compositions created by human composers. I do not find Jonathan Berger's intimation (discussed later) that the program's works are "models" any more palatable.

Early in 1992 I had Experiments in Musical Intelligence compose 5000 works using a small database of Stravinsky's music and then insert the program's output into the database, replacing the original Stravinsky (see Cope 1996, chapter 7, for examples of output). I hoped that the program would develop its own style which I believe that it did, ultimately. This past year, having both listened to and converted a number of the works (including a symphony and five piano sonatas) into music notation, I personally composed a work *in the style of Experiments in Musical Intelligence*. In effect, I reversed the process by which my program creates music. My question is, Which of these two works are the "simulations?" The tables have turned—thus I presume my imitative work is the simulation. However, being human and having spent a significant amount of time composing this new work, I flatly reject that label. I argue that my work has more inspiration and intuition than Experiments in Musical Intelligence works have. However, if you maintain that the program's works are simulations, then we can deduce the true rationale for using the term "simulation" instead of "composition": machine programs cannot, in this narrow view, compose real music—a singularly homocentric and seriously limited view of creativity.

In his book *Fluid Concepts and Creative Analogies* (1995) Doug Hofstadter discusses creativity in terms similar to my own. Here, he references his Letter Spirit program, which models central aspects of human creativity on a computer.

In genuine human creation (and in our slowly-coming-into-being Letter Spirit architecture), any design decision made during the creation of one letter has some chance of influencing the design of all the other letters in the gridfont—even supposedly "finished" ones. Indeed, one single tiny decision, made just when one thought one was finally approaching the *end* of the process, can trigger a cascade of related decisions throughout the alphabet and thus lead to an avalanche, forcing total reconsideration of every decision made, and the possible reconstruction of every single letter. This inherent unpredictability and instability of what one is doing is precisely the excitement and magic of the genuine creative act. It is closely related to the idea we described earlier, of a system's *making its own decisions*.   (p. 463)

Though Experiments in Musical Intelligence does not quite work in this way, SPEAC decisions can in fact create a "cascade of related decisions." The recursive version of the program, which I discuss briefly in chapter 3, reevaluates controller levels on failed output, thus causing reconsideration of many decisions during composition. The overarching goal of Letter Spirit is to impart "a sense of deep style to a machine." (Hofstadter 1995, p. 407) Indeed, that is the goal for Experiments in Musical Intelligence as well.

Jim Aikin frames Eleanor's last question from a slightly different vantage point:

No, the question that interests me is subtler. The question is, is it even theoretically possible for a computer program, no matter how sophisticated, to produce good Mozart? I claim it's not. The reason is because Mozart—the real Mozart—was a holistic analog phenomenon, not a reductionist digital phenomenon. The real Mozart had unconscious drives, turbulent flashes of emotion, and a sly sense of humor.   (Aikin 1993, p. 25)

Interestingly, Aikin reveals his bias toward programs like Experiments in Musical Intelligence and virtual music in general; even before hearing a work, he categorically rejects any effectiveness it might otherwise have. Aikin also confuses Mozart's music with Mozart the person, a common misperception (see particularly The Role of Intention in chapter 18).

In an interview, noted American composer George Crumb comments on style imitations in which he argues that even human composers cannot compose effective style imitations:

G.C. I personally don't think that such music would be viable; it would be second-hand, derivative. Any good composer can of course duplicate the external characteristics of any given style, but it would be impossible for such music to be anything more than an academic exercise. I can imagine using a short passage of traditional music as a quotation or quasi-quotation, juxtaposed with other music, but anything in excess of this would lack validity in my opinion. (Shuffett 1980, p. 30)

Clearly Crumb would agree with Aikin in his contention that computer-composed music in the styles of certain composers cannot, a priori, be successful. I find such closed-mindedness rampant when I speak on Experiments in Musical Intelligence to audiences with different amounts of musical education: musically sophisticated audiences react in basically the same way as musically naive audiences.

Let me state the obvious: Experiments in Musical Intelligence does not hear, see, or feel. At its simplest level, the program only adds and subtracts, the binary sine qua non of computers. However, I contend that the works of Experiments in Musical Intelligence have a rich and deep context, similar to the contexts provided by human composers. While the program is not visceral or self-aware, this context can provide listeners with a wealth of comparable, if not equivalent, contexts for their listening experiences. For example, as a result of the manner in which Experiments in Musical Intelligence composes new works, the music in the database at the time of composition contributes to the overall meaning of the program's compositions. As well, different virtual music programs will, by virtue of their coding, create different types of output even when emulating the same composer. Therefore, Experiments in Musical Intelligence has a style of its own. No matter how effectively it may compose in the style of a particular composer, I can hear elements of the program that add a distinctive quality, unmistakably the result of the manner in which the program composes. Music composed in known styles will also, regardless of human or machine origin, contextualize a composition (see and listen to the machine-composed Scarlatti, Brahms, Joplin, and Bartók in appendix D as examples of this contextualization). Possibly most important, like human-composed music, virtual music has performers who invest performance practice and personal interpretation into their performances. These critically important aspects of musical perception should not be dismissed.

Eleanor expresses her assessment of the role of the programmer:

The program could not have invented itself. It is entirely dependent on human existence for its own existence. To consider that what Experiments in Musical Intelligence does is an entirely automatic process is to miss the fact of this dependency. The program's functional context remains bounded by human values.

Though it is hard to disagree with this assertion, I should point out the obvious: Mozart also did not invent himself, nor was he unbounded by the human values of his culture and historical context.

One of the more important aspects of Eleanor's contribution is her articulation of one of the basic tenets of the Experiments in Musical Intelligence program:

What is most conspicuous in the comparison of Experiments in Musical Intelligence to most other systems is that Experiments in Musical Intelligence opts for more data and fewer rules. In a sense it invests almost all of its capacity for specificity in patterns and very little in procedure.

From the earliest days following my first attempts at four-part Bach-style rules-based composition, I have attempted to have the program rely as exclusively as possible on the data in its database rather than on rules that I provided. Whenever I was faced with questions of how to handle particular compositional processes (cadence, points of arrival, form, etc.), I focused on the analysis of music in the database. It was this approach that I felt, and still feel today, would provide the most authentic approach to style inheritance.

Interestingly, both Doug and Eleanor invoke the name of Hegel in their contributions, but for very different reasons. Doug uses a Hegel quote as a template for n-gram-frequency generations as examples for his thoughts on computer-generated prose. Doug's Hegel quote, a particularly opaque fragment, seems well suited to demonstrate a kind of style inheritance—the computer-created prose appearing as indecipherable as the original Hegel initially appears to be. Eleanor in contrast, relates a particularly lucid quote from Hegel:

The objection that works of art elude the treatment of scientific thought because they originate out of *unregulated fancy* and *out of feelings* ... and therefore take effect only on feelings and imagination ... raises a problem ...

She further notes that Hegel believed that a "concrete universal was entirely possible in music." I agree with Hegel to the extent that to shroud works of art in the mysteries of emotion is delusionary. This type of thinking has often kept the study of art in the Dark Ages. It is not that I believe that art and music can be explained completely and empirically, but only that we have barely scratched the surface of what we *can* understand.

Bernie Greenberg

Bernie begins his commentary by asserting that

Artistic beauty is in the eye, ear, and mind of the beholder, not necessarily the artist, let alone the art.

I agree with this comment and particularly with Bernie's careful use of the phrase "not necessarily." However, he often speaks about emotional content, a reference which Doug Hofstadter makes as well. For example, Bernie notes that

While Cope makes significant headway on the modeling of formal architecture (the program's Mozartean works, the operatic overture in particular, achieve quite remarkable success in this regard), that notion remains tantalizingly distinct from emotional architecture.

and

Without some attempt at modeling the space of emotional dynamics, that is, drama, one cannot hope to create emotionally fulfilling art.

Bernie alludes to some difficult terrain. I have no idea what "emotional architecture" is, no less how to program it. I do not think, however, that Bernie questions the possibility that computers will eventually produce music he can emotionally appreciate. In fact, he already seems to find emotional content in some of the Experiments in Musical Intelligence output:

The program's melding of Bach and Beethoven in its resynthesis of the *Moonlight Sonata* needs no credentials beyond its own manifest beauty. When I heard it on National Public Radio some weeks before the symposium absent any revelation of its genesis, I was moved by it as pure music.

Of course, I assume that being "moved" by this work equates to being "emotionally moved."

I am often struck by the emotional connection which many have to "In the Mood," a popular song from the 1940s performed most notably by the Glenn Miller Band. This repetitive and banal melody—if it can be called a melody at all—has, to my thinking at least, almost no intrinsic musical value. However, to someone who lived during the 1940s, this music seems to embody the wartime spirit in America and the era of swing music (see Miller 1999, 2000). As basically an exercise in simple triadic outlines on a syncopated rhythmic palette, there is nothing about this music that would suggest its popularity. Jazz bandleaders that I know complain of its inordinate difficulty compared to its musical worth and the disproportionate number of requests they get to perform it compared to more musically rewarding swing music. Clearly the context for this music does not arise entirely from the intentionality of its composer but rather from the circumstances and attendant emotions of its performances during World War II. Indeed, the success of "In the Mood" most likely derives from blind luck rather than intention.

As another example of the importance of this kind of context, I was recently hired to use the Experiments in Musical Intelligence program to create a world anthem. I used 186 national anthems as models for the program. In order to properly translate this music to a database I had to check each anthem for errors, a task I completed by ear. Two things struck me during the dozens of hours I sat listening to these anthems. First, to me, anthems represent the simplest, most derivative, and dullest repertoire in the world. The two or three anthems that held my attention did so by contrast to the blandness of the others, not by any true uniqueness or beauty of their own. Second, and with little doubt, anthems have the most devoted following of any music in the world. Anthems endure as long as countries endure and produce rapt attention and emotional reactions like few other musical forms. Anthems survive their various demeaning orchestrations and the often fickle shifts of popular styles. For me at least, the musical quality of anthems often seems inversely proportional to the esteem with which they are held.

In both of these cases, Miller's "In the Mood" and national anthems, the effect of the music clearly derives from listener-perceived context and has little or nothing to do with the music itself. There are, of course, many other examples of this sort of contextual persuasion. I believe that to some degree we hear *all* music with similar kinds of context. For example, the context in which we hear a work for the first time greatly influences our perception of it on subsequent hearings. Composer or performer intention often has little or nothing to do with this perception. Without the prejudgment created by foreknowledge that a work was created by a machine program, virtual music can engender just as much of this context—and hence perceived meaning—as any piece of human-composed music. (See chapter 18 under Music Cognition for further thoughts.)

Bernie's comments on the shortcomings of many of the program's works are very well taken. For example, he notes that

> In short, the counterpoint evidenced in the output of Cope's composing program is far too timid for Bach.

This is certainly true. As mentioned in chapter 6, counterpoint is not inherited from databases in Experiments in Musical Intelligence. Counterpoint results from a separate subprogram which has many shortcomings. Ultimately, however, I hope to devise a technique whereby Experiments in Musical Intelligence will inherit contrapuntal forms from the music in its database as it does other aspects of composition.

Steve Larson

In a lively series of letters to a perceived—human—student, Steve argues that

> the order of keys and meters you use differs only very slightly from Bach's ... why didn't you follow his scheme more exactly?

As Eleanor Selfridge-Field points out in her commentary, "these works are not in Bb. It is only these specific realizations which are in this key." I choose keys for Experiments in Musical Intelligence in order to make the program's works more playable. In the instance to which Steve refers, the key differences are exclusively the result of such attempts.

Steve further observes:

> ... in some places, you quote big chunks of motivically distinctive material. For example, your Invention no. 8 ... begins very much like Bach's Invention no. 9.

I note here how Steve inadvertently conflates the word "quote" with "very much like." Quotations do occasionally occur in Experiments in Musical Intelligence output as a natural consequence of the processes used for composition. Of course, Bach often uses quotation himself (as in the chorales and cantatas where, usually, at least part of one line is a quotation from a hymn or other sacred melody). Steve later acknowledges aspects of Bach's own quotation:

> And Bach *recycled* his own material, too.

Doug Hofstadter accurately describes Experiments in Musical Intelligence's quotation a little differently:

Admittedly, there are episodes in some of Emmy's two-part inventions that clearly come from specific Bach inventions, but that is probably because only a couple of inventions were being drawn on in those cases.

The smaller the database, the more potential there is for quotation in Experiments in Musical Intelligence output. In fact, while fifteen inventions seems like a great deal of music, it actually represents a very small amount of data.

However, I don't share the aversion to quotation that many critics apparently have. Quotation can be as difficult to effectively place as creating original material. For example, one could imagine a new play being written by a computer program in similar fashion to Experiments in Musical Intelligence. Such a program could have access to a database of similar-style plays (using Shakespeare and Tennessee Williams would obviously not work well). Next, the program would have to fashion a new plot that makes sense and define a set of characters to engage that plot. Then, this program would have to create realistic dialogue between those characters that equally fit the style of the original plays in the database. This dialogue would also have to move the direction of the plot toward its desired end. If, in the progress of interlacing these complicated and often competing elements, there were moments when a character, for a moment or two, seemed to be quoting or paraphrasing one of the characters in one of the plays in the database, it could be forgiven, especially if the play otherwise succeeded. After all, imagine the complexities of getting "My kingdom for a horse" to work even half so well in new surroundings as it does in the original. It seems equally complex to logically integrate a musical quote into the fabric of a new composition, particularly an invention or fugue with all of their attendant constraints.

Steve articulates another view of quotation in his commentary:

I always feel more creative (or at least that my "theft" is less recognizable as such) when I steal Bach's "instructions" (altering the "ingredients") rather than when I steal his "ingredients" (especially if we equate ingredients with specific melodic material instead of underlying patterns of rhythm or pitch).

I suggest that voice-leading represents Bach's instructions and hence, while Steve implies that Experiments in Musical Intelligence uses ingredients, I assert that the program actually uses instructions. Unfortunately, using instructions does not exclude the possibility of quotation. The program's Invention no. 2 using fourth-species counterpoint is just such an example. Following Bach's—and Fux's—voice-leading instructions produced an example that almost duplicates Bach's own solution in his Invention no. 6 (see Bach in appendix D).

Signatures represent another type of quotation. Steve describes signatures in a revealing but oblique way:

I don't think composers really work with anything as microscopic as notes. Perhaps the ingredients include motives or, even better, the pitch and rhythm patterns that make up motives or that combine them in various ways.

I can't imagine that composers actually think in terms of individual notes either. I personally compose more often in terms of motives and consider that Experiments in Musical Intelligence, by virtue of its approach to transformational recombinancy and signatures, uses motives for composing as well. I further examine quotation and the degree to which it affects music cognition in chapter 18.

Jonathan Berger

Jonathan Berger's commentary casts a somewhat different light on Experiments in Musical Intelligence's approach to composition. He proposes

that creativity is in the ear of the beholder.

Steve, interestingly, seems to agree somewhat with Jonathan:

I think that this is where the essence of real musical creativity lies: in the ability to listen discerningly.

and to some extent so does Bernie as I mention earlier:

Artistic beauty is in the eye, ear, and mind of the beholder, not necessarily the artist, let alone the art.

Certainly Doug Hofstadter would disagree with this point of view. Doug argues (in chapter 16) that "to claim that the active involvement of our recipient brains transfers all credit for greatness and depth from the creator to the recipient is nonsense." I again argue (see chapter 3) that greatness is not an empirical judgment.

While I do not agree with Jonathan's assertion that creativity occurs exclusively in the ear of the beholder, I genuinely appreciate his focus on the listener's contribution to the musical experience.

Composition at its best provides a framework within which a listener's attention is drawn, sometimes by seduction, other times by force, but always by manipulation of expectations and realizations.

Here, Jonathan mirrors my own processes with SPEAC and, to some extent, earmarks. Doug Hofstadter terms this "the *tension-resolution status*" (italics mine). Jonathan adds that:

We not only expect *what* will happen, but also *when* it will happen.

I further engage the important issues raised by the relationships of listeners to Experiments in Musical Intelligence music under Music Cognition in chapter 18.

Dan Dennett

I find Dan Dennett's following statement extremely enlightening:

Life on earth has been generated over billions of years in a single branching tree—the Tree of Life—by one algorithmic process or another.

Not only does Dan relate algorithmic processing to the work of human composers (as I do here and in Cope 2000) but he connects it to life itself.

Dan continues:

Many find this vision of creativity deeply unsettling—some would add that it is not just unsettling; it is crass, shallow, philistine, despicable, or even obscene.

In contrast, I find this vision not only supportive of the approaches that I have taken in Experiments in Musical Intelligence but natural and completely logical.

However, after describing the virtual worlds of Karl Sims, Dan subsequently argues that

What's missing in Sims's world of evolving virtual creatures, is, in a word, *concreteness*.

This argument relates as well to Experiments in Musical Intelligence's lack of experience in the real world for which its output is destined. If we compare artificial creativity only to human models, then such discrepancies will no doubt prosper and even continue to widen. I submit that using models other than human ones might be useful objectives for our computer-generated virtual realities. Only hubris would suggest that human-perceived reality represents the only reality worth our attempts to imitate. However, Dan provides a good rationale for various types of realities:

... the shortcomings—such as they are—of Experiments in Musical Intelligence have nothing to do with carbon vs. silicon, biology vs. engineering, humanity vs. robotity. Concentrating on these familiar—indeed threadbare—candidates for crucial disqualifiers is succumbing to misdirection.

Doug agrees with Dan and comments that he

can imagine ideas and meanings and emotions and a first-person awareness of the world (an "inner light," a "ghost in the machine") emerging from electronic circuitry as easily as from proteins and nucleic acids.

Comparing these thoughts to Eleanor Selfridge-Field's comments (see my earlier references in this chapter) on the importance of relating Experiments in Musical Intelligence only to human creativity highlights another difference in viewpoints among the commentaries in this book.

Alan Turing (1950) warns us that while machines might suffer from inadequacies in some arenas, they certainly excel in others:

We do not wish to penalize the machine for its inability to shine in beauty competitions, nor to penalize a man for losing in a race against an airplane.   (p. 435)

Dan further draws the important corollary that

... when you're modeling creativity, there should be junk lying around that your creative processes can bump into, noises that your creative processes can't help overhearing.

and posits

noise as a potential source of signal, as something that it *might* turn, by the alchemy of the creative algorithm, into function, into art, into meaning.

I have recently added extraneous but not unrelated music to otherwise consistent Experiments in Musical Intelligence databases with the hope of creating something similar to this "noise." My efforts, however, have not produced successful results thus far.

Dan's assertion that

Human music doesn't mean anything, however wonderful it is.

seems far too simplistic. For example, Jonathan would argue that music means whatever the listener wants it to mean. Doug, on the other hand, hears "meaning all over the place in music." To Bernie Greenberg, Bach's music captures deep religious angst. Dan might argue, however, that Bernie hears these profound utterances by virtue of knowing about Bach's life and Bach's beliefs, and thus that Bernie hears only what he wishes to hear rather than what is actually present.

To Lewis Carroll (1975)—in *Alice's Adventures in Wonderland*—meaning seems equally evasive:

"Then you should say what you mean," the March Hare went on.
"I do," Alice hastily replied; "at least—at least I mean what I say—that's the same thing, you know."
"Not the same thing a bit!" said the Hatter. "Why, you might just as well say that 'I see what I eat' is the same thing as 'I eat what I see!'"
"You might just as well say," added the March Hare, "that 'I like what I get' is the same thing as 'I get what I like!'"
"You might just as well say," added the Dormouse, which seemed to be talking in his sleep, "that 'I breathe when I sleep' is the same thing as 'I sleep when I breathe!'"   (p. 84)

Dan's comment about music not having meaning reminds me of the deceptiveness of language. We assign names to both actions and things and then believe that by so doing we have divined their meaning. All we actually have done is create a catalog of names. When our catalog becomes very complex and these names develop evolving histories filled with cross-references, we can be fooled into thinking that all of this cataloging actually provides an understanding of the world around us. This is only a subterfuge.

Music on the other hand, does not name things, but rather consists of abstract relationships—a kind of aural architecture. Music therefore fails at giving us an effective catalog of names. In contrast to language, music's coherence and structure depend on balance and resolution of tension. However, music *does* share with language the evolving histories filled with cross-references. As one example, there is a moment near the end of Gustav Mahler's Eighth Symphony, the so-called *Symphony of a Thousand*, that I am convinced summarizes many similar moments in Western music—endings of large works by composers whose music Mahler had intimate familiarity with as a conductor. I hear Beethoven, Mozart, and Bach in Mahler's music, a veritable who's who of music history. Listeners not steeped in such literature cannot begin to understand how Mahler's music works. Those listeners who do have this background, however, can savor these moments, which are rooted in and allude to an extraordinary lineage of composers and musical ideas. These lineages represent a form of musical meaning. By virtue of the processes it uses to compose, Experiments in Musical Intelligence's music holds many of these same treasures. While some may argue that the program's examples lack intention, I suggest that Mahler was probably unaware of much of the interplay of history in his own music as well.

Meaning in music also depends on many related conditions: the cultural background of listeners, the previous musical experience of listeners, the quality of performance, the mood of listeners, the physical health of listeners, and so on. To suggest that there is one coherent meaning or experience shared by all to a single work ignores these and other important human variables.

Doug Hofstadter

I have responded to many of Doug's comments elsewhere in this book, particularly in chapter 3. However, one particular comment in chapter 16 deserves further discussion. Doug's questioner states rather emphatically:

... all a composer can do is create a situation in which music will happen in some of the audience members' minds.

Doug responds:

I think this is a grotesque twist on the truth.

Like Doug, I cannot simply ascribe all the meaning I derive from music to myself. Here is one of my favorite examples of such musical meaning. At a certain point in Tchaikovsky's overture to *Romeo and Juliet*, the music arrives at a dominant-seventh chord in the key of C major. This G–B–D–F chord lingers almost interminably while a motivic fragment repeats ominously. At one point, unbeknownst to the audience, Tchaikovsky respells the F of the dominant-seventh chord as an E-sharp, making it a German augmented-sixth chord in the key of B major or B minor. The actual sound of the chord does not change, only its spelling in the score. Tchaikovsky then moves this German augmented-sixth chord to the tonic six-four chord in B major. As if falling through a hidden trap door, the music moves from a key signature of no sharps or flats to a key signature of five sharps. These kinds of key relations occur in many late Romantic works. However, Tchaikovsky makes unique use of the modulation by his long-held preparatory dominant-seventh chord.

As a child, having no knowledge of Shakespeare's *Romeo and Juliet*, little previous experience with Tchaikovsky's music, and certainly no understanding of key signatures or music theory, this powerful moment spoke to me in ways that fifty years later I can still vividly remember. Telling me that what I felt was a figment of my listener's imagination is laughable. So powerful was my experience with this work that I, at age twelve, went directly to a music store and purchased their last piano score to *Romeo and Juliet* with my life savings. I had to know what it was that held so much *meaning* for me. Whether my interpretation of this music coincided precisely with the composer's intentions seems unimportant. That I could understand the actual musical events that caused my perception *is* important.

This story recalls Doug Hofstadter's remarks which I mentioned earlier in this chapter in response to Dan's comments on music lacking meaning:

I personally think that I hear meaning all over the place in music, but it is very hard for me to explain this meaningfulness in words.

I take up the subject of this wonderful quote again in more depth in chapter 18.

The Commentaries as a Group

The commentaries disagree most intensely on the definition and role of machine creativity. For example, Doug Hofstadter remarks:

... *if* audiences clamored for more and more of them [Experiments in Musical Intelligence works], then I would feel I would have to despondently throw in the towel as a researcher who is seeking the mechanisms of creativity.

I would, in contrast, be all the *more* interested in seeking the "mechanisms of creativity" were this the case. Eleanor Selfridge-Field notes that creativity has both understandable and vague domains:

Creativity lies both within and without the domain of cognitive studies

while Steve Larson relates creativity almost entirely to cognition:

I think that this is where the essence of real musical creativity lies: in the ability to listen discerningly.

Jonathan Berger relates creativity almost solely to the listening experience:

Thus an understanding of expectations enlightens our understanding of creativity

while Dan Dennett views creativity as accidental:

The exploitation of accidents is the key to creativity, whether what is being made is a new genome, a new behavior, or a new melody.

Many of the commentaries, certainly Doug's and Bernie's, argue for the "deep," "emotional," "soul" of human-created art. My problem remains however: how to react to such vague and undefined terms with anything but vague and undefined responses. I don't mean to denigrate these ideas; indeed, the terms have probably been used as properly and elegantly as they can be. For me, however, using words like "deep," "emotional," and "soul"—repositories for what we *can't* explain— to *explain* ideas seems contradictory.

18 Perspectives and the Future

As verified by the sheer volume of articles and interviews about Experiments in Musical Intelligence which have appeared since 1987, the program continues to challenge many listeners' assumptions about creativity, inspiration, and how and why we listen to music. Such challenges, it seems to me, are healthy and reveal many facets of how we perceive music. In this chapter I discuss some aspects of Experiments in Musical Intelligence's relevance to artificial intelligence, artificial creativity, and music cognition, as well as provide a few thoughts about the future. I apologize for occasionally lapsing into rhapsodic collages; so many of these issues interrelate that it is often difficult to clearly separate one from another.

Artificial Intelligence and Artificial Creativity

Current approaches to artificial intelligence include (1) expert (rule-based) systems; (2) fuzzy sets; (3) genetic algorithms; (4) intelligent agents; and (5) neural networks. In some ways Experiments in Musical Intelligence represents a hybrid of many of these processes. For example, pattern-matching can be seen as a simple form of fuzzy sets. Experiments in Musical Intelligence uses a small expert system for counterpoint. Association nets (discussed shortly) broadly resemble the connectivity of neural nets. In most ways, however, the processes that Experiments in Musical Intelligence uses are unlike any of these approaches to artificial intelligence. The program is, rather, database dependent with parsing (analysis) and generational (composing) components. Many of my writings also refer to the program's primary engine as an ATN (augmented transition network; see Cope 1996, chapters 1 and 5 for in-depth descriptions of this process) grammar.

As a grammar, Experiments in Musical Intelligence inherits both its attributes and drawbacks from natural language processes. The principal advantage of using such grammars, for me at least, is that programs using these grammars develop both their syntax and semantics from examples (data), thus remaining relatively unbiased. The principal weakness of using language models is the need to segment music into groupings (beats, motives, measures, phrases, etc.) which may very well be artificial.

Linguist Benjamin Whorf (1956) resonates with my musical worries in expressing his own more general concerns about the efficacy of segmentation:

We cut up and organize the spread and flow of events as we do, largely because, through our mother tongue, we are parties to an agreement to do so, not because nature itself is segmented in exactly that way for all to see. Languages differ not only in how they build their sentences but also in how they break down nature to secure elements to put in those sentences ... By these more or less distinct terms we ascribe a semifictitious isolation to parts of experience ... Indeed this is the implicit picture of classical physics and astronomy—that the universe is essentially a collection of detached objects of different sizes ... The real question is: What do different languages do, not with those artificially isolated objects but with the flowing face of nature in its motion, color, and changing form; with clouds, beaches, and yonder flight of birds? For, as goes our segmentation of the face of nature, so goes our physics of the Cosmos.   (pp. 240–1)

This insightful passage brings into question whether or not our use of language fundamentally distorts our interpretation of the universe (see also my response to Dan Dennett in chapter 17). Without question, Whorf's arguments pose serious concerns about the processes used by the Experiments in Musical Intelligence program. Music is analog or continuous in nature, not digital or fragmented, and any method of segmenting it into separate groupings may impose a degree of artificiality and arbitrariness to it.

At the same time, natural language processes offer important opportunities for understanding and analyzing music. I recently spoke to a professional biologist who is in the process of creating a video game to teach young people about biology. His tack involves a kind of virtual reality wherein users "become" a particular animal or insect and then, following a kind of genetic algorithm, attempt to survive in a world filled with punishments and rewards. He first described how the user, in this case acting as a bee, would leave the hive, find a field of flowers, and then return to communicate its find to its fellow bees. I asked this biologist what kind of language bees used to communicate such information. He then described a dance where the bee indicates direction by aligning its body with the field. He continued by demonstrating the bee's motion to communicate distance, which he called "wiggling its butt." Each wiggle represents a unit of distance measurement which other bees understand. The animals this biologist had programmed included lizards, which I subsequently learned communicate, in part, through the language of head-bobbing. This biologist convinced me that we encounter languages in many different forms everywhere we look. Music may be one of these languages, one which we simply have not yet fully plumbed, and one that may yet reveal important truths from its depths.

Beyond its focus on language and grammar, Experiments in Musical Intelligence holds other interesting correlations with artificial intelligence. First, finding voice-leading rules in databases and then applying those rules to create new instances of stylistically related output was, in 1980 at least, a somewhat unusual approach to composing music. As I pointed out in chapter 1, most researchers in this area (e.g., Hiller and Isaacson 1959, Schottstaedt 1989, Ebcioğlu 1987, 1992) use expert systems where rules are supplied by the program's creator rather than derived from music in a database. Second, while pattern-matching was, and is, a common staple of the artificial intelligence community, finding and reintroducing matched patterns (signatures) in new instances of output remains fairly unusual. I continue to find the lack of interest in this highly rewarding process astounding. Third, and possibly most important, my introduction and use of association nets remains unique to my work. Association nets are simple yet powerful tools for inductive learning and thus deserve explanation here.

I use an association net in a program I created in the early 1990s called BackTalk (see Cope 2000). BackTalk "learns" from positive and negative input provided by a human collaborator. While I refrain from calling this process intelligent—preferring to believe that intelligence requires life—I do refer to BackTalk's use of an association net as "intelligent-like."

Association nets resemble neural nets in some respects (Loy and Todd 1991; Hörnel and Menzel 1998). However, there are a number of important differences between these two processes. Neural nets are generally fixed in terms of their nodal content while association nets can have an unlimited number of interconnected nodes. Neural nets also require training through a process known as "backpropagation," which redirects output back through the net as input as many times as necessary to train the net to match or approximate its input. While association nets can chain backward as well as forward, they do not backpropagate as do neural nets. Association nets do not, therefore, require the same kind of training as neural nets. Finally, and possibly most important, association nets do not have hidden units, as do neural nets. The nodes in association nets can be accessed at any time, revealing all of their explicit and implicit associations.

BackTalk takes many types of input. For example, the program can "learn" any language, including artificial languages. Here is a brief example of the beginning of an English language conversation with BackTalk taken from chapter 2 of *The Algorithmic Composer* (Cope 2000).

U: What is your name?

U: My name is David!

C: name?

U: Your name is Computer!

C: name?

U: What is your name?

C: Computer!

U: What is my name?

C: David!

	what	is	your	name?	my	name	david!	computer!
what		3.7	1.4	7.61	1.0	1.0	1.72	1.72
is	1.6		2.5	7.43	1.7	1.2	3.27	3.17
your	1.3	2.1		6.9	1.0	1.5	1.72	2.57
name?	1.2	2.0	1.2		1.0	1.0	1.72	1.72
my	1.0	1.8	1.0	4.69		1.4	2.57	1.62
name	1.0	2.7	1.0	3.24	0.9		2.19	2.47
david!	0.9	1.4	0.9	3.14	0.6	0.6		1.52
computer!	0.9	1.0	0.6	3.14	0.5	0.2	0.1	

Figure 18.1
A grid showing the weightings for all word connections in BackTalk.

BackTalk has no foreknowledge of *any* language and thus at the beginning of this conversation it has no knowledge of the English language. However, BackTalk does not simply parrot the user's input. The program consists of multiconnected nodes and weightings which help it to slowly adapt to its input. The use of a single word for No (indicated by the use of an asterisk) helps BackTalk recalculate its weights and conform to users' preferences. Thus the program could be said to learn. Figure 18.1 shows BackTalk's weightings for the conversation just given. The words "what" and "is" have almost identical weightings between "david!" and "computer!" However, the words "your" and "name?" favor "computer!" while the weights for "my" and "name?" favor "david!"

Experiments in Musical Intelligence currently uses an association net similar to the one in BackTalk. Therefore, whatever intelligent-like behavior one might ascribe to BackTalk must be similarly ascribed to Experiments in Musical Intelligence. Musically, the program equates user rejection of works with the use of an asterisk. Thus, by virtue of its ability to adapt, Experiments in Musical Intelligence achieves a measure of the user's aesthetic differentiation. I believe that some of the program's more recent compositions, particularly its larger-scale works in the forms of symphonies and concerti, have been effective primarily because of the presence of an association net.

Artificial creativity, a subclass of artificial intelligence, centers on studies of human creative processes. Human creativity is typically defined as "novel and useful solutions to problems" (Koestler 1964; Wallas 1926; Weisberg 1986). For Experiments in Musical Intelligence, the main problem is how to create effective new music from old models. The solutions to this problem—the music that the program produces—obviously vary in degree of quality. However, the program has challenged listeners with its unique results, many of which give the impression of having been composed creatively.

Creativity requires the ability to think "outside of the box." For example, here is a classic artificial intelligence puzzle that requires a certain amount of creativity to solve:

Puzzle: Of eight gold coins, one weighs slightly more than the rest. You must, using a balance scale and only two weighings, find the heavier coin.

The obvious first step, that of splitting the eight coins into two groups of four coins and weighing them against one another, and thus eliminating four coins from the puzzle, results in three weighings to achieve an answer, not two. The solution lies in the creative decision to leave some coins out of the weighing—a solution that reveals a hidden variable in the weighing process.

Solution: Put two coins aside and weigh the remaining two groups of three coins against one another. If the scale balances, then weigh the two set-aside coins to find the heaviest. Otherwise, take the heaviest group of three coins, set one aside, and then weigh the remaining two. Either the scale will balance, indicating the set-aside coin as the heaviest, or the scale will indicate the heaviest coin.

A computer program can easily be written to solve this puzzle. The problem, however, is that such a program will not be able to solve new puzzles unless these puzzles conform to the same basic structure as the one just described. For example, the following variation on the classic so-called Missionaries and Cannibals puzzle requires the same basic process as the coin puzzle (thinking outside of the box), but does not conform to it structurally:

Puzzle: A rancher has a chicken, a fox, and a bag of grain. Using a boat that will allow only one of these to accompany him, he must transport all three to the other side of a river. Unfortunately, if left unattended together, the fox will eat the chicken. Likewise, if left unattended, the chicken will eat the grain. The rancher does not want either of these to occur. How does the rancher transport all three to the other side of the river safely?

The principle found in the first puzzle, that of expanding the possibilities, will produce a successful solution to this rancher puzzle as well. The solution requires taking advantage of unused opportunities.

Solution: The rancher takes the chicken across the river first since the fox will not eat the grain while he's gone. When the rancher returns, he takes the fox across the river. The rancher then returns *with the chicken* since otherwise the fox would eat the chicken. The rancher then deposits the chicken back on the original side, transports the grain across the river, and then returns for the chicken.

In both of these puzzles, the creative solution lies in fully understanding the limits of the problem and carefully measuring the alternative solutions at each transition point in the puzzle using as few assumptions as possible. Computers can be programmed to deal with either puzzle and with different numbers of coins or different types of animals and grains. A single program that could solve both puzzles as well as others of a similar general type on its own would merit being called independently creative.

When I give these puzzles to students, I usually wait five minutes and call for a show of hands from those who think they have solved it. I usually get a 5 to 10 percent response. Before providing an answer, I ask the students to try again. This time, however, I suggest (in regard to the second puzzle, for example) that instead of regarding this as an abstract game, that they use some "method acting"—*become* the rancher who has to transport his chicken, his fox, and his grain across the river intact. I ask that they imaginatively place themselves in the boat. After another five minutes or so, I again call for a show of hands from those who think they have solved the problem. This time I usually get a 90 percent response and most of those who raise their hands have solved it correctly.

The difference, I believe, between the first approach—of abstracting the puzzle mathematically—and the second approach—of visualizing the actual events as they unfold—tells us something about creativity. When students take the rancher's role they no longer have a choice but to think without assumptions. Here's how:

1. They take the chicken across the river or else the fox eats the chicken or the chicken eats the grain;

2. They come back and get either the grain or the fox—either will do;

3. When they arrive at the other side the only alternative is to bring one of them back. They can't bring back the same one they just brought over, since that produces no net gain. Therefore, what had never occurred to them in the abstract becomes a necessity when the stakes seem real;

4. They exchange whatever they bring back to the original side with the remaining choice and the puzzle is solved.

The coin puzzle unravels almost as neatly when it becomes clear (as it must) that it can only be solved by three groups of coins.

Creativity, it seems to me, requires the engagement of real objects and real events and not their abstractions. Abstraction, which is a requirement for mathematics, language, and understanding most of the world around us, does not lend itself well to creativity. Interestingly, association nets do not abstract well. The simplest kinds of mathematics cause BackTalk no end of trouble. For example, when the program encounters nonlanguage problems such as those posed by mathematics, the net lacks the ability to deduce new solutions based on previous experience. For example, the program fails to derive the correct answer when the following are input:

one plus one is two!

two minus one is one!

one plus two is three!

what is three minus one?

Of course, an association net can be taught the correct answer to this question. However, when given the same basic problem but with different numbers, the program must learn from scratch rather than deduce an answer based on logic. Such calculations require the abstraction of words into concepts and principles—inductive reasoning—which association nets, by virtue of their rudimentary parsing system, can only vaguely approximate.

Importantly, however, as unlikely as it may seem given that these nets have no sense of the real world, no self-awareness, and no ability to method-act, association nets have their own reality. Given a fairly extended conversation upon which to build such a reality and provided with these two puzzles, association nets can usually solve them as well as many other problems of a similar type. Experiments in Musical Intelligence's musical problems often demand the same kind of creative solutions. To reach these solutions, I have the program's association net directly control certain variables that affect—particularly—pattern-matching for signatures, fine-tuning of SPEAC meanings, and the amount of unifications and "templagiarism" used in the output. In short, the program adapts in order to change certain aspects of its output (see Cope 1992b for more information about this approach). I believe that this kind of processing qualifies as creative, even using the most conservative meaning of that word.

However, a sense of the real world surely does not constitute the entire essence of creativity. All of us know people who work almost exclusively with the real world and who seemingly have very little creativity. One element missing from our considerations of creativity, it seems to me, concerns assumptions. Creativity questions assumptions so that solutions that might otherwise remain hidden reveal themselves. Here is another puzzle to help prove this point:

Puzzle: You must produce eight separate pieces from a newly baked cake while slicing it only three times with a bread knife.

Given the two previous puzzles and the advice above about assumptions, this puzzle should be relatively easy. Cakes may be sliced in many ways and method-acting will help solve the puzzle. Ultimately, however, one must remove the assumptions of how cakes can be sliced to solve this puzzle.

Solution: Cut the cake twice from the top down being sure to intersect the slices and then cut the cake once horizontally, breaking the resulting four slices into two pieces each for a total of eight pieces.

One would think that computers lack assumptions and that this aspect of creativity would be natural for them. However, the opposite is true: programmers who program those computers assume a great deal about their programming languages, their ultimate users, the problems their applications are meant to solve, and so on. I have attempted to avoid some of these pitfalls in my programming of Experiments in Musical Intelligence by relying whenever possible on the music in a database rather than on my own, heavily influenced by assumptions, biases.

For me, jazz improvisation provides an especially good example of creativity. Working within the boundaries created by the structured form of a given melody and harmony template, jazz improvisers guide their instruments through minefields of assumptions which the best of them constantly question. It would be hard to imagine a gifted jazz improviser sitting at a desk without an instrument and notating the intricate rhythmic nuances and pitch inflections innate to jazz. Anyone having improvised themselves would realize the futility by just imagining this. Anyone having heard a rote improvisation which doesn't question assumptions would immediately hear its lack of inspiration. For the gifted and truly creative jazz improviser, both the act of performing and questioning are necessary for the true art to emerge.

There is, then, a "what if" quality to creativity. What if this constraint did not exist? What if I could do such and such? Combining these qualities with a true sense of the problem through what I term method acting, can help solve otherwise intractable problems. I do not doubt that there are many other aspects of creativity that I have not covered here. However, the two I have discussed represent what I have tried to program into Experiments in Musical Intelligence.

Scott Turner, in his book *The Creative Process: A Computer Model of Storytelling* (1994), comments optimistically:

Someday computers will be artists. They'll be able to write amusing and original stories, invent and play games of unsurpassed complexity and inventiveness, tell jokes, and suffer writer's block. (p. ix)

I find this last comment particularly ironic, even Pirandelloesque, since it was just such a "writer's block" that led me to create Experiments in Musical Intelligence in the first place.

Music Cognition

The term "cognition" has become the word of choice recently to describe the process of *knowing*, or more succinctly: perceiving. Music cognition refers to how we perceive music and, more fundamentally, how we perceive meaning in music. Dowling and Harwood, in their book *Music Cognition* (1986), follow a classification system devised by the nineteenth-century philosopher Charles Peirce (1931–5, vol. 2). I have also found this approach quite useful in attempting to understand both perception and creativity. Peirce uses three basic categories: index, icon, and symbol. An *index* indicates an association which a listener has with a particular musical experience. In its simplest musical form, an index might be a recognizable quote—the ominous use of *Dies Irae*, for example, in music by Berlioz and Rachmaninoff. In more complex forms, an index can indicate a personal association a listener might feel, for example, on experiencing a work originally heard under special circumstances. An *icon* indicates an actual similarity of experiences. In its most obvious forms, icons could appear as tempo or metric imitations of running, dancing, and so on. In more subtle forms, icons can be closely tied to the recognition of commonly used patterns, and so on. A *symbol* achieves meaning through its syntax rather than association or recognition. Meaning is derived contextually from an event's relationship with neighboring symbols. For example, the play of tension and release over time in music depends on such syntactic relations and hence reveals symbols.

My own versions of Peirce's index, icon, and symbol involve associative context: universal, global, and local. Universal contexts parallel Peirce's indexes and involve paraphrasing and quotation from other composers and results from recombinance in Experiments in Musical Intelligence. Global contexts resemble Peirce's icons and in Experiments in Musical Intelligence take the form of signatures, earmarks, and other stylistic and formal patterns. Local contexts follow Peirce's idea of symbols in that context derives from preceding and following events. SPEAC accounts for local contexts in Experiments in Musical Intelligence.

In chapter 3 of my book *Experiments in Musical Intelligence* (1996), I describe a listening test given to college music majors with foreknowledge of the basic composing processes used by Experiments in Musical Intelligence. This foreknowledge included pattern-matching for signatures, a good example of Peirce's icon classification. Music by Mozart was mixed with computer-composed music in the style of Mozart by Experiments in Musical Intelligence, some of which contained signatures. The results indicated that signatures play a significant role in style recognition. Computer-composed works with signatures fared nearly as well as actual Mozart, while computer-composed music without signatures rated quite poorly.

In my experience, listeners tend to focus primarily on one of Peirce's three approaches to perception, although listening is dynamic, with context and multidimensionality playing significant roles. For example, listeners without a great deal of experience with a certain type of music will tend toward an indexical approach, at least in their initial experience, hearing whatever associations their interpretation allows. Listeners with a strong affinity for, but not a great knowledge of, a certain type of music will be more apt to hear music iconically, reacting to what they perceive as emotional or physical interconnections. Listeners having significant experience with a certain type of music will more likely react to the symbolic—or syntactical—relationships present. In other words, these listeners will hear patterns contextually. Interestingly, the more listeners understand the syntax of such symbols, the less perceptual and emotional sway it may hold over them.

Experiments in Musical Intelligence output, especially if listeners are aware of the computational source of its compositions, can conflict with Peirce's three categories because of a perceived lack of intention. For example, listeners to an Experiments in Musical Intelligence work who lack experience with classical music often forego their usual indexical relationship because they feel that without intent such indexes can't really exist. These listeners complain of receiving no emotional or perceptual information from these works because they have no other source upon which to draw. Other listeners, who typically hear symbolically, react to the contextual relationships in the music and are disturbed that music composed by a computer program can have this sort of persuasiveness. Still other listeners, who have a significant body of knowledge of music theory and syntax and who might otherwise listen to music symbolically, while possibly impressed by the program's arrangement of symbols, are not swayed perceptually or generally moved emotionally. All of these reactions occur, even though Experiments in Musical Intelligence music possesses as much potential for indexical, iconic, and symbolic meaning as does music created by human composers.

Context can play further important roles in how we perceive music. For example, as a boy of twelve or thirteen, I listened to a great deal of classical music. My only source for this music in Phoenix, Arizona at the time was our local library which had a rather large collection of 78 rpm recordings. In order to borrow these recordings, however, I had to walk to the library, usually pulling my small four-wheel red wagon to help cart them home—a 40-minute walk. I would then play the recordings over and over since the library lent them for only twenty-four hours at a time. I repeated this scenario day after day. Because the recordings were 78 rpm, many sides were required, even for a single short movement. Since my record player was not automatic, this meant that I had to replace each disk by hand when its short playing time had elapsed.

My favorite work of the time, Rachmaninoff's Second Piano Concerto, required many 78 rpm disks and thus many manual disk exchanges. The recording company had, luckily for me, gauged the music so that each record-side fragment began with a distinctly different musical section and ended with some type of cadence. Thus, each record side had a kind of independence and integrity of its own while still contributing to Rachmaninoff's larger concerto. Since it took me a fairly long time, maybe a minute, to exchange the disks, my perception of Rachmaninoff's concerto was that of a series of small episodes fitting wonderfully into a more magical whole which I could only imagine. When the opportunity came for me to hear Rachmaninoff's Second Piano Concerto in performance and in three continuous movements, I was terribly disappointed. Where with my library recordings there had been extraordinary moments of anticipation during the silent moments while changing disks, delicious moments where I could hear the next section only in my mind and have my mind's ear then confirmed, there now was nonstop music.

Though my experience here represents an extreme example, every listener filters music through similar kinds of contexts: cultural, experiential, and situational. Rather than suggesting we avoid such contexts, for, in part, they make us who we are, I suggest that we attempt to understand them. Only then can we begin to put the fragments together and hear music as a whole.

Ultimately, however, we listen to music multidimensionally, with no two moments exactly alike. One instant the timbre may rise to prominence, another instant a harmony, the next instant a rhythm or a motive. What's more, composers, performers, and audiences each have their own perceptions. In other words, perception is dynamic and not only changes from one instant to the next but varies by point of view.

Listeners to Experiments in Musical Intelligence music who know of its source are constrained by extraordinary contexts. To fully appreciate the music they hear, these listeners must understand this context and place it in proper perspective. However, listeners too often dismiss the program's output because of a perceived lack of intention. For these listeners, computer composition will always be second rate.

The Role of Intention

Lack of intention continues to be the single most cited reason why listeners to the music of Experiments in Musical Intelligence refuse to accept its output as *true* composition, on a par with music composed by human beings. Eleanor Selfridge-Field's reference to "simulations" and Jonathan Berger's use of the term "models" seem, at the least, the result of a perceived lack of intention in computer-created music. Other often-used terms include "re-creations," "caricatures," "pastiches," and "compilations." Though I must frankly admit to calling these works "recombinations," "replicants," and even "style imitations" on occasion, I argue here that these *compositions* should receive at least the same *kind* of respect that their database cousins receive.

Here is an example of a reaction to the music of Experiments in Musical Intelligence that begs the question of intention:

Q: ... do you think computers are capable of creating great art? What do you think of David Cope's work with the program that simulates the styles of classical composers?

A: Let's imagine you and I are in a relationship and for years I've written you wonderful love letters. And I'm a computer scientist and one day I say, "You know, I'm going to prove my prowess by getting my computer to analyze all my love letters, dig out the most profound parts, and put them together to make the best love letter of all." Which would you rather get in the mail?

The point isn't the achievement, the output. The point is the actual connection. You have to remember that even great music like Bach's is only barely adequate to bridge the terrible interpersonal gap that separates people. The last thing you want to do is create an emphasis on the artifact rather than the authentic human connection. Show me a new way to be authentic and I'll get excited about that. A new way to be inauthentic, by having computer-simulated Bach, why that's as easy as lying. Truth is what's hard. (McKenna 1999, p. 29)

The respondent here, interestingly, is Jaron Lanier, often given credit for the creation of *virtual reality*—the term if not its first realization. Lanier's incendiary remarks will no doubt resonate with many readers. Of course, Lanier's defensive arguments are loaded with emotional baggage that deflects us from the real issues. First, his comparison of music to love letters diverts our attention from important

Figure 18.2
A phrase from one of the mazurkas created by Experiments in Musical Intelligence found in chapter 1 (see figure 1.13).

issues of musical creativity. One might just as well ask "... whether you'd rather have a real relationship or watch one in a play?" I hardly think a preference for the former should jeopardize our love for Shakespeare, for example, or the movies of Hitchcock. Fiction can reveal substance and purpose that otherwise may remain hidden. Second, by focusing on some imaginary relationship or "connection" he supposedly has with composers, he distracts us from the only tangible and analyzable reference we have— the music itself. These diversions from the core issues warrant further analysis, particularly since they represent often-repeated arguments against artificial creativity in general and Experiments in Musical Intelligence in particular.

Lanier's comparison of music to love letters trivializes music composition by relegating it to the status of a byproduct of what he perceives as more important person-to-person relationships. In contrast, with Experiments in Musical Intelligence I am attempting to create music as profound as that composed by any human composer, only with different tools. The following discussion provides one example of such creation.

Figure 18.2 shows the first phrase from one of the mazurkas created by Experiments in Musical Intelligence found in chapter 1. Figure 18.3 then shows the Chopin mazurka that I believe the program used as a model for its output. These two mazurkas clearly have distinct lives of their own, with the former not simply an arrangement or a depiction of the latter. To make this point even clearer, figures 18.4 and 18.5 show two phrases from two different Chopin mazurkas which, to me at least, resemble one another more closely than the Experiments in Musical Intelligence mazurka and the original Chopin after which it was modeled resemble one another. On the basis of originality alone, I would argue that the computer-composed phrase has at least an equal right to be labeled an original composition as Chopin's posthumously published mazurka phrase, which resembles, however unintentionally, another of his mazurkas.

Figure 18.3
The clarified beginning of the Chopin mazurka which Experiments in Musical Intelligence program used as
a model for figure 18.2 (op. 30, no. 2, 1836).

Figure 18.4
The clarified beginning of Chopin mazurka, op. 7, no. 1 (1830).

Figure 18.5
The clarified beginning of Chopin mazurka (posthumous), 1826.

Figure 18.6
"Sliding" chromaticism in Chopin's op. 6, no. 1, 1830 (mm. 6–9).

Figure 18.7
A similar passage to figure 18.6 in op. 67, no. 2, 1849, published posthumously (mm. 22–5).

Figures 18.6 and 18.7 present another "borrowing" from the many that could be shown. In these examples, the mazurkas span the entire period of Chopin's mazurka-creating life (nineteen years) and yet the passages show uncanny resemblance. To some this idea may seem heretical—that composers use and reuse materials extensively in different works during their careers. I feel that, given *most* composers' predilection for inheriting style, materials, and even quotations from their own compositions (no less other composers' music), to call one a simulation and the other a true composition merely demonstrates bias, not intelligent judgment. Theorist Leonard Meyer (1989) speaks of such paraphrasing in his *Style and Music*:

Paraphrase, modeling, and borrowing of the sort that I have in mind have been prevalent in all periods ... Handel's extensive borrowings from the works of Telemann and Keiser or of Mozart's Overture in the Style of Handel from the Suite in C Major (K. 399), of Schubert's use of Beethoven's works as models and sources, of Schoenberg's orchestration of Brahms's Piano Quartet in G Minor, and of the many parodies and borrowings of twentieth-century composers: Prokofiev being "Classical"; Stravinsky being "Baroque," "Classic," and "Gothic," or using Gesualdo and Pergolesi; Bartók using folk materials ..." (p. 55)

This represents the type of stylistic composition that Experiments in Musical Intelligence creates.

Lanier, as was the case with Eleanor Selfridge-Field, Bernie Greenberg (as quoted by Doug Hofstadter in chapter 2), and Dan Dennett (e.g., *musalot*) would have you believe that Experiments in Musical Intelligence imitates the style, but not the substance, of the originals upon which it bases its compositions. I, on the other hand, would have you believe that human composers also imitate styles; in fact, therein lies much of their art. Beethoven's second symphony follows the style of his first symphony, but is no less valid for it. Those who suggest that Beethoven lacks the *intent* to create such style imitation should note that many critics base their principal arguments against Experiments in Musical Intelligence on just such a lack of intent.

Lanier treats human-composed as well as computer-composed musical compositions as artifacts that then play secondary roles to what he describes as the true "connection." Bach's *Matthäuspassion*, of which Bernie Greenberg speaks so eloquently in chapter 12, is just such an artifact, according to Lanier. Unfortunately, while we can romantically imagine Bach's thoughts, his intentions, and his dreams, his scores and the resulting performances of his music are what we actually have. However, I agree with at least part of what Lanier *seems* to be saying here. A musical score is only a representation of a work, not the work itself. Performers bring music alive with sound by incorporating many different elements—performance practice, analysis, knowledge of the composer's life and possible intentions, personal interpretation, and so on. This then becomes the work, or at least one iteration of the many possible. Lanier's argument fails, however, when he alludes to some kind of imagined relationship between a listener and a composer. I am reminded of an old Zen Buddhist adage: "The finger pointing at the moon is not the moon." For me, Lanier seems fixated on the finger—the composer behind the work—rather than the work itself.

Interestingly, Doug Hofstadter tells of a professional composer at McGill University who commented, after a presentation on Experiments in Musical Intelligence, that he liked the program's Bach inventions *far better* than he liked the Bach inventions on which they were based. Certainly this listener has not been persuaded by Western civilization's identification of certain works and composers as irrefutably superior. While I don't personally agree that the Experiments in Musical Intelligence inventions are superior to those of Bach, I applaud this listener's fortitude in revealing what surely represents an unpopular opinion.

Lanier further reduces an extremely complicated program, Experiments in Musical Intelligence, to a simple stereotype:

... dig out the most profound parts, and put them together to make the best love letter of all. Which would you rather get in the mail?

and

... why that's as easy as lying.

These comments seem particularly unfortunate. Experiments in Musical Intelligence has taken over nineteen years to develop and represents something more, I feel, than a creator of lies.

As a member of my collegiate debating team, I was once asked to defend both sides of a particular issue and, in rare form that day, won both matches. However, after basking in congratulations for a day or two, I considered exactly what it was that I had achieved. I concluded that the truth was the truth, regardless of my debating victories. At least in one case, possibly two, I had successfully defended a lie. Thinking this not to be an achievement at all, I resigned from the team. I remember my resignation vividly: "I think I will stick to music," I said. "Music does not lie." Lanier would probably not appreciate this story. For him, apparently, even if many of us cannot tell the difference, some music is a lie while other music is not.

Peeling away more layers of Lanier's rhetoric reveals a simple core: his perceived lack of *intention* in the music of Experiments in Musical Intelligence. Human composers have ears, come from cultures, and so on. Therefore, human borrowings, whether conscious or unconscious, result from intention. Human compositions provide information about cultural lineage and serve as pointers to signs and symbols that reflect the composer and the composer's culture and traditions. Experiments in Musical Intelligence borrowings, on the other hand, result only from its processes of composition and therefore lack intention.

Jim Aikin, in an article on Experiments in Musical Intelligence, noted that "Human composers exhibit intentionality. Intentionality is audible." (Aikin 1996, p. 6) Were intentionality audible, I doubt seriously that the controversy surrounding my work would exist. Certainly, if we can hear intentionality, then we should be able to easily differentiate computer-created works from human-composed works. From the results of The Game in this book's first chapter and the many times The Game has been played, I can only conclude that intentionality is *not* audible. It is possible, however, that every one of the Experiments in Musical Intelligence program's compositions has intentionality: *mine.* I intend for each one of its works to exist and I, through my programming, intend for each one of its works to be as convincing as possible. Programming for me *is* composing, and I cannot separate my notes-on-paper intentionality from my programming intentionality.

When people speak about intention I am reminded of a visit to Independence Pass, which is directly west of Independence, California. The trail ascends, and slowly a vista, which hitherto had been without trees, quite stark, and almost brutal, becomes a lush, green, and lake-filled panorama. I remember sitting at the pass and eating tuna fish out of a can and thinking: What an extraordinary moment in my life! And as I sat there, a seventy-year-old man came puffing up the trail wearing a heart-monitoring device and sat down. He noted that he had not been to the pass for thirty years. He had come back to that one spot because of its beauty. He said: "My God, look at this. I've risked my life to see this." However, nothing in that view *intended* to be beautiful, nor cared a whit about what we thought.

For many, part of the appreciation of a work apparently results from recognizing its human achievement. Remember, however, that humans designed and built the computer on which Experiments in Musical Intelligence runs; a human devised all of the software that creates the program's music; humans composed the music that the program uses as a database; and, possibly most important, humans perform, listen to, and evaluate the output. There is, in fact, almost nothing in the supposedly automatic and uninspired process that is not human-created.

With the exception of Experiments in Musical Intelligence composing 5000 works in its own style (see Cope 1996, chapter 7), I have steadfastly adhered to a simple principle in regard to the program's output: *the music is more important than the process that created it.* I have singled out certain works and had them discussed, performed, recorded, and published rather than having the program spew out hundreds of new works a day—which it could easily accomplish.

Doug comments on this in chapter 2:

What will such nitpicky details matter, when new Bach and Chopin masterpieces applauded by all come gushing out of silicon circuitry at a rate faster than H_2O pours over the edge of Niagara? Will that wondrous new golden age of music not be "truly a thing of beauty?" Won't it be sweet to swoon in a sea of synthetic sublimity?

While a proliferation of style-specific music might astonish and even intimidate some, I am not interested in producing a carnival act. I have been, and continue to be, interested in creating and experiencing what I consider good music. Focusing on the artistic quality of some of the program's output seems more accountable to this goal than flooding the world with music to prove my program's potential for prodigious creativity. I suppose in many ways that I continue to adhere to the principle that important art, whether human-, nature-, or machine-created, in some ways achieves its status through scarcity—through the one and not the many.

All works by Experiments in Musical Intelligence are attributed to "David Cope with Experiments in Musical Intelligence" and my personal documentation lists these works alongside my other non–computer-related works without discrimination. Why these works should be treated any differently than computer works by Hiller and Xenakis, for example, confounds me.

Music Composition and Theory

I find it hard to imagine that any composer who listens intelligently to music could resist the conscious or subconscious desire to imitate a particularly special moment in their own music, however embellished or varied that imitation might be. In *Experiments in Musical Intelligence* (Cope 1996, chapter 1) I discuss numerous examples of such borrowing in music history (see also Cooke 1959). In many ways, I believe that the musical language of Western art music depends on such recombinancy, the fundamental principle behind the Experiments in Musical Intelligence program.

I have developed a program called Sorcerer to detect such imitations in music. Sorcerer—named because of the sources it finds—is given a target work and a series of probable sources as a database and matches patterns from this target work against patterns in each of the probable sources. I believe that the resulting matched patterns represent an incredibly rich series of connections for analysts and musicologists to study. These borrowings—I call them *allusions*—give their constituent notes a deeper meaning. An awareness of these allusions can provide evidence for the deep communication which many feel certain music possesses (see Doug Hofstadter's comments in chapter 2, for example).

As an example, one of my favorite works, Stravinsky's *Firebird Suite* (1910), would provide an incredible spectrum of possibilities for Sorcerer and, hopefully, confirm the existence of non–computer-based recombinancy. For example, I know already that Stravinsky uses two folksong quotations (*khorovods* or round dances) from the collection *One Hundred Russian Folk Songs* (1877) by his teacher Nikolai Rimsky-Korsakov. One of these folksongs—"U Vorot Sosna Raskachalasya (The Pine Tree by the Gate)—forms the foundation of the grand finale of *Firebird*. Stravinsky also uses parts of Rimsky-Korsakov's *Golden Cockerel* (1908), as well as music from Anatol Liadov's *Baba Yaga* (op. 56, 1907). Liadov was, interestingly, offered the commission for *Firebird* before Stravinsky but turned it down. None of this analysis is intended to denigrate the brilliance of *Firebird*. On the contrary, knowledge of these quotations and influences imbues this work with a deep cultural heritage and context and thus adds powerful expressivity and meaning to the work.

American composer George Rochberg (1969) comments on such quotation:

The center piece of my *Music for the Magic Theatre* is a transcription, that is, a completely new version, of a Mozart adagio. I decided to repeat it in my own way because I loved it. People who understand, love it because they know it began with Mozart and ended with me. People who don't understand think it's by Mozart.   (p. 87)

I have an ulterior motive for developing Sorcerer: I hope to use it to indicate to Experiments in Musical Intelligence some of the logic and meaning behind the original uses of the quotations and paraphrases it sometimes incorporates in its compositions. To evolve these meanings, the program will require two databases—one for composition in its normal mode and another for informing the program of what in its compositional database originated in its second database, the one used by Sorcerer. This "informing" will include the character, location, context, and so on, as well as the makeup of events. Experiments in Musical Intelligence will then attempt to quote and paraphrase in much the same ways as the original music upon which it models its compositions, and as a consequence, hopefully, inherit more of the musical meaning that drives the originals.

An important and somewhat new subfield of music semiotics has emerged called *musical hermeneutics*, which involves studies of signifiers—pointers toward musical meaning (see Agawu 1996). While hermeneutics relates more to nonmusical sources, the concept, that of seeking the origins of what "meets the ear," has similar goals to the discovery of musical sources of meaning.

Virtual music can offer insights into certain aspects of music theory that unfortunately have generally been ignored to date. For example, music theory has, for decades, used codified rules based on implied statistical probabilities. These probability-based rules generally ignore the unique or seldom-used exceptions that, I believe, often separate inspired composition from routine composition. Students using such rules generally create average compositions. Experiments in Musical Intelligence, on the other hand, produces music that *includes* exceptions. This fact often leads, I feel, to the program's more true-to-style and hence more genuinely musical output.

Signatures offer another potentially important contribution to music theory. While the notion of patterns common to two or more works of a composer is not new—often called clichés—the use of signatures in Experiments in Musical Intelligence represents a somewhat different approach to musical analysis. Collecting, authenticating, and comparing signatures will eventually, I feel, become an important component in both music theory and musicology. Signatures, along with earmarks and unifications, all pose important questions regarding the role that patterns play in our understanding and recognition of musical style and meaning.

SPEAC—see chapter 5—incorporates what I feel is a useful approach to musical analysis. SPEAC often indicates different functional shadings for two chords that consist of exactly the same notes but have different contexts. This type of differentiation more accurately represents how we hear music—not as a static succession of chords but as a dynamic flow of relationships between hierarchically connected harmonies and harmonic regions.

I am often asked for the smoking gun behind the Experiments in Musical Intelligence program's works—the simple formulae for their success. These three interlocking, but nonetheless independent, processes—use of exceptions to rules, importance of certain patterns, and SPEAC analysis—represent these formulae.

Using most or even all of these concepts in analysis would not, I believe, require a major overhaul of current approaches to music theory. In fact, many of these processes would enhance traditional techniques rather than replace them. For example, I believe that the inclusion of exceptions would improve our rules-based approach to teaching music theory—the exceptions proving the rule so to speak. Evaluating signatures would fortify that which our ears already perceive and would help capture more musical essence in our analyses. SPEAC can reveal meaning in harmonic analyses when harmonic analysis alone refuses to produce the insights we otherwise perceive in music.

Even if the descriptions of these approaches do not inspire theorists to experiment with such possibilities, I hope the results of their use will. While Experiments in Musical Intelligence has created and continues to create controversy, few listeners can ignore the quality of some of its output.

The Future

I do not consider myself a card-carrying futurologist any more than Doug Hofstadter does. However, since many critics of Experiments in Musical Intelligence see the program as one of the harbingers of things to come, it seems only right that I address its future as well its past.

Experiments in Musical Intelligence does not currently offer collaborative opportunities for composers. With this in mind, I created Alice (*algorithmically integrated composing environment*). Alice composes as much relevant music as desired—from a single note to an entire piece—in a composer's general style as evidenced in previously composed music provided in its database and in the style of the work currently being composed. Alice creates this music as either connective material or as extensions that maintain the stylistic continuity and appropriate formal logic of the music already present. The program composes in much the same manner as Experiments in Musical Intelligence, using an association net, SPEAC, pattern-matching, and the various other techniques described in this book. Alice differs from Experiments in Musical Intelligence in that it uses a form of inherited rules recombinancy.

In the future, composers may be more apt to use programs like Alice, since such programs do not presuppose anything about a composer's style or approach to composition. Alice strives to work *with* rather than *apart* from its user. Ultimately, the program attempts to be as invisible as possible in output. I describe Alice in detail in my book *The Algorithmic Composer* (Cope 2000) and include a form of it on the accompanying CD-ROM of that book.

Future composers will, I believe, use programs like Alice routinely, leaving the choice of many of the actual notes to its algorithms. I think that most composers would appreciate hearing possible solutions to problems, fresh perspectives on a just-composed or just-about-completed passage, or experimental extensions to a new phrase. These composers will always make the ultimate decision as to whether or not to use such music. Even if all the output proposed by an Alice-like program fails to please, it might still inspire, if only by its failure to persuade.

However, even such a minimal use of computers may be off-putting to some. At the beginning of his book *The Fourth Discontinuity*, Bruce Mazlish recounts Sigmund Freud's contention that there have been three great pivotal points in human history where major crises have contradicted humanity's naive feelings of self-importance.

First was Copernicus, who, according to Freud, taught that our earth "was not the centre of the universe but only a tiny fragment of a cosmic system of scarcely imaginable vastness." Second was Darwin, who "destroyed man's supposedly privileged place in creation and proved his descent from the animal kingdom." Third was Freud himself. On his own account, Freud admitted, or claimed, that psychoanalysis "seeks to prove to the ego that it is not even the master in its own house, but must content itself with scanty information of what is going on unconsciously in the mind." (Mazlish 1993, p. 3, quoting Freud 1974, pp. 284–5)

Mazlish goes on to discuss the work of American psychologist Jerome Bruner, who adds a fourth discontinuity to Freud's list: "... a fourth and major discontinuity or dichotomy still exists in our time: the discontinuity between humans and machines" (Mazlish 1993, p. 4).

A similar view was expressed by Gary Kasparov during his match with the chess-playing program called Deep Blue (see also Hofstadter's account in chapter 2): "In one respect, I think I am trying to save the dignity of mankind by playing in this match" (Kasparov 1996). Many felt that Deep Blue's ultimate victory over Kasparov represented a sad day for humanity. I felt then and still feel today that this outcome represents yet one more victory for humanity: not only can we devise an extraordinary game such as chess and play that game at incredible levels of sophistication but we can also program computers so that they can beat the very best of us at that game. I believe that we may also one day make the same claim about music composition: not only can we compose great music but we can also program computers to compose great music. In both instances, chess and music, I believe that the latter achievements eclipse the former.

Thus, I do not agree with either Bruner or Kasparov. Machines do not represent another discontinuity. Computers and computer programs like Experiments in Musical Intelligence represent extensions of the human intellect, tools that allow us to achieve yet greater accomplishments.

When I began Experiments in Musical Intelligence in 1980–1, I had but one dream, that of resolving a composer's block. Interestingly, composer colleagues now often ask me whether or not I miss composing, or what I might have composed had I not been coding Experiments in Musical Intelligence for the past eighteen years. I generally respond that I *have* been composing these eighteen years, and I refer them to the more than six thousand works that would not have existed without my program.

I am enjoying the most productive period of my creative life, not *in spite of*, but *because of*, virtual music.

And this is just the beginning.

Bibliography

Agawu, V. Kofi. 1991. *Playing with Signs*. Princeton, NJ: Princeton University Press.

————. 1996. "Music Analysis versus Musical Hermeneutics." *The American Journal of Semiotics* 13/1: 9–24.

Aikin, Jim. 1996. "The Limitations of EMI." *Computer Music Journal* 20/3: 5–7.

————. 1993. "Ghost in the Machine." Keyboard 19/9: 25–28.

Ames, Charles. 1987. "Automated Composition in Retrospect: 1956–1986." *Leonardo* 10/2: 169–85.

Ames, Charles, and Michael Domino. 1992. "Cybernetic Composer: An Overview." In *Understanding Music with AI*, edited by Mira Balaban, Kemal Ebcioğlu, and Otto Laske. Cambridge, MA: MIT Press.

Anderson, John. 1973. *Human Associative Memory*. New York: Wiley.

————. 1983. *The Architecture of Cognition*. Cambridge, MA: Harvard University Press.

Babbitt, Milton. 1964. "Who Cares if You Listen?" *Stereo Review*, May, pp. 38–40.

Bach, J. S. 1941. *371 Harmonized Chorales and 69 Chorale Melodies with Figured Bass*, edited by Albert Riemenschneider. New York: Schirmer.

Baker, Nicholson. 1996. "Changes of Mind." (originally published in *Atlantic Monthly*). In *The Size of Thoughts: Essays and Other Lumber*, pp. 3–9.

Berggren, Ulf. 1995. *Ars Combinatoria: Algorithmic Construction of Sonata Movements by Means of Building Blocks Derived from W. A. Mozart's Piano Sonatas*. Uppsala, Sweden: Uppsala University, Department of Music.

Bernstein, Leonard. 1959. *The Joy of Music*. New York: Simon & Schuster.

Bharucha, Jamshed, and Peter Todd. 1989. "Modeling the Perception of Tonal Structure with Neural Nets." *Computer Music Journal* 13/4: 44–53.

Boethius, Anicius Manlius Severinus. n.d. *De institutione musica*, book I [text] with illustrations from Trinity College, Cambridge, MS R. 15.22, found in the electronic *Thesaurus Musicarum Latinarum* under the rubric www.music.indiana.edu/tml/6th–8th/BOEMUSIC_ with the continuations MCTC944.html and 13GF.gif.

Carroll, Lewis. 1865/1975. *Alice's Adventures in Wonderland*. New York: Viking Press.

Common Music. 1998. Available at: http://ccrma.www.stanford.edu/CCRMA/Software/cm/cm.html.

Cooke, Deryck. 1959. *The Language of Music*. New York: Oxford University Press.

Cope, David. 1991a. *Computers and Musical Style*. Madison, WI: A-R Editions.

————. 1991b. "Recombinant Music." *Computer* 24/7: 22–8.

————. 1992a. "A Computer Model of Composition." In *Machine Models of Music*, edited by Stephan M. Schwanauer and David A. Levitt. Cambridge, MA: MIT Press, pp. 403–25.

————. 1992b. "Computer Modeling of Musical Intelligence in EMI." *Computer Music Journal* 16/2 (summer): 69–83.

————. 1993. "Virtual Music." *Electronic Musician*, 9/5: 80–5.

————. 1994. *Bach by Design*. CD. Baton Rouge, LA: Centaur Records.

————. 1996. *Experiments in Musical Intelligence*. Madison, WI: A-R Editions.

————. 1997a. "CUE." *Computer Music Journal* 21/3(fall): 69–83.

————. 1997b. *Classical Music Composed by Computer*. CD. Baton Rouge, LA: Centaur Records.

————. 1999. *Virtual Mozart*. CD. Baton Rouge, LA: Centaur Records.

————. 2000. *The Algorithmic Composer*. Madison,WI: A-R Editions.

Dennett, Daniel C. 1975. "Why the Law of Effect Will Not Go Away." *Journal of the Theory of Social Behavior* 5: 169–87.

————. 1995. *Darwin's Dangerous Idea*. New York: Simon & Schuster.

———. Forthcoming. "The Evolution of Evaluators." [In a volume on evolutionary economics.]

Dowling, Jay, and Dane Harwood. 1986. *Music Cognition.* New York: Academic Press.

Ebcioğlu, Kemal. 1987. *CHORAL Project: An Expert System for Harmonizing Four-Part Chorales.* Yorktown Heights, NY: IBM Thomas J. Watson Research Center.

———. 1992. "An Expert System for Harmonizing Chorales." In *Understanding Music with AI,* edited by Mira Balaban, Kemal Ebcioğlu, and Otto Laske. Cambridge, MA: MIT Press.

———. 1993. "An Expert System for Harmonizing Chorales in the Style of J. S. Bach." In *Understanding Music with AI,* edited by Mira Balaban, Kemal Ebcioğlu, and Otto Laske. Cambridge, MA: MIT Press, pp. 294–334.

Edelman, Gerald M. 1987. *Neural Darwinism: The Theory of Neuronal Group Selection.* New York: Basic Books.

Fodor, Jerry. 1983. *The Modularity of Mind.* Cambridge, MA: MIT Press.

Freud, Sigmund. 1974. *The Standard Edition of the Complete Works of Sigmund Freud.* Vol. 16, translated from the German under the general editorship of James Strachey. London: Hogarth Press.

Fry, Christopher. 1993. "Flavors Band: A Language for Specifying Musical Style." In *Machine Models of Music,* edited by Stephan Schwanauer and David Levitt. Cambridge, MA: MIT Press.

Fux, Johann Joseph. 1725. *Gradus ad Parnassum.* Currently available as *The Study of Counterpoint,* edited by Alfred Mann. New York: Norton, 1943.

Gherdingen, Robert. 1988. *A Classic Turn of Phrase.* Philadelphia: University of Pennsylvania Press.

Grey, J. M. 1977. "Multidimensional Perceptual Scaling of Musical Timbres." *Journal of the Acoustical Society of America* 61/5: 1270–77.

Hadamard, Jacques. 1949. *The Psychology of Inventing in the Mathematical Field.* Princeton, NJ: Princeton University Press.

Hearst, Eliot. 1977. "Man and Machine: Chess Achievements and Chess Thinking." In *Chess Skill in Man and Machine,* edited by Peter W. Frey. New York: Springer-Verlag.

Hegel, G. W. F. 1970. *On Art, Religion, Philosophy,* edited by J. Glenn Gray (the section "On Art" translated by Bernard Bosanquet [London, 1905] from Hegel's *Vorlesgungen über die Aesthetik,* I. derived from Hegel's "Introductory Lectures on the Art of the Absolute Spirit"). New York: Harper & Row.

Hiller, Lejaren, and Leonard Isaacson. 1959. *Experimental Music.* New York: McGraw-Hill.

Hofstadter, Douglas R. 1979. *Gödel, Escher, Bach: An Eternal Golden Braid.* New York: Basic Books.

———. 1985. *Metamagical Themas.* New York: Basic Books.

———. 1995. *Fluid Concepts and Creative Analogies.* New York: Basic Books.

———. 1997. *Le Ton Beau de Marot.* New York: Basic Books.

Holland, John. 1995. *Hidden Order: How Adaption Builds Complexity.* Reading, MA: Addison-Wesley.

Hörnel, Dominik, and Wolfram Menzel. 1998. "Learning Musical Structure and Style with Neural Networks." *Computer Music Journal* 22/4: 44–62.

Iverson, Eric, and Roger Hartley. 1990. "Metabolizing Music." In *Proceedings of the 1990 International Computer Music Conference.* San Francisco: International Computer Music Association.

Jackendoff, Ray. 1992. *Languages of the Mind.* Cambridge, MA: MIT Press.

Kasparov, Gary. 1996. "Kasparov Speaks." Available at: www.ibm.com.

Keene, Sonya. 1989. *Object-Oriented Programming in Common Lisp: A Programmer's Guide to CLOS.* New York: Addison-Wesley.

Keislar, Doug, E. Wold, and T. Blum. 1996. "Content-Based Classification, Search, and Retrieval of Audio." *IEEE Multimedia* 3: 27–36.

Kirnberger, Johann Philipp. 1757. *Der allezeit fertige Polonaisen- und Menuettenkomponist.* Berlin.

Kivy, Peter. 1990. *Music Alone: Philosophical Reflections on the Purely Musical Experience*. Ithaca, NY: Cornell University Press.

Koch, Heinrich Christoph. 1983. *Introductory Essay on Composition [Versuch einer Anleitung zur Composition* (Rudolfstadt and Leipzig, 1782–93)], translated by Nancy Kovaleff Baker. New Haven, CT: Yale University Press.

Koestler, Arthur. 1964. *The Act of Creation*. New York: Dell.

Kohonen, Teuvo. 1984. *Self-Organization and Associative Memory*. Berlin: Springer-Verlag.

Ledbetter, Huddie. 1976. "Good Mornin' Blues." From *Leadbelly*. New York: Folkways.

Leibnitz, Gottfried Wilhelm. 1666. *Dissertatio de arte combinatoria*. Leipzig: J. S. Fickium V. J. P. Seuboldum.

Lester, Joel. 1986. *The Rhythms of Tonal Music*. Carbondale, IL: Southern Illinois University Press.

————. 1998. "J. S. Bach Teaches How to Compose: Four Pattern Preludes of the *Well-Tempered Clavier*," *College Music Symposium* 38: 33–46.

Loy, Gareth, and Peter Todd. 1991. *Music and Connectionism*. Cambridge, MA: MIT Press.

MacKay, Donald. 1970. *Information, Mechanism and Meaning*. Cambridge, MA: MIT Press.

Mahling, A. 1991. "How to Feed Musical Gestures into Compositions." In *Proceedings of the 1991 International Computer Music Conference*. San Francisco: International Computer Music Association.

Mazlish, Bruce. 1993. *The Fourth Discontinuity*. New Haven, CT: Yale University Press.

McKenna, Barbara. 1999. "Jason Lanier Gets Real." *Arts and Ideas* 1/1: 23–30.

Meyer, Leonard. 1956. *Emotion and Meaning in Music*. Chicago: University of Chicago Press.

————. 1989. *Style and Music*. Chicago: University of Chicago Press.

Miller, Glenn. 1999. *The Fabulous Glenn Miller*. CD. New York: BMG Music.

————. 2000. Available at: http://members.xoom.com/bojans/glenn.htm.

Morehen, John. 1993–4. "Aiding Authentic Performance: A Fingering Databank for Elizabethan Keyboard Music," *Computing in Musicology: An International Directory of Applications* 9: 81–92.

Morell, Virginia. 1997. "Microbiology's Scarred Revolutionary." *Science* 276/2(May): 699–702.

Mozart, Wolfgang Amadeus. 1956. *Sonatas*. Bryn Mawr, PA: Theodore Presser.

————. 1968. *Piano Sonatas*. New York: Edwin Kalmus.

————. 1986. "Piano Sonatas." *Neue Mozart-Ausgabe*. Kassel, Germany: Bärenreiter-Verlag.

Nagel, Thomas. 1979. *Mortal Questions*. Cambridge, UK: Cambridge University Press.

Narmour, Eugene. 1992. *The Analysis and Cognition of Melodic Complexity: The Implication-Realization Model*. Chicago: University of Chicago Press.

Nyman, Michael. 1974. *Experimental Music: Cage and Beyond*. New York: Schirmers.

Orwell, George. 1949. *1984-A Novel*. New York: Harcourt Brace Jovanovich.

Patchwork. 1998. Available at: http://www.ircam.fr/produits-real/logiciels/patchwork-e.html.

Peirce, Charles. 1931–5. *Collected Papers*, Vols. 1–6, edited by C. Hartshorne and P. Weiss. Cambridge, MA: Harvard University Press.

Rameau, Jean-Philip. 1985. *Treatise on Harmony*, translated by Philip Gossett. New York: Dover.

Ratner, Leonard. 1970. "Ars Combinatoria Chance and Choice in Eighteenth-Century Music." In *Studies in Eighteenth Century Music Essays Presented to Karl Geiringer on the Occasion of his 70th Birthday*, edited by H. C. Robbins Landon. New York: Oxford University Press.

Repp, Bruno H. 1989. "Expressive Microstructure in Music: A Preliminary Perceptual Assessment of Four Composers' Pulses." *Music Perception* 6: 243–74.

————. 1996. "Patterns of Note Onset Asynchronies in Expressive Piano Performance." *Journal of the Acoustical Society of America* 100: 3917–32.

Réti, Rudolph. 1962. *The Thematic Process in Music*. New York: Macmillan.

Reybrouck, M. 1995. "Music and the Higher Functions of the Brain." *Interface Journal of New Music Research* 18: 73–88.

Riemann, Hugo. 1911. *Harmony Simplified: The Theory of the Tonal Function of Chords*. London: Augener.

Riepel, Joseph. 1755. *Grundregeln zur Tonordnung insgemein*. Frankfurt.

Rochberg, George. 1969. "No Center." *Composer* 1/2: 86–9.

Rowe, Robert. 1993. *Interactive Music Systems: Machine Listening and Composing*. Cambridge, MA: MIT Press.

Schank, Roger C. 1982. *Dynamic Memory*. Cambridge, UK: Cambridge University Press.

Schank, Roger C., and Abelson, R. P. 1977. *Scripts, Plans, Goals, and Understanding*. Lawrence Erlbaum.

Schenker, Heinrich. 1926. *The Masterwork in Music*. Vol. 1, translated by Ian Bent et al. London: Cambridge University Press.

————. 1935. *Free Composition* [*Der freie Satz*. Vienna: Universal Edition], translated and edited by Ernst Oster. New York: Longman, 1979.

————. 1954. *Harmony*, edited by Oswald Jones; translated by Elizabeth Mann Borgese. Chicago: University of Chicago Press.

Schmuckler, Mark A. 1989. "Expectation in Music: Additivity of Melodic and Harmonic Processes." *Music Perception* 7: 109–50.

Schoenberg, Arnold, 1948. *Fundamentals of Musical Composition*, edited by Gerald Strang. New York: St. Martin's Press.

Schottstaedt, William. 1989. "Automatic Counterpoint." In Current *Directions in Computer Music Research*, edited by Max Mathews and John Pierce. Cambridge, MA: MIT Press.

Schweitzer, Albert 1905/1966. *J. S. Bach*. Vol. 2, translated by Ernest Newman. New York: Dover.

Selfridge-Field, Eleanor. 1992. "Review of David Cope, Computers and Musical Style." *Journal of the American Musicological Society* 45/3(fall): 535–48.

————. 1996. "The Music of J. S. Bach: New Paradigms for the Age of Technology." In *Vorträge und Berichte vom KlangArt-Kongress 1993* (*Neue Musiktechnologie II*), edited by Bernd Enders. Mainz: Schott (with a CD including live performances of four works simulated by computer in the style of J. S. Bach), pp. 133–47.

Serafini, Luigi. 1981. *Codex Seraphinianus*. Milan: Franco Maria Ricci.

Shuffett, Robert. 1980. "Interviews with George Crumb." *Composer* 10/11: 29–42.

Sims, Karl. 1994a. "Evolving Virtual Creatures." *Computer Graphic Proceedings* SIGGRAPH ACM-0-89791-667-0/9.4/007/0015: 15–22.

————. 1994b. "Evolving 3D Morphology and Behavior by Competition." In *Artificial Life IV Proceedings*, edited by R. Brooks and P. Maes. Cambridge, MA: MIT Press, pp. 28–39.

Smoliar, Stephen. 1994. "Computers Compose Music, But Do We Listen?" *Music Theory Online*/6.

Spitta, Phillip. 1873–80/1951, *Johann Sebastian Bach*, New York: Dover.

Stevens, Catherine, and C. Latimer. 1992. "A Comparison of Connectionist Models of Music Recognition and Human Performance." *Minds and Machines* 2/3: 79–400.

Stevens, Catherine, and C. Latimer. 1993. "Recognition of Short Tonal Compositions by Connectionist Models and Listeners: Effects of Feature Manipulation and Training." In *Musikometrika-5: Fundamentals of Musical Language: An Interdisciplinary Approach*, edited by M. G. Boroda. Bochum, Germany: Brockmeyer, pp. 197–224.

Stravinsky, Igor. 1975. *An Autobiography*. London: Calder and Boyars.

Sundberg, J., A. Askenfelt, and Fryden L. 1983. "Musical Performance: A Synthesis-by-Rule Approach." *Computer Music Journal* 7: 37–43.

Swift, Jonathan. 1726. *Gulliver's Travels*. London: Benjamin Motte.

Symbolic Composer. 1997. Available at: http://www.xs4all.nl/~psto/.

Thalmann, N. Magnenat, and D. Thalmann. 1990. *Synthetic Actors in Computer-Generated 3D Films*. New York: Springer-Verlag.

Turing, Alan M. 1950. "Computing Machinery and Intelligence." *Mind* 59: 434–460, no. 236. Reprinted in *Mechanical Intelligence*. 1992, edited by D. C. Ince. New York: North Holland, pp. 133–60.

Turner, Scott. 1994. *The Creative Process: A Computer Model of Storytelling*. Hillsdale, NJ: Lawrence Erlbaum.

Vantomme, Jason. 1995. "David Cope: Bach by Design—Experiments in Musical Intelligence", *Computer Music Journal* 19/3: 66–8.

Wallach, Amei. 1995. "Strokes of Genius, or Flailings in the Dark?" *New York Times*, Sunday, September 24, 1995, Arts and Leisure section: 34–6.

Wallas, G. 1926. *The Art of Thought*. New York: Harcourt Brace.

Webster's College Dictionary. 1991. New York: Random House.

Webster's New World Dictionary. 1984. New York: Warner Books.

Weisberg, D. 1986. *Creativity: Genius and Other Myths*. New York: W. H. Freeman.

Weizenbaum, Joseph. 1976. *Computer Power and Human Reason*. San Francisco: W. H. Freeman.

Whorf, Benjamin. 1941/1956. "Languages and Logic." In *Language, Thought, and Reality: Selected Writings of Benjamin Lee Whorf*, edited by John B. Carroll. Cambridge, MA: MIT Press, pp. 233–45.

Williams, Peter. 1980. *The Organ Music of J. S. Bach*, Vol. 2 (chorale preludes). Cambridge, UK: Cambridge University Press.

Xenakis, Iannis. 1971. *Formalized Music*. Bloomington, IN: Indiana University Press.

Zarlino, Gioseffe. 1558. *Le istitutioni harmoniche*. Venice.

Ziporyn, Evan. 1998. "Who Listens if You Care." In *Source Readings in Music History*, edited by Robert P. Morgan. New York: W. W. Norton, pp. 41–8.

APPENDIXES

A Mozart Databases

K. 284

K. 310

K. 330

K. 333

K. 545

B An Experiment in Musical Intelligence: Mozart Movement

C An Experiment in Musical Intelligence: Mozart Reject

D Virtual Music

Scarlatti Sonata

Domenico Scarlatti (1685–1757), son of famous opera composer Alessandro Scarlatti, composed more than 550 keyboard sonatas. These harpsichord works represent a benchmark of idiomatic writing for that instrument. Scarlatti's sonatas are characterized by two-voice imitative textures with frequent abrupt dynamic contrasts—often referred to as terraced dynamics. Most of the sonatas follow a simple one-movement binary form with each of the two sections immediately repeated. The first section usually cadences in the key a fifth above the initial key. The second section, after modulating to various keys, returns to the original key of the work. This schematic is followed exactly by the Experiments in Musical Intelligence Scarlatti sonata found here.

Due to the availability of more than five hundred of Scarlatti's sonatas on transportable MIDI files and the relative brevity of each work, I was able to include over fifty sonatas in the database of each Scarlatti-like sonata Experiments in Musical Intelligence composed. Therefore, finding the exact derivation of this sonata (1997) is most difficult. For those interested enough to seek out possible sources, I have identified nine candidates which seem likely contributors: Longo nos. 165, 181, 183, 252, 254, 255, 261, 337, and 325. The dynamics and articulations as shown in this sonata were inherited from the original music by Scarlatti and not added later.

Bach Inventions

Scarlatti's prolific repertoire of sonatas dwarf, at least in number, Bach's (1685–1750) mere fifteen inventions. Thus, hearing the database in machine-composed Bach inventions is far more likely than in machine-composed Scarlatti sonatas. However, inventions—and contrapuntal forms in general—can overshadow much of this paraphrasing since the structure tends to contradict recombinancy by requiring almost constant imitation. Inventions also do not typically demand the larger structural attention that many homophonic forms require.

Bach composed his fifteen two-part inventions in 1723 just prior to his move to Leipzig. He used these works to teach keyboard technique though they have since become standard classics of the form. The inventions follow an ascending scale–like key scheme from C major to B minor with some form of each key (major or minor) represented. In each invention the opening subject, or melodic idea, serves as a germinal motive for the work as a whole.

The inventions in the style of Bach created by the Experiments in Musical Intelligence program in 1987–8 retain some of the imagination which seems to have sparked the originals and exemplify the imitative style of inventions. Five of these inventions were recorded on Experiments in Musical Intelligence's first CD, *Bach by Design* (Cope, 1994) and three more were later recorded on *Classical Music Composed by Computer* (Cope 1997b).

Since Experiments in Musical Intelligence has to choose a measure of initial music, in this case most likely the beginning of an original Bach invention, it is not surprising that many of the program's inventions model a particular Bach invention. The computer-composed Invention no. 2, for example, follows closely Bach's own Invention no. 6—a case of what theorists and music historians know as fourth-species counterpoint. The computer-composed Invention no. 5 and Bach Invention no. 8 represent another close correlation. Other resemblances include Invention no. 7 and Bach Invention no. 12, Invention no. 10 and Bach Invention no. 15, and Invention no. 13 and Bach Invention no. 14. The beginnings of each of these Bach models appears in figure D.1. Other relationships between the two sets of inventions exist beyond these simple comparisons, but I will leave such discoveries to the reader.

While the Bach inventions can be occasionally difficult to play due to the independence of parts, the Experiments in Musical Intelligence Bach inventions are difficult to play because the program has so little connection with the constraints imposed by the size, shape, and flexibility of the human hand. Whatever limited information the program possesses about such performance limitations has been gleaned from Bach's music itself. I have attempted here to choose keys based on resultant ease of performance and, at least generally, Bach's model of key order and choice in his own inventions.

Analysts who take Experiments in Musical Intelligence's inventions seriously will delight in finding some of the same kinds of motivic development (motives turned upside down and backward, sequenced, etc.) that the Bach inventions possess. These variations emanate directly from the hierarchical processes the program uses in its recombinative approach to composition. Unlike the Bach inventions, however, these computer-composed inventions are not examples of important music. However, they do have, at times, a charm often lacking in human imitations of Bach's masterpieces (see chapter 13 for more on these inventions).

Figure D.1
The beginnings of Bach Inventions (a) 6; (b) 8; (c) 12; (d) 14; and (e) 15.

1

2

4

5

6

7

8

9

10

11

12

13

15

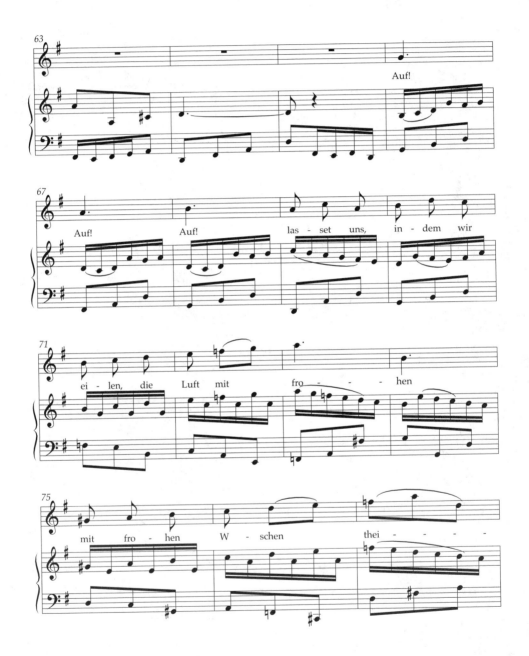

Mozart Sonata

Mozart's (1756–1791) melodic and harmonic textures differ significantly from Bach's intense counterpoint. Mozart's sonatas typically follow a three-movement (fast–slow–fast) structure with sonata-allegro (AB-development-AB) first movements, song-form (AB or ABA) second movements, and rondo third movements (ABACA......, etc.), thereby differing substantially from the forms found, for example, in Scarlatti's sonatas discussed earlier. Mozart occasionally uses variations form as well. Experiments in Musical Intelligence's sonata (1997) follows the basic scheme of sonata-allegro (mvt. 1), theme with variations (mvt. 2), and rondo (mvt. 3).

The computer-composed sonata's first movement draws from many different sources. For example, the program's measures 1–2 result from a combination of measure 6 and measure 9 from Mozart's K. 279 (1774), first movement. The program's measure 3 derives from Mozart's K. 309 (1777), third movement, measures 33–4. Measures 17–8 of the new sonata movement emanate from Mozart's K. 283 (1774), first movement, measures 24–5. Each of these references appear in order in figure D.2. Measure 4 of the program's first movement replication shows a typical Mozart signature, as does the final bar, a variation of the signature shown earlier (see figure 9.1).

The main theme of Experiments in Musical Intelligence's second movement represents a classic example of the program's recombinative processes. Figure D.3 shows this recombination of Mozart's K. 331 (1778), first movement (my choice to include in a database otherwise consisting of second movements). The lines from the original music to the newly composed phrase (at the bottom) indicate the origins and how, through the recombination process, the originals become reorganized while retaining their individual shape. This new music varies from the originating music while maintaining many aspects of its logic and coherence. Almost any other recombination of the segments shown here will produce musical gibberish.

The variations of this computer-composed second movement theme all stem from those by Mozart in his K. 331, first movement. For example, variation 1 of the program's movement follows closely that of the original Mozart variation 1. Variation 2 of the program's composition beginning in measure 33 resembles that of Mozart's variation 2. Measure 49 in the program's new movement derives from Mozart's variation 3, and so on. Some of these sources are shown in figure D.4.

The Experiments in Musical Intelligence Mozart third movement has multiple origins. For example, the beginning of the first theme of the new movement resembles the pickup to movement 2 of K. 310 (1778) and measures 33–5 of the second movement of K. 309 (1777). Measures 11–4 of the program's third movement draw from

Figure D.2
From Mozart's (a) K. 279 (1774), mvt. 1, m. 6; (b) K. 279 (1774), mvt. 1, m. 9; (c) K. 309 (1777), mvt. 3, mm. 33–4; (d) K. 283 (1774), mvt. 1, mm. 24–5.

Figure D.3
Theme from Mozart's K. 331, mvt. 1, with lines to show Experiments in Musical Intelligence derivations.

Figure D.4
Variation types in Mozart's K. 331, mvt. 1.

Figure D.5

From Mozart's (a) K. 310 (1778), mvt. 2, pickup; (b) K. 309 (1777), mvt. 2, pickup to mm. 33–5; (c) K. 280 (1774), mvt. 1, mm. 43; (d) K. 309 (1777), mvt. 2, mm. 36–7; (e) K. 331 (1778), trio, beginning.

measures 43–5 of movement 1 of Mozart's K. 280 (1774). Measures 60–1 of the computer-composed sonata third movement resemble Mozart's second movement of K. 309 (1777), measures 36–7. Measure 62 of the new music imitates the opening of the trio of K. 331 (1778). Some of the originating Mozart examples appear in figure D.5. Measure 8 of the computer-composed third movement contains a variation of a signature on beats 2 and 3 (see figure 5.1 of Cope 2000).

With all of these references pointing toward the original Mozart sonatas, one might imagine that the resulting Experiments in Musical Intelligence sonata would sound like a pastiche of quotes and clichés. However, even after listening carefully to the music in figures D.2 to D.5, most listeners will find the computer-composed replication substantially original in design, if not content. I believe this is due to the complicated formal logic the program utilizes during composition, as discussed in chapter 6.

Interestingly, the connections between Mozart's original music and the just-described computer-composed sonata represent merely a beginning to this kind of source analysis. Readers who own copies of Mozart's piano sonatas may wish to draw further relations between Mozart's music and the Experiments in Musical Intelligence replications. Readers may also be interested in relating such material to music within Mozart's sonatas themselves for, after a few hours of trying to discover sources for the computer-composed music, the similarity between many of Mozart's own choices and other of his music will become apparent.

I. Allegro Moderato

II. Andante

III.   Allegro

tas. The rocking motion of the left-hand accompaniment occurs in both the *Pathétique* and *Appassionata* sonatas. However, the right-hand material clearly represents an inversion of op. 2, no. 1 (1793–5), possibly the result of voice exchanges with another section of that same sonata. This composite, as with the opening material, represents a good example of music derived from a database honed by selecting similar material for recombinant composition.

Interestingly, the transition from theme 1 to theme 2 (mm. 52–9) of the Experiments in Musical Intelligence Beethoven first movement resembles Mozart's C minor *Fantasy* (K. 475, 1785, m. 18 with the hands reversed and the rhythm augmented; see Mozart 1986) more than any of the Beethoven's sonatas in the database. Beethoven was particularly fond of Mozart's *Fantasy*. In terms of inheritance from Beethoven, the computer-composed transition resembles the music in the left hand of the transition to the recapitulation in Beethoven's op. 2, no. 1, first movement (mm. 94–109). The complexity of the responsible code makes the absolute identification of the sources impossible.

The second theme of the machine-composed Beethoven first movement (beginning in m. 60) represents a composite of many different Beethoven themes. Therefore it is difficult, given the various competing processes involved, to determine an explicit inheritance. Interestingly, this theme most resembles the main theme of a work Beethoven originally wrote as a second movement to his *Waldstein* sonata, op. 53 (1803–4), but later discarded. This latter theme bears an uncanny resemblance to the second entrance of the theme beginning in measure 70 in the computer-composed example. It is uncanny because this theme was not in the database at the time of composition.

Signatures may well be present in the computer-composed music, but they prove quite difficult to find in this movement. At its best, Experiments in Musical Intelligence produces music with transparent seams between recombinant and signature elements and this seems to be the case here. The closing theme of the program's movement (beginning six measures from the end of the movement) appears to be an amalgam of various of Beethoven's concluding ideas.

This computer-composed Beethoven first movement has moments of obvious sources, almost quotations. However, there are also occasions of spontaneity and ingenuity as the program interweaves inherited materials. In many instances, this combination of inheritance and originality produces music of worth beyond that of simple imitation. This kind of innovative composition occurs as the result of interplay and, most important, balance between the various constituent processes of the program. The music sounds in the style of the original and not as a pastiche of recognizable sources.

The use of a multicomposer database in the Experiments in Musical Intelligence Beethoven second movement provides a source of materials not unlike sources available to human composers. Though dominated by their own sensibilities and by inheritance from their own previous work, human composers demonstrate the influences of many other composers' works which subtly affect their own style. It is hard to imagine a program supposedly exhibiting intelligent-like behavior *not* having access to the diversity of musical materials made available by multicomposer databases.

I discuss a method of combining more than one style in *Computers and Musical Style* (Cope 1991a, chapter 5) in the creation of *Mozart in Bali*, an orchestrated version of which has now been recorded (Cope 1997b). For the most part, this work and others (such as *For Keith*, also discussed in Cope 1991a) exemplify a kind of brute-force method of combining styles where each style retains its individuality. Not all style integrations need be so harsh.

The multicomposer database used for the Experiments in Musical Intelligence Beethoven second movement consisted of the second movement of Beethoven's *Moonlight Sonata* (op. 27, no. 2, 1801) and Bach's first prelude from his *Well-Tempered Clavier*. The resemblance of the Experiments in Musical Intelligence's second movement to Beethoven's sonata movement is obvious when compared to the original shown in figure D.6. However, the chord progression results from Bach's

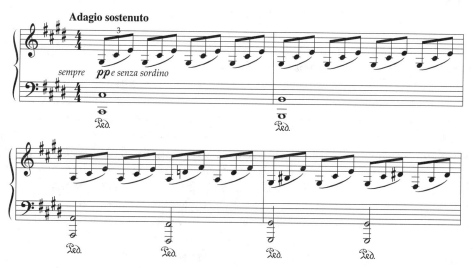

Figure D.6
The beginning of Beethoven's Sonata, op. 27, no. 2.

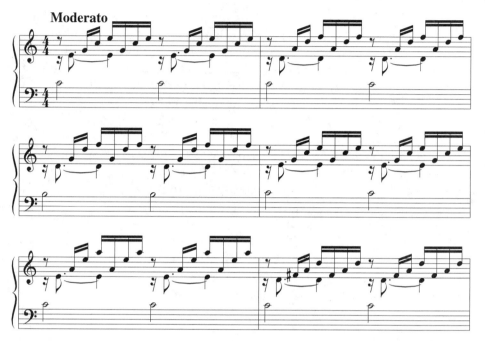

Figure D.7
The beginning of the first prelude of Bach's *Well-Tempered Clavier*.

prelude as shown in figure D.7. The new music of figure D.8, while derivative, nonetheless has a life characteristically its own. This form of style combination melds some of the parameters of one composer's music in a database with different parameters of another composer's music in the same database. One might further imagine the dynamics of Mahler combined with the rhythms of Debussy, the harmonies of Brahms, and so on.

Careful selection of music for databases, particularly for databases that consist of fragments of works, can play an important role in user intention in Experiments in Musical Intelligence output. This second movement—the so-called Bach-Beethoven movement to which Bernie Greenberg refers so glowingly in his commentary (see chapter 12)—resulted from such human control over the database at the time of composition.

The computer-composed Beethoven third movement presents an intriguing variation of Beethoven's third movement theme (beginning m. 11) of his *Sonate Charatéristique: Les Adieux* (op. 81a, 1809–10). Other themes and ideas of this movement

Figure D.8
The beginning of a slow movement, arguably in the style of Beethoven.

have less clear roots, though no doubt they attribute their characteristic Beethoven sound to inheritance from specific Beethoven movements. As with the faster material of the computer-composed first movement, however, the textures here seem unnaturally thin, even for Beethoven fast movements.

The first and second movements of this sonata appear on the CD, *Classical Music Composed by Computer* (Cope 1997b).

I

II.   Andante Sostenuto

III. Allegretto

Mendelssohn Song without Words

Like Schubert, Mendelssohn (1809–1847) composed a large number of *Songs without Words* (eight books, 48 actual works) of which Experiments in Musical Intelligence used ten to create its music. Among those the program used were nos. 7 ("Contemplation," op. 30, no. 1, 1834) and 20 ("The Fleecy Clouds," op. 53, no. 2, 1841). The computer-composed "Song without Words" is possibly the most derivative in this collection. I have included this song not because it represents particularly effective composition, but because it demonstrates one extreme of output. I often save music such as this to provide listeners and readers with examples of the program's less effective composing. Even so, this song has its unique moments and special musicality which separate it somewhat from the originals upon which it is based.

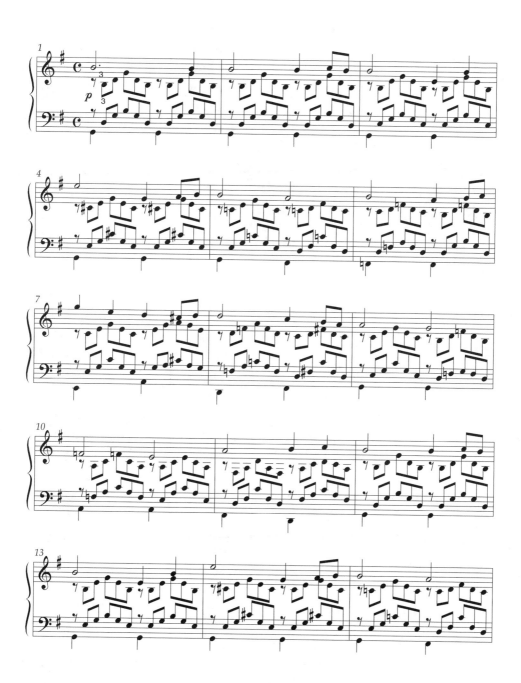

Chopin Mazurka

The lack of originality of the computer-composed Mendelssohn "Song without Words" is contrasted by the program's numerous more original output of mazurkas in the style of Chopin. Experiments in Musical Intelligence composed over one hundred mazurkas in the style of Frédéric Chopin (1810–1849) during the winter of 1987. I selected one of these for performance and recording, and published it in my book *Computers and Musical Style* (Cope 1991a). My choice was made quickly because of time constraints and I based my decision almost entirely on ease of performance and structural simplicity. I have revisited this set of mazurkas in recent years and have been amazed by the overall quality of the works, general authenticity of style, and the appearance of inspired creativity. The mazurka which appears here equals or surpasses the quality of the one chosen for publication in Cope 1991a.

The mazurka style generally follows a three-part triple-meter form, with, at least in Chopin's examples, an emphasis on dotted rhythms and triplets. These characteristics are easily recognizable in this mazurka. The um-pah-pah left hand and straightforward right-hand melody, while not obligatory, further characterize the mazurka style. As well, the rhythm is quite flexible in performance since a piano mazurka is not performed as a true dance. Some of Chopin's mazurkas remain fixed diatonically to the initial key while others evolve chromatically. The middle section of this mazurka, like most of Chopin's mazurka middle sections, contrasts the outer sections. Twelve of the fifty-one Chopin mazurkas were used for this particular replicant.

Like the original music, the Experiments in Musical Intelligence mazurka is not a mere collection of patterns or simply reordered compilations of Chopin's originals. In fact, comparing the harmonic progressions, the melodic contours, and the chromaticism of the mazurka published here with those of Chopin's originals proves the originality and uniqueness of the computer-composed music. Finding derivations is often difficult just as it would be when comparing one of the Chopin mazurkas with other Chopin mazurkas.

for Doug Hofstadter

Chopin Nocturne

Chopin composed nineteen nocturnes over a period of sixteen years (1830–1846).
Keys of these nocturnes vary, but major keys slightly outnumber minor keys—eleven
to ten—with two nocturnes each in the keys of C, C-sharp, G, and B minor and
E-flat major. For the most part Chopin composed these nocturnes in small sets of
two or three (op. 9 and 15 have three each, and op. 27, 32, 37, 48, 55, and 62 have
two each—one published posthumously). The nocturne has a generally free (though
ABA is typical) musical form with a slow lyrical melody accompanied by repeating
arpeggios. Meters vary but 4/4 predominates.

As with its inventions in the style of Bach, Experiments in Musical Intelligence's
nocturne in the style of Chopin uses a particular model for its initial material and
general form: op. 72, no. 1 (1827) shown in part in figure D.9. Note how the program
has varied the main thematic idea by extending it downward an octave and then
continuing in a different manner from the original. The theme of the B section of the
computer-composed Chopin (beginning in m. 30) derives from the middle theme of
Chopin's Nocturne, op. 48, no. 2 (1841) beginning in measure 57 (see figure D.10). A
somewhat different Chopin signature than found in figure 5.3 occurs frequently in

Figure D.9
The beginning of Chopin's Nocturne, op. 72, no. 1 (1827).

Figure D.10
Measure 57 from Chopin's Nocturne, op. 48, no. 2 (1841).

various guises in the Experiments in Musical Intelligence nocturne (see mm. 8, 12, 15, etc.) and a variant of this signature forms a significant part of the second theme (see m. 30).

The chromaticism that appears in measure 3 between the right and left hands in the Experiments in Musical Intelligence Chopin nocturne creates a temporary dissonance (G-sharp against G-natural). Out of context, this dissonance seems quite atypical of Chopin's music. However, as is often the case with computer-composed replications, careful examination of Chopin's style reveals many equivalent instances. For example, in op. 72, no. 1, E occurs with E-sharp in measure 21, beat 4, and in measure 37 F-sharp sounds against F-natural on beat 4 (see figure D.11). Both of these passages use the chromaticism as passing scales just as in the computer-composed example.

Figure D.11
From Chopin's op. 72, no. 1 (1827): (a) m. 21; (b) m. 37.

Brahms Intermezzo

Like the Experiments in Musical Intelligence program's Chopin nocturne, the program's Brahms (1833–1897) *Intermezzo* (1997) relies almost entirely on a single piece, op. 117, no. 1 (1892), for its model, even though two other intermezzi were present in the database at the time of composition. This is curious in that, while the new work obviously resembles its model, it has many differences. Only rarely does the original clearly reveal itself in the new music, notably measure 28 of the computer-composed music, which nearly quotes from measure 38 of the original. This paraphrasing results, in part, from the program's use of various cross-measure transformations, as in the beginning of theme 2 in measure 17, where the hemiola between the hands collides; Brahms would more likely keep the octaves synchronous in such situations.

Mahler Song

The opera *Mahler* (1997), from which this song derives, follows the life of the composer and conductor Gustav Mahler (1860–1911) whose career conducting operas is legendary, though he never composed an opera himself. The libretto is formed from letters and writings by Mahler, his wife Alma, and many of Mahler's friends and acquaintances, including Anton Bruckner, Hans von Bülow, Alma Mahler, Thomas Mann, Arnold Schoenberg, Richard Strauss, Bruno Walter, and Anton von Webern, among others. *Mahler* is the second opera (*Mozart* was the first, *Scriabin* the next) in a series of operas composed by the Experiments in Musical Intelligence program on librettos based on the writings of well-known composers. This Alma Mahler song occurs in the second act of the opera.

The accompaniment at the beginning of this aria resembles Mahler's song "Frülingsmorgen" (1880–3) though a note-by-note comparison proves the former's originality. Interestingly, the beginning of the melody in the voice part here originates in the accompaniment part of "Frülingsmorgen." A careful comparison of the harmonies of both the computer program's music and "Frülingsmorgen" reveals how the program extends and varies the harmonic progressions while maintaining stylistic integrity (see mm. 4–5 of "Frülingsmorgen" and mm. 7–8 of the song presented here).

The second theme of the Experiments in Musical Intelligence aria (see m. 42) has many elements in common with Mahler's "Hans und Grethe" (1880–3), though what are fragments in Mahler's original spin out as full melodies in the computer-generated music. Aside from these paraphrasings, the music of this aria seems genuinely original and conforms to Mahler's style quite effectively.

Setting texts to Experiments in Musical Intelligence music poses interesting challenges. Most composers set music to text rather than vice versa. This results from the requirement that musical meter should, for the most part, match poetic meter and for most composers it seems easier to have the text before writing the music. My program, however, does not set texts particularly well so this process must be reversed. I often have the advantage, however, of using translatable texts. I make several different translations to English and choose the one which best meets the criteria for an effective song setting.

cresc.

we   walked   on   home.

Rachmaninoff Suite

The Experiments in Musical Intelligence Rachmaninoff *Suite* (1993) evolved from a Rachmaninoff (1873–1943) database consisting of his *Second Suite*, op. 17 (1901), his song "Before My Window," op. 26, no. 10, and fragments from his second piano concerto. This computer-composed Rachmaninoff suite movement demonstrates many transformational properties that contribute to its original sound. This suite movement typifies how subtly signatures can be embedded in otherwise completely recombinant music. When properly placed, approached, and exited contextually, signatures can add immeasurably to stylistic integrity. These signatures must occur in the right numbers and be of the right length and yet not fix so much music in place that the original work becomes recognizable.

The Rachmaninoff *Suite* appears on the CD, *Classical Music Composed by Computer* (Cope 1997b).

Joplin Rag

As Mahler's style differs from that of Rachmaninoff, so do the rags of Scott Joplin
(1868–1917) differ from the style of Mahler. *Another Rag* (1988) derives its rhythms,
harmonic progressions, and melodic configurations from a number of similar Joplin
rags. These original rags begin in octaves (introduction) which include syncopated
tied sixteenth-notes both across and within beats. The main body of the rags typically
contain a duple-metered um-pah left-hand figuration in eighth-notes.

Note how the Experiments in Musical Intelligence program's rag has kept introductory (mm. 1–4) material intact even though this material often has the same initiating number of notes as the main theme appearing in measure 5. For example, the

rag begins with three simultaneous notes, the same number as begins measure 5. Measure 2 begins with two notes, the same number as that initiating measure 11. Yet none of this contextual material gets improperly mixed. Both the introduction and the main theme retain a musical consistency similar to the original Joplin models upon which this new work is based. Aside from the connective integrity provided by the recombinant process itself, the use of SPEAC, discussed in chapter 6, provides the necessary mechanism for achieving this consistency.

This Joplin rag appears on the CD, *Classical Music Composed by Computer* (Cope 1997b).

Bartók Bulgarian Danse

The Experiments in Musical Intelligence Bartók Bulgarian Danse (1998) seems modeled after Bartók's (1881–1945) *Sechs Tänze in bulgarischen Rhythmen*, no. 152 of the *Mikrokosmos* (1926–39, vol. 6). The $2 + 2 + 2 + 3$ meter, scalar melodic line, and basic textures clearly derive from Bartók's original. There are, however, a number of novel idiosyncrasies in the computer-composed composition. First, the scale, while related to Bartók's polymodal scale, has its own life here. As well, the use of the scale—almost everywhere one looks—deviates significantly from Bartók's more subtle use. The ending, however, owes to Bartók's original: a thrice-repeating measure which abruptly cadences.

While not eminently successful, the computer-composed music does show a number of stylistic similarities with other works in Bartók's *Mikrokosmos*. The composite meter, for example, is typical of music by Bartók. As well, the switching of textures between hands appears often in Bartók's music for piano and provides effective interplay. One principal element of Bartók's style that does not surface in this machine replication is nonscale chromaticism which Bartók's music has in abundance. The strictly diatonic use of the scale here adds to the machine work's stagnancy, while Bartók's music has more vibrancy.

Prokofiev Sonata

The quasi-tonal or nontonal harmonic progressions that one finds in some contemporary music might lead one to expect that a fundamental revision of code would be necessary to create convincing replications. This is not the case, however. For example, even though Prokofiev's (1891–1953) style differs markedly from the music presented thus far, the fact that the program bases its composing on the voice-leading it discovers in its database makes creating Prokofiev as straightforward as creating Mozart.

This computer-composed Prokofiev sonata was completed in 1989 using primarily Prokofiev's sonatas nos. 3 (1917), 5 (1923), and 7 (1939–42) as a database (parts of sonatas nos. 4, 6, and 8 were also used). The program's first movement (not shown here) was inspired by Prokofiev's own attempt to compose his Tenth Piano Sonata, an attempt thwarted by his death. As such, the movement represents another of the many potential uses of programs such as Experiments in Musical Intelligence—the completion of unfinished works.

The beginning of the second movement of the computer-composed Prokofiev sonata follows closely the triadic accompaniments of both of the middle movements of his fifth and seventh sonatas. Each of Prokofiev's originals has repeating major triads as a backdrop to their main themes. The initial melody here, however, resembles one from *Peter and the Wolf* though that work was not in the database at the time of composition. Like so many similar examples found in Experiments in Musical Intelligence's algorithmic composition, elements embedded in a composer's style often mirror actual works not used by the program during composition. Cope (1991a) provides various signatures and other sources for the music in this movement.

As mentioned in chapter 6, this movement has a double binary form of A–B–A–B, where the second B is an extended version of the first B section. The A section begins in measure 1 and again in measure 22, while the B section begins in measure 10 and again in measure 27.

E The Game Key

Answers to The Game

Game 1

Work 1: César Cui (1835–1918), from Twelve Miniatures, op. 20
Work 2: Experiments in Musical Intelligence
Work 3: Experiments in Musical Intelligence
Work 4: Bedřich Smetana (1824–84), Andante in Es-Dur (1856)

Game 2

Chorale 1: J. S. Bach (1685–1750), Chorale no. 12
Chorale 2: Experiments in Musical Intelligence
Chorale 3: J. S. Bach, Chorale no. 6
Chorale 4: Experiments in Musical Intelligence

Game 3

Mazurka 1: Experiments in Musical Intelligence
Mazurka 2: Frédéric Chopin (1810–49), Mazurka op. 67, no. 1
Mazurka 3: Frédéric Chopin, Mazurka op. 33, no. 1
Mazurka 4: Experiments in Musical Intelligence

Index